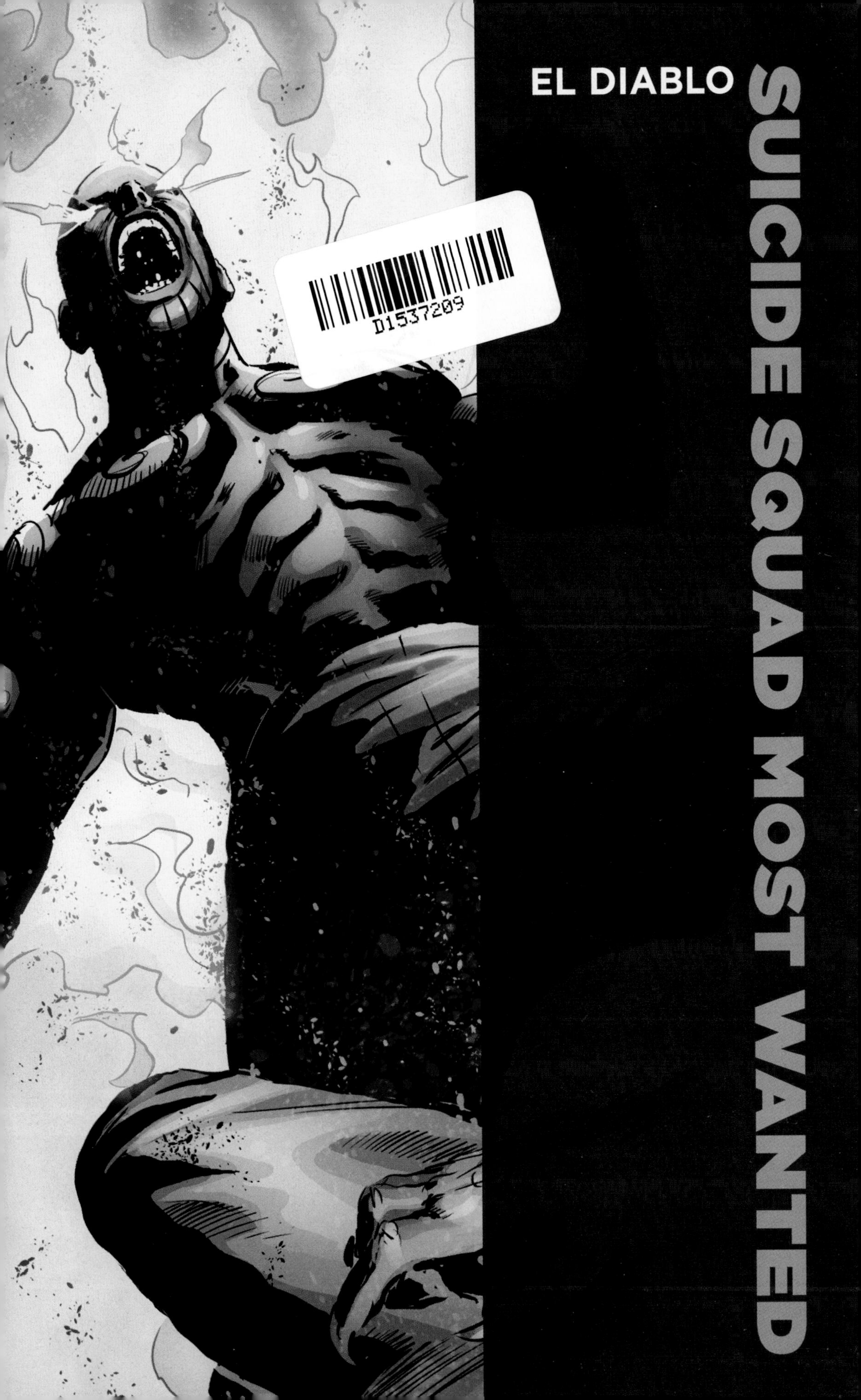

EL DIABLO

SUICIDE SQUAD MOST WANTED

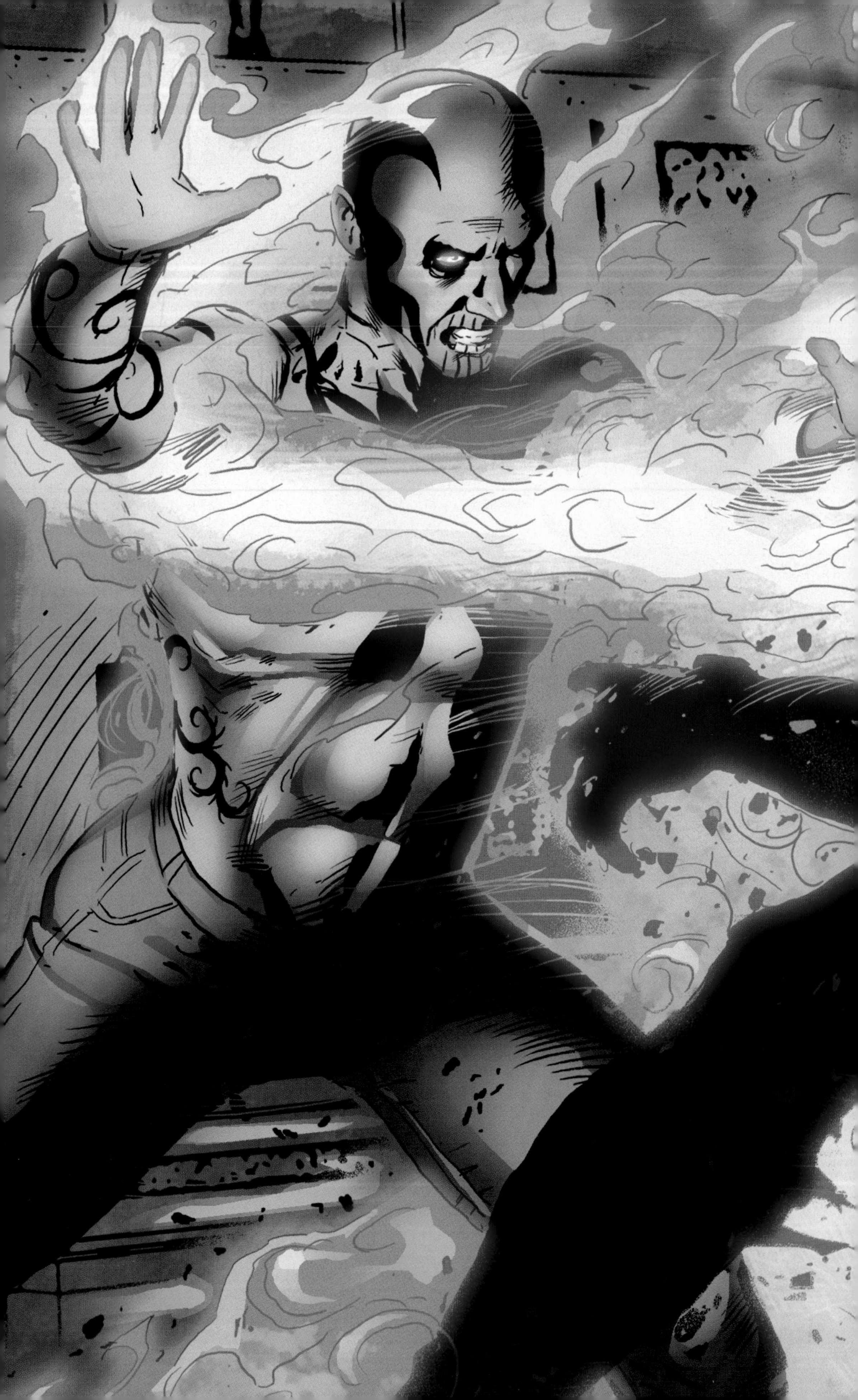

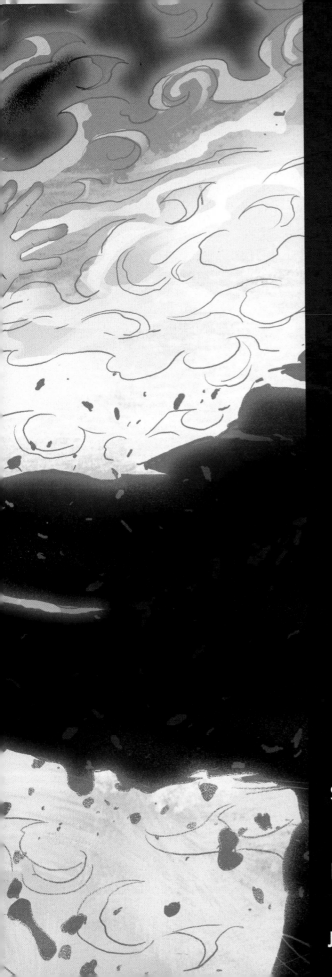

EL DIABLO

SUICIDE SQUAD MOST WANTED

WRITTEN BY
JAI NITZ

ARTIST
CLIFF RICHARDS

COLORIST
HI-FI

LETTERER
JOSH REED

SERIES & COLLECTION COVER ART BY
MIKE HUDDLESTON & RICO RENZI

BATMAN CREATED BY
BOB KANE with BILL FINGER

AMANDA WALLER CREATED BY
JOHN OSTRANDER & JOHN BYRNE

HARVEY RICHARDS, DAVID WOHL Editors - Original Series
JEB WOODARD Group Editor - Collected Editions
ERIKA ROTHBERG Editor - Collected Edition
STEVE COOK Design Director - Books
DAMIAN RYLAND Publication Design

BOB HARRAS Senior VP - Editor-in-Chief, DC Comics
DIANE NELSON President
DAN DiDIO Publisher
JIM LEE Publisher
GEOFF JOHNS President & Chief Creative Officer
AMIT DESAI Executive VP - Business & Marketing Strategy, Direct to Consumer & Global Franchise Management
SAM ADES Senior VP - Direct to Consumer
BOBBIE CHASE VP - Talent Development
MARK CHIARELLO Senior VP - Art, Design & Collected Editions
JOHN CUNNINGHAM Senior VP - Sales & Trade Marketing
ANNE DePIES Senior VP - Business Strategy, Finance & Administration
DON FALLETTI VP - Manufacturing Operations
LAWRENCE GANEM VP - Editorial Administration & Talent Relations
ALISON GILL Senior VP - Manufacturing & Operations
HANK KANALZ Senior VP - Editorial Strategy & Administration
JAY KOGAN VP - Legal Affairs
THOMAS LOFTUS VP - Business Affairs
JACK MAHAN VP - Business Affairs
NICK J. NAPOLITANO VP - Manufacturing Administration
EDDIE SCANNELL VP - Consumer Marketing
COURTNEY SIMMONS Senior VP - Publicity & Communications
JIM (SKI) SOKOLOWSKI VP - Comic Book Specialty Sales & Trade Marketing
NANCY SPEARS VP - Mass, Book, Digital Sales & Trade Marketing

SUICIDE SQUAD MOST WANTED: EL DIABLO

DC Comics, 2900 West Alameda Ave., Burbank, CA 91505
Printed by Vanguard Graphics, LLC, Ithaca, NY, USA. 3/17/17. First Printing.
ISBN: 978-1-4012-6865-7

Library of Congress Cataloging-in-Publication Data

FSC
www.fsc.org
MIX
Paper from responsible sources
FSC® C016956

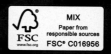

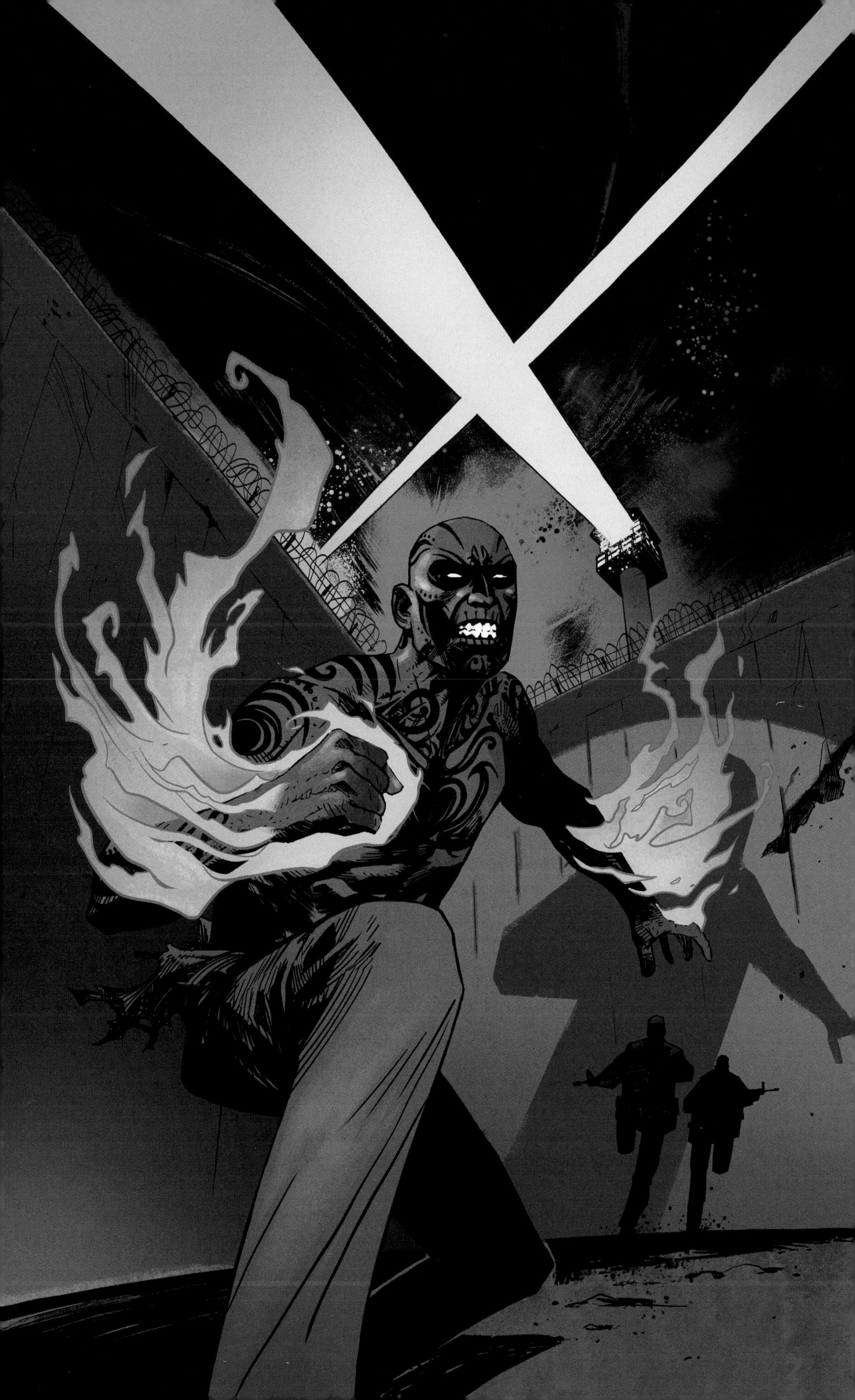

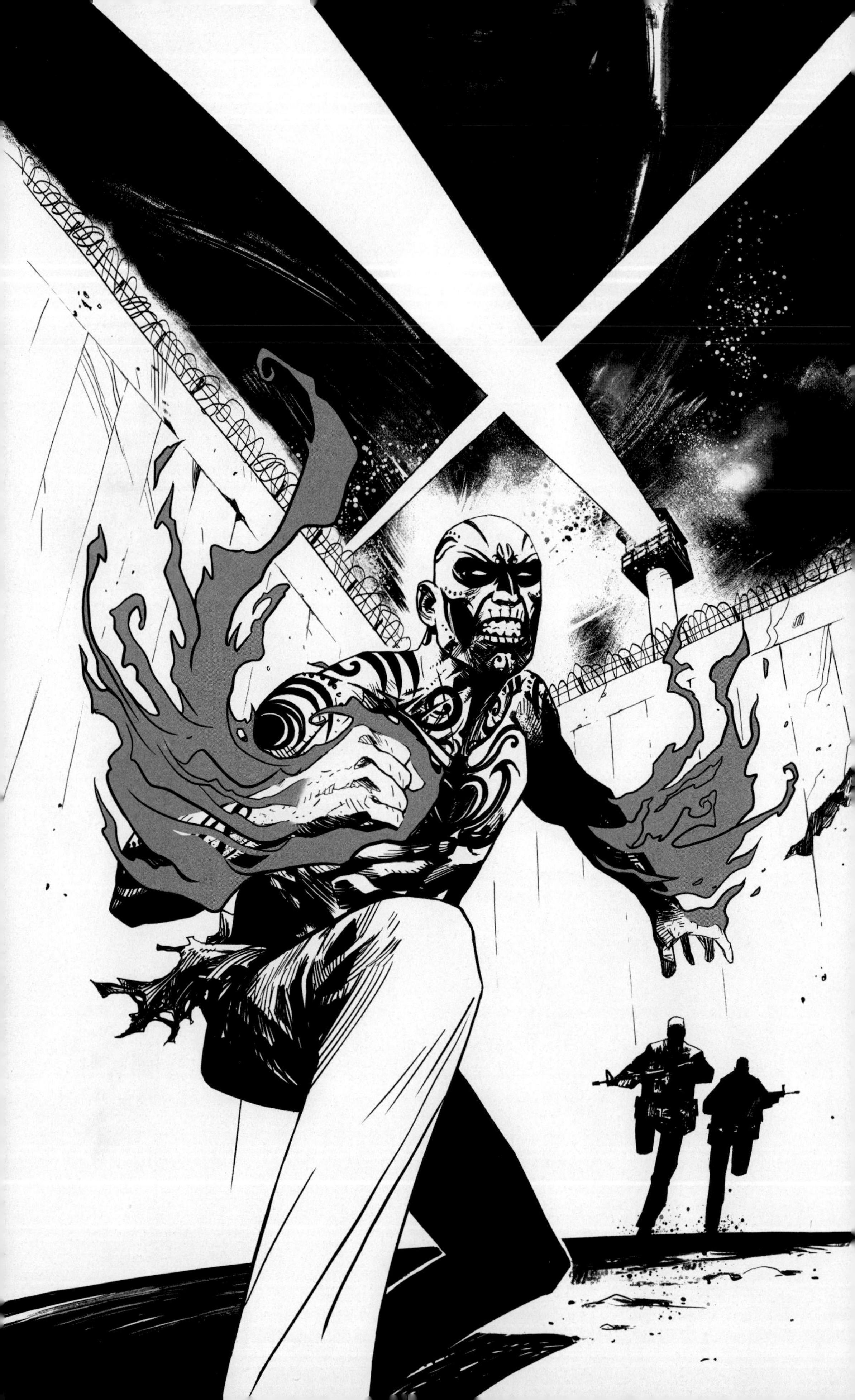

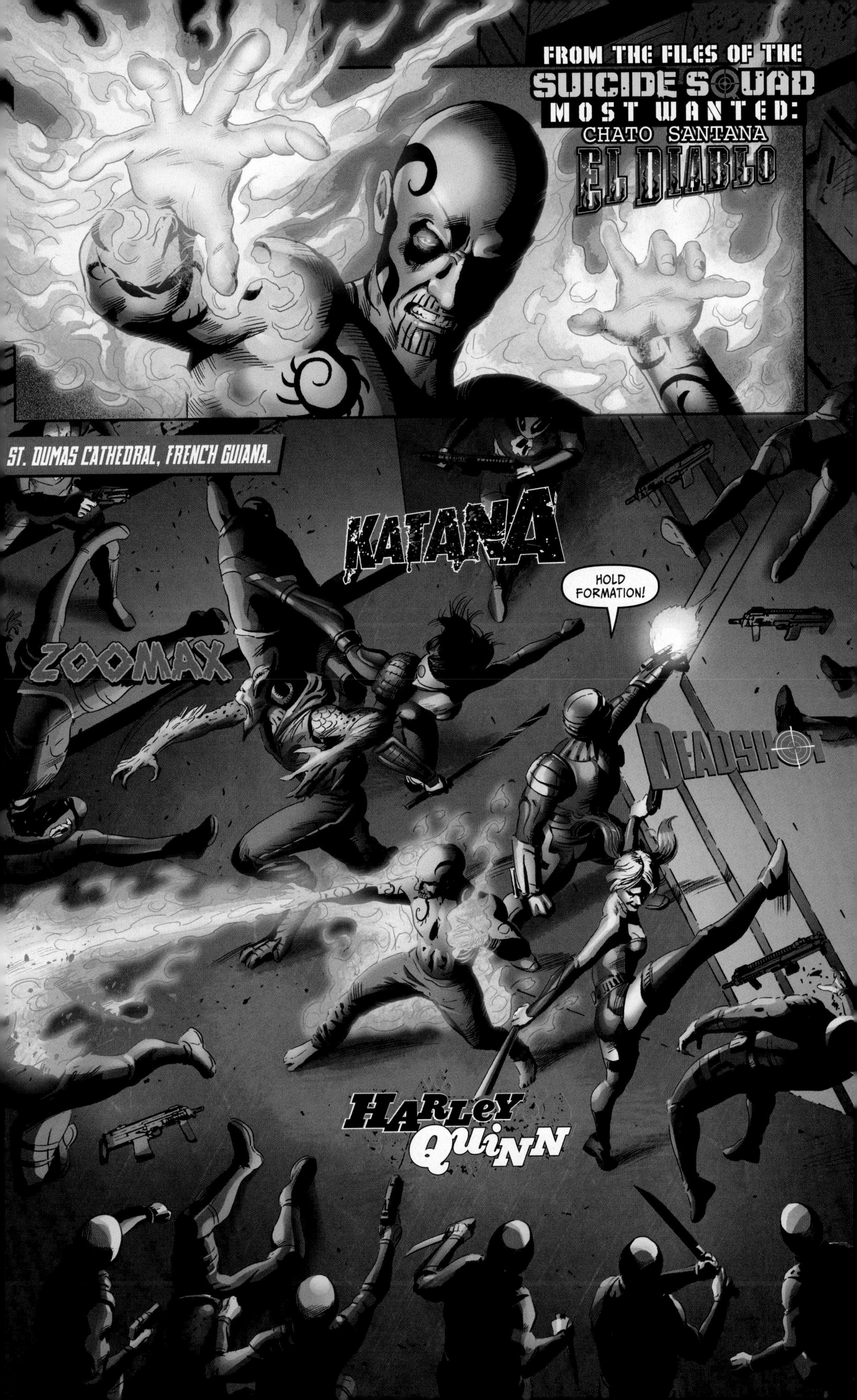
FROM THE FILES OF THE
SUICIDE SQUAD
MOST WANTED:
CHATO SANTANA
EL DIABLO
ST. DUMAS CATHEDRAL, FRENCH GUIANA.
KATANA
HOLD FORMATION!
ZOOMAX
DEADSHOT
HARLEY QUINN

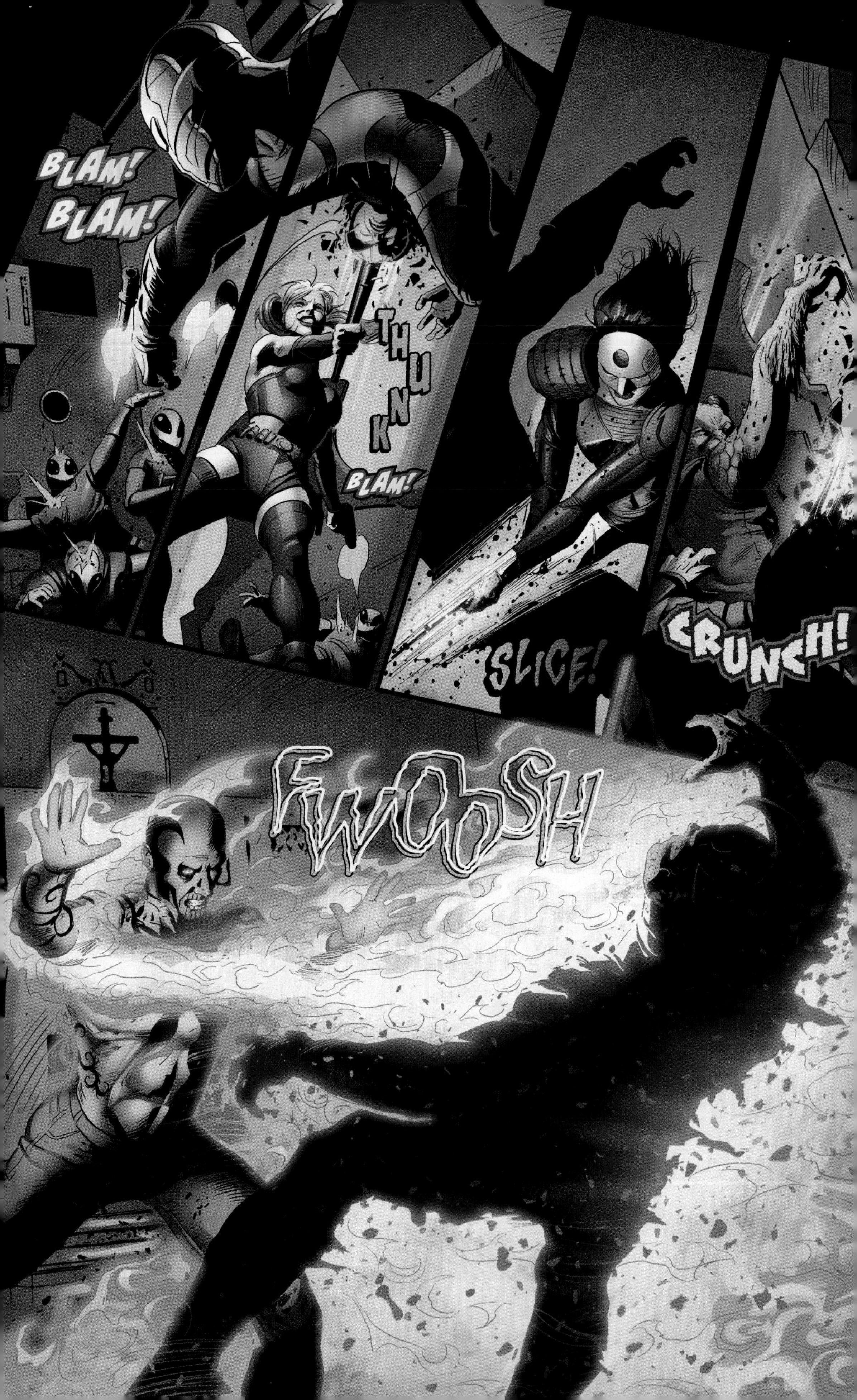
BLAM!
BLAM!
THUNK
BLAM!
SLICE!
CRUNCH!
FWOOSH

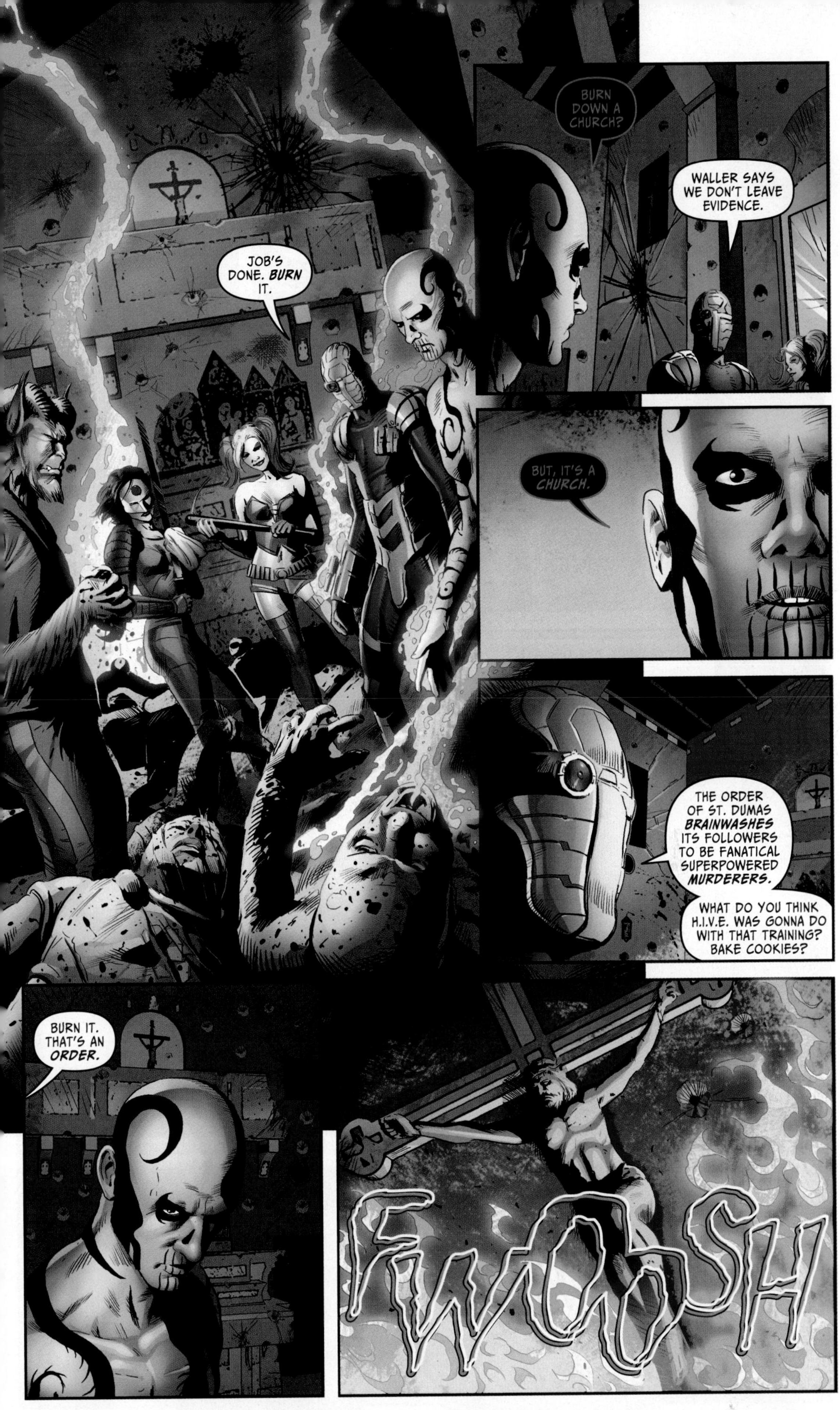
JOB'S DONE. BURN IT.
BURN DOWN A CHURCH?
WALLER SAYS WE DON'T LEAVE EVIDENCE.
BUT, IT'S A CHURCH.
THE ORDER OF ST. DUMAS BRAINWASHES ITS FOLLOWERS TO BE FANATICAL SUPERPOWERED MURDERERS.
WHAT DO YOU THINK H.I.V.E. WAS GONNA DO WITH THAT TRAINING? BAKE COOKIES?
BURN IT. THAT'S AN ORDER.
FWOOSH

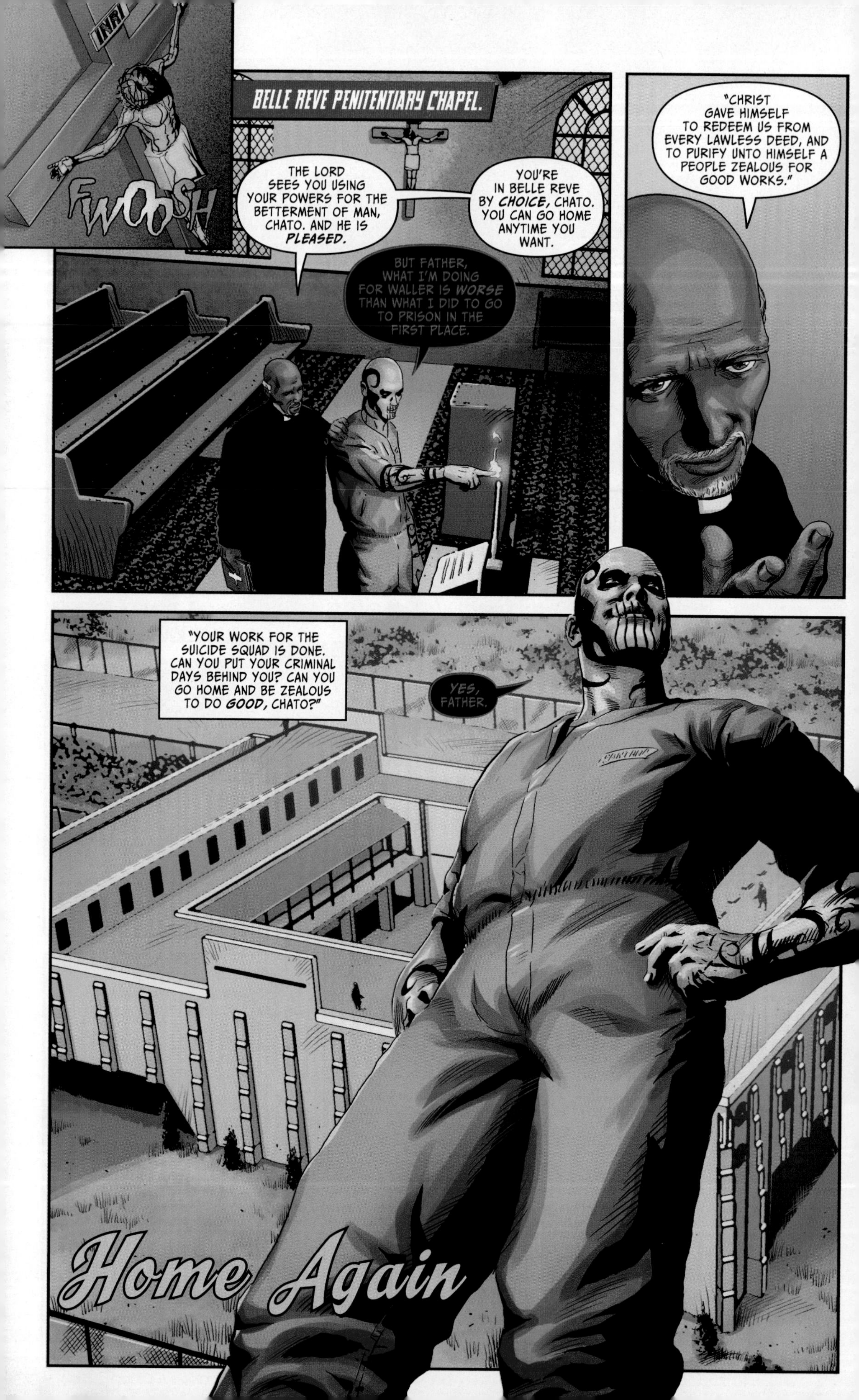
FWOOSH
BELLE REVE PENITENTIARY CHAPEL.
THE LORD SEES YOU USING YOUR POWERS FOR THE BETTERMENT OF MAN, CHATO. AND HE IS *PLEASED.*
YOU'RE IN BELLE REVE BY *CHOICE,* CHATO. YOU CAN GO HOME ANYTIME YOU WANT.
BUT FATHER, WHAT I'M DOING FOR WALLER IS *WORSE* THAN WHAT I DID TO GO TO PRISON IN THE FIRST PLACE.
"CHRIST GAVE HIMSELF TO REDEEM US FROM EVERY LAWLESS DEED, AND TO PURIFY UNTO HIMSELF A PEOPLE ZEALOUS FOR GOOD WORKS."
"YOUR WORK FOR THE SUICIDE SQUAD IS DONE. CAN YOU PUT YOUR CRIMINAL DAYS BEHIND YOU? CAN YOU GO HOME AND BE ZEALOUS TO DO *GOOD,* CHATO?"
YES, FATHER.
Home Again

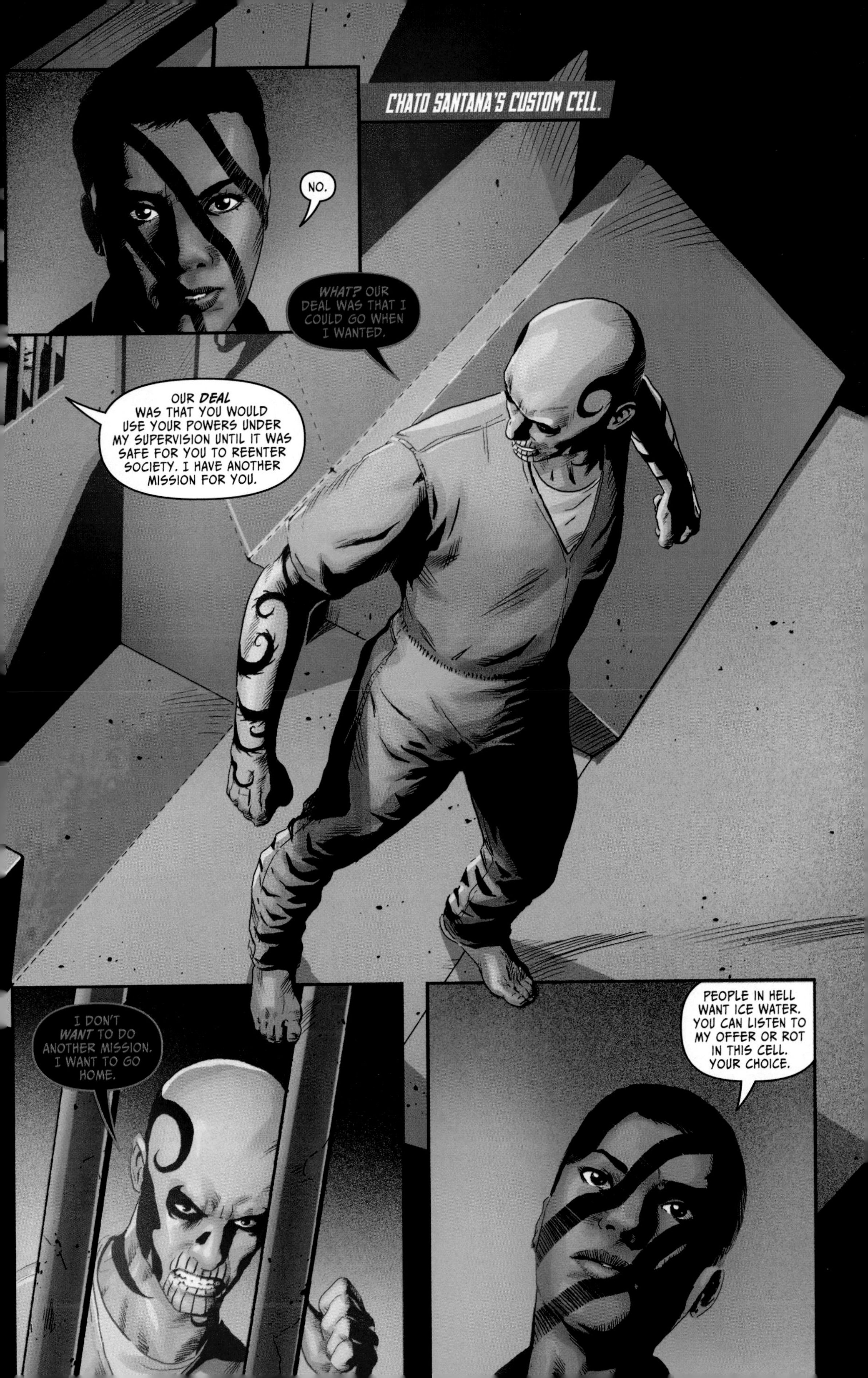
CHATO SANTANA'S CUSTOM CELL.
NO.
WHAT? OUR DEAL WAS THAT I COULD GO WHEN I WANTED.
OUR DEAL WAS THAT YOU WOULD USE YOUR POWERS UNDER MY SUPERVISION UNTIL IT WAS SAFE FOR YOU TO REENTER SOCIETY. I HAVE ANOTHER MISSION FOR YOU.
I DON'T WANT TO DO ANOTHER MISSION. I WANT TO GO HOME.
PEOPLE IN HELL WANT ICE WATER. YOU CAN LISTEN TO MY OFFER OR ROT IN THIS CELL. YOUR CHOICE.

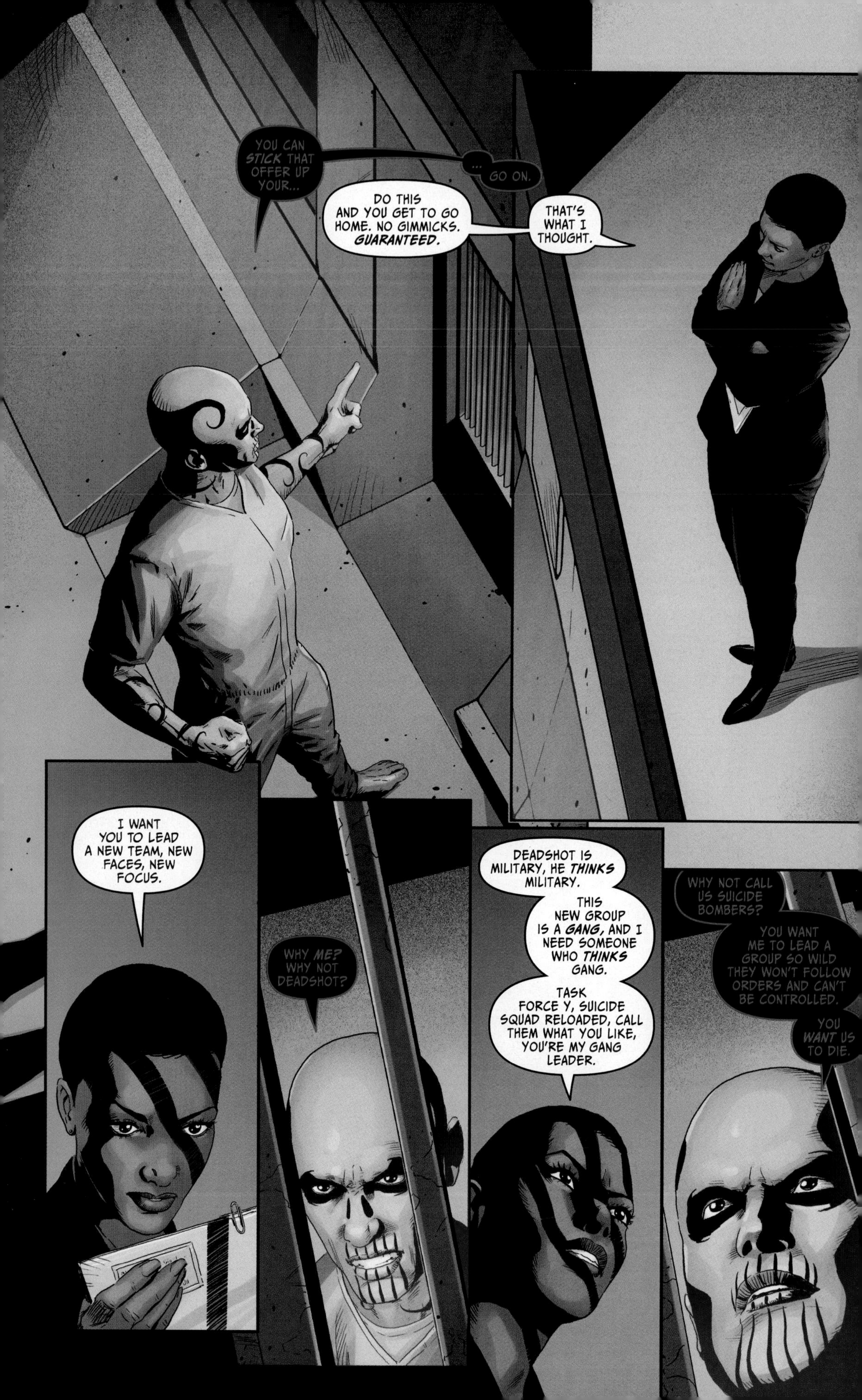

YOU CAN STICK THAT OFFER UP YOUR...
...
GO ON.
DO THIS AND YOU GET TO GO HOME. NO GIMMICKS. GUARANTEED.
THAT'S WHAT I THOUGHT.
I WANT YOU TO LEAD A NEW TEAM, NEW FACES, NEW FOCUS.
WHY ME? WHY NOT DEADSHOT?
DEADSHOT IS MILITARY, HE THINKS MILITARY.
THIS NEW GROUP IS A GANG, AND I NEED SOMEONE WHO THINKS GANG.
TASK FORCE Y, SUICIDE SQUAD RELOADED, CALL THEM WHAT YOU LIKE, YOU'RE MY GANG LEADER.
WHY NOT CALL US SUICIDE BOMBERS?
YOU WANT ME TO LEAD A GROUP SO WILD THEY WON'T FOLLOW ORDERS AND CAN'T BE CONTROLLED.
YOU WANT US TO DIE.

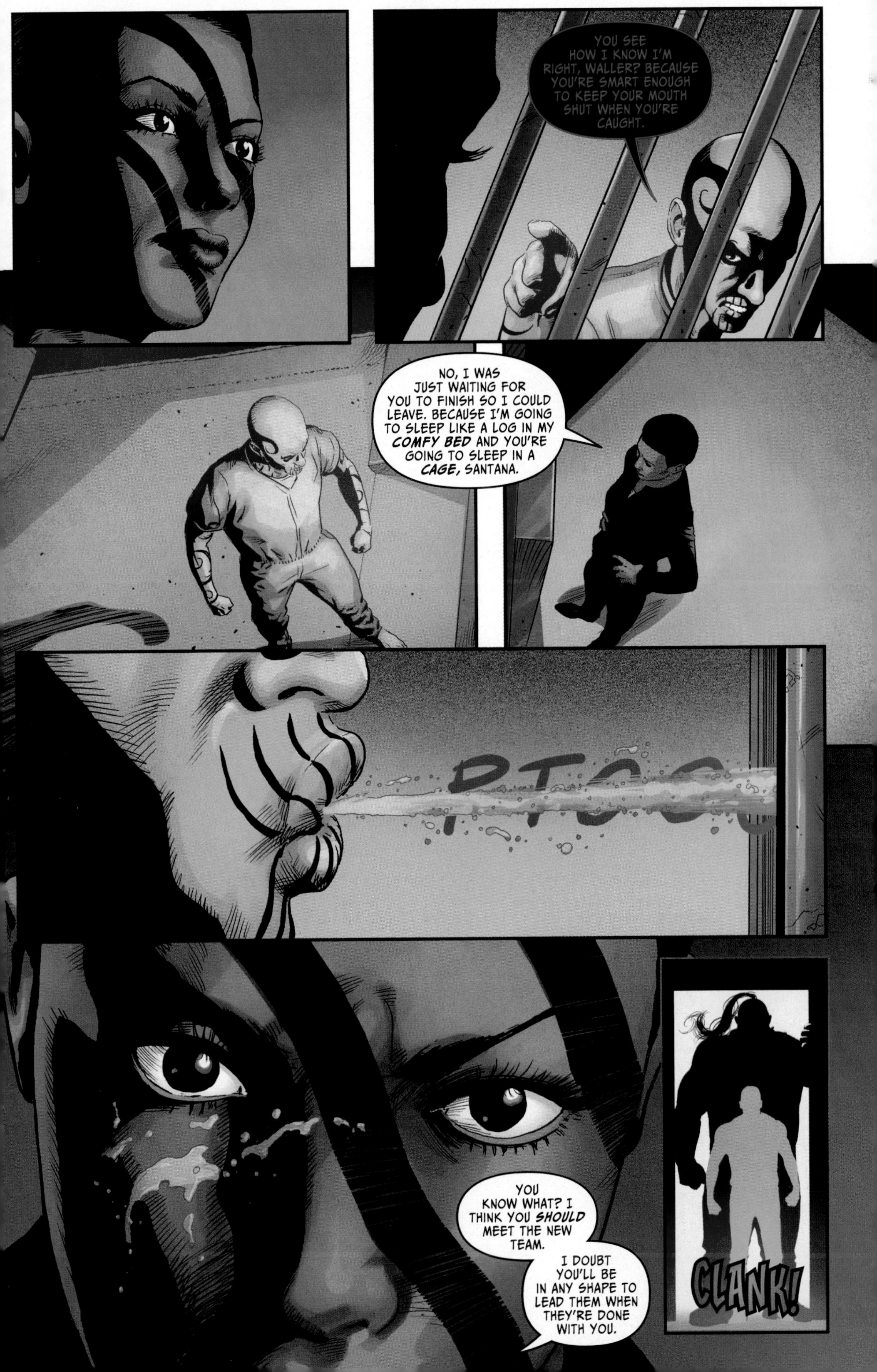
YOU SEE HOW I KNOW I'M RIGHT, WALLER? BECAUSE YOU'RE SMART ENOUGH TO KEEP YOUR MOUTH SHUT WHEN YOU'RE CAUGHT.
NO, I WAS JUST WAITING FOR YOU TO FINISH SO I COULD LEAVE. BECAUSE I'M GOING TO SLEEP LIKE A LOG IN MY COMFY BED AND YOU'RE GOING TO SLEEP IN A CAGE, SANTANA.
PTOO
YOU KNOW WHAT? I THINK YOU SHOULD MEET THE NEW TEAM.
I DOUBT YOU'LL BE IN ANY SHAPE TO LEAD THEM WHEN THEY'RE DONE WITH YOU.
CLANK!

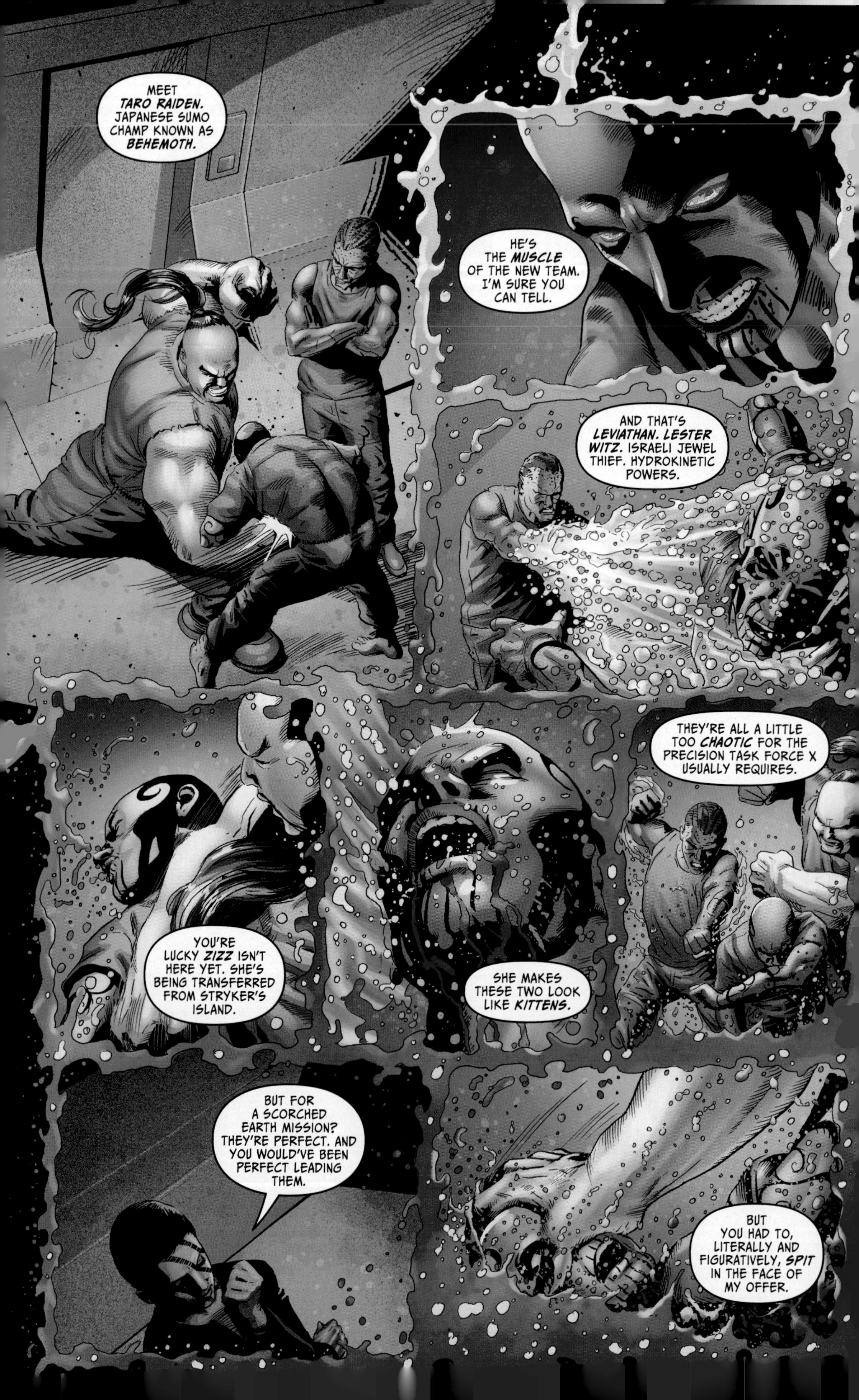
MEET *TARO RAIDEN.* JAPANESE SUMO CHAMP KNOWN AS *BEHEMOTH.*
HE'S THE *MUSCLE* OF THE NEW TEAM. I'M SURE YOU CAN TELL.
AND THAT'S *LEVIATHAN. LESTER WITZ.* ISRAELI JEWEL THIEF. HYDROKINETIC POWERS.
YOU'RE LUCKY *ZIZZ* ISN'T HERE YET. SHE'S BEING TRANSFERRED FROM STRYKER'S ISLAND.
SHE MAKES THESE TWO LOOK LIKE *KITTENS.*
THEY'RE ALL A LITTLE TOO *CHAOTIC* FOR THE PRECISION TASK FORCE X USUALLY REQUIRES.
BUT FOR A SCORCHED EARTH MISSION? THEY'RE PERFECT. AND YOU WOULD'VE BEEN PERFECT LEADING THEM.
BUT YOU HAD TO, LITERALLY AND FIGURATIVELY, *SPIT* IN THE FACE OF MY OFFER.

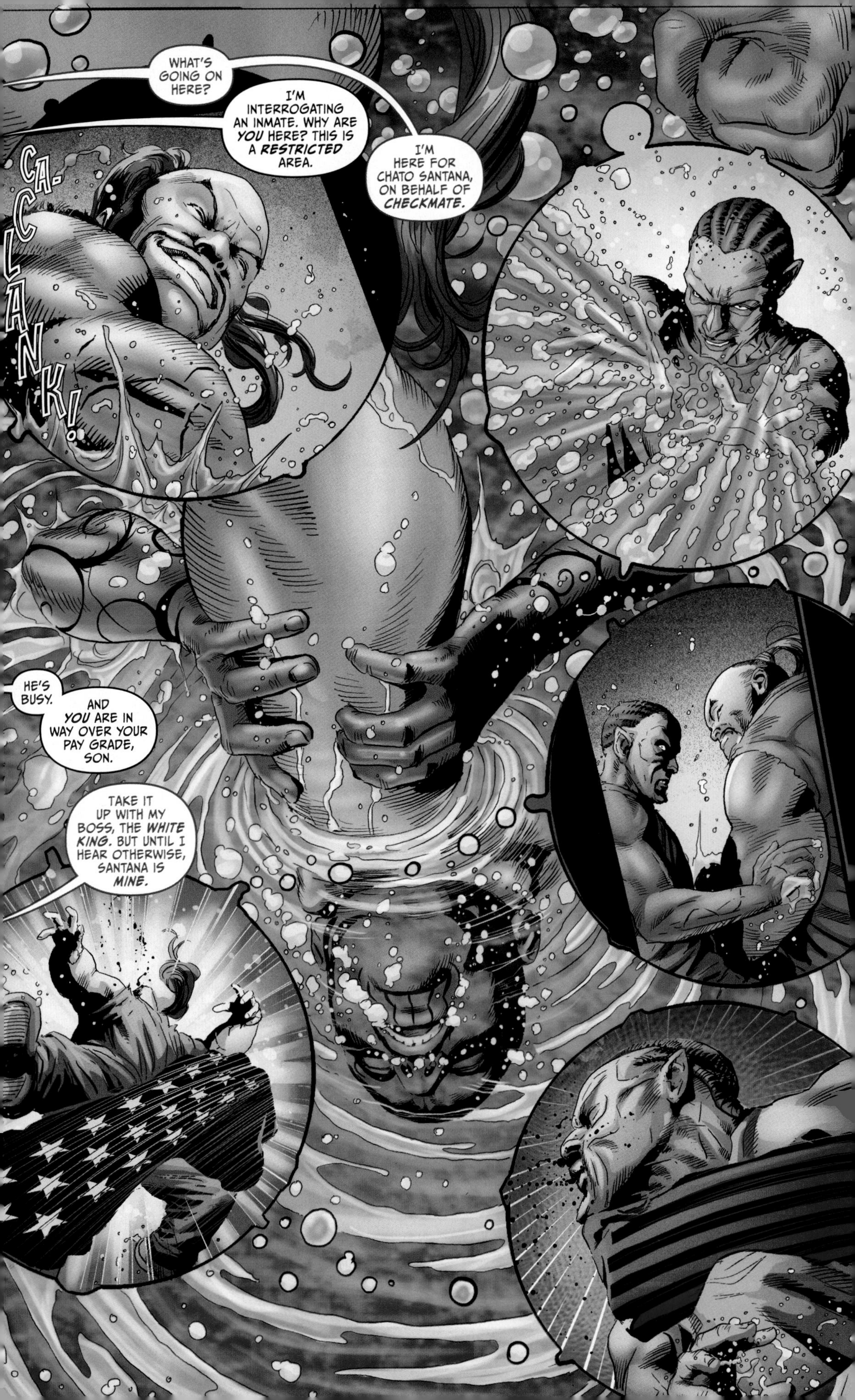
WHAT'S GOING ON HERE?
I'M INTERROGATING AN INMATE. WHY ARE YOU HERE? THIS IS A RESTRICTED AREA.
I'M HERE FOR CHATO SANTANA, ON BEHALF OF CHECKMATE.
CA-CLANK!
HE'S BUSY.
AND YOU ARE IN WAY OVER YOUR PAY GRADE, SON.
TAKE IT UP WITH MY BOSS, THE WHITE KING. BUT UNTIL I HEAR OTHERWISE, SANTANA IS MINE.

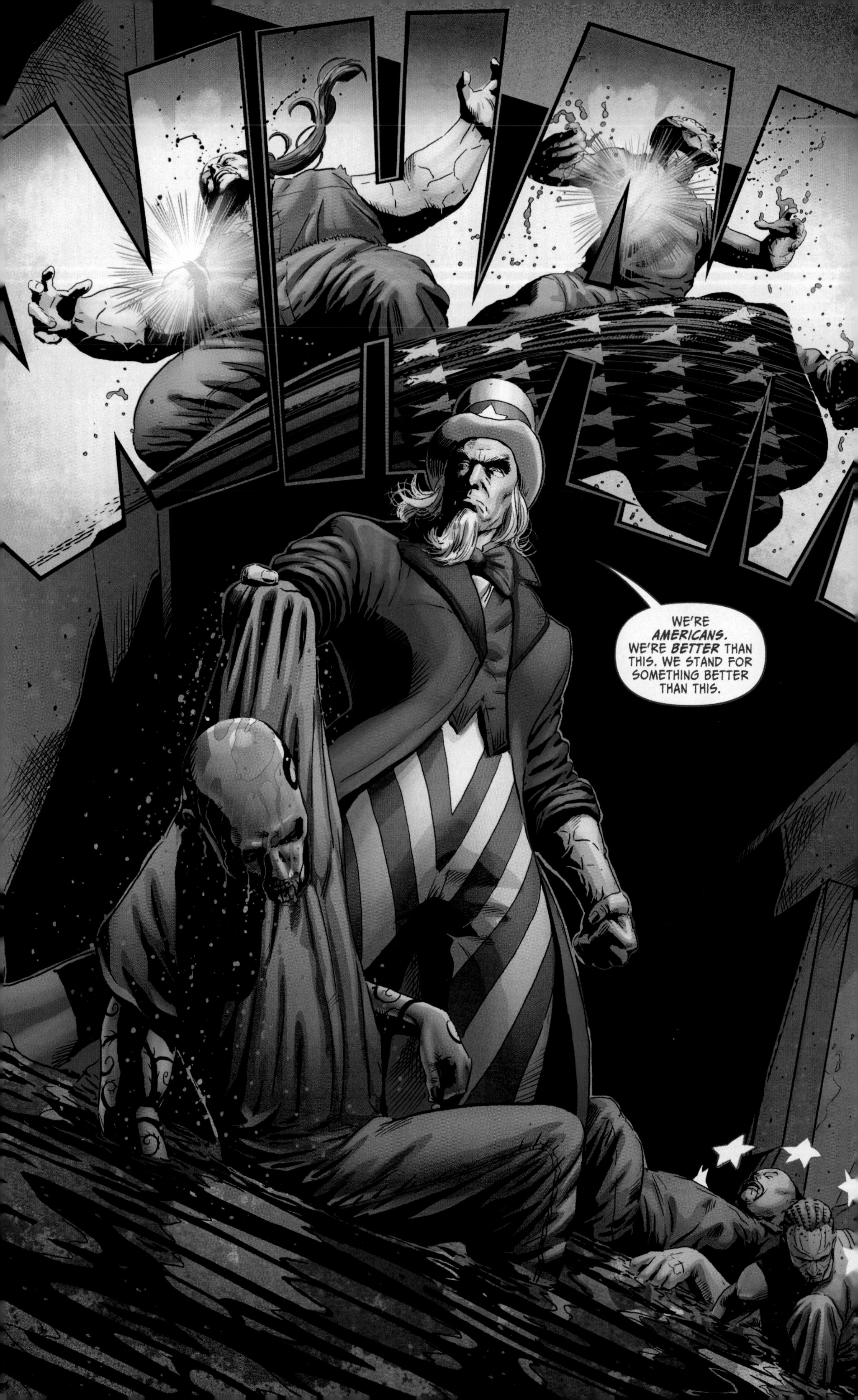
WE'RE *AMERICANS.* WE'RE *BETTER* THAN THIS. WE STAND FOR SOMETHING BETTER THAN THIS.

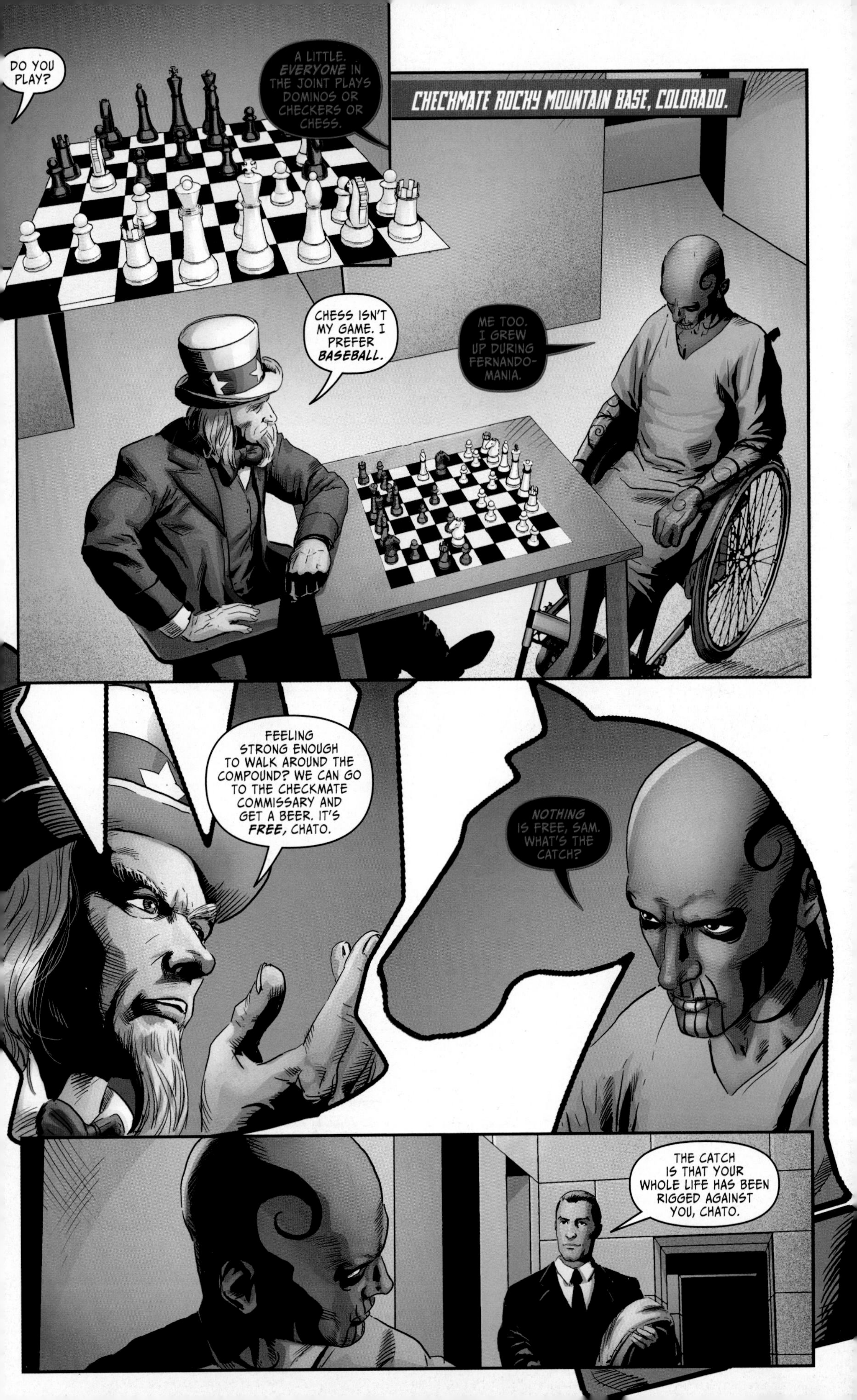
DO YOU PLAY?
A LITTLE. EVERYONE IN THE JOINT PLAYS DOMINOS OR CHECKERS OR CHESS.
CHECKMATE ROCKY MOUNTAIN BASE, COLORADO.
CHESS ISN'T MY GAME. I PREFER BASEBALL.
ME TOO. I GREW UP DURING FERNANDO-MANIA.
FEELING STRONG ENOUGH TO WALK AROUND THE COMPOUND? WE CAN GO TO THE CHECKMATE COMMISSARY AND GET A BEER. IT'S FREE, CHATO.
NOTHING IS FREE, SAM. WHAT'S THE CATCH?
THE CATCH IS THAT YOUR WHOLE LIFE HAS BEEN RIGGED AGAINST YOU, CHATO.

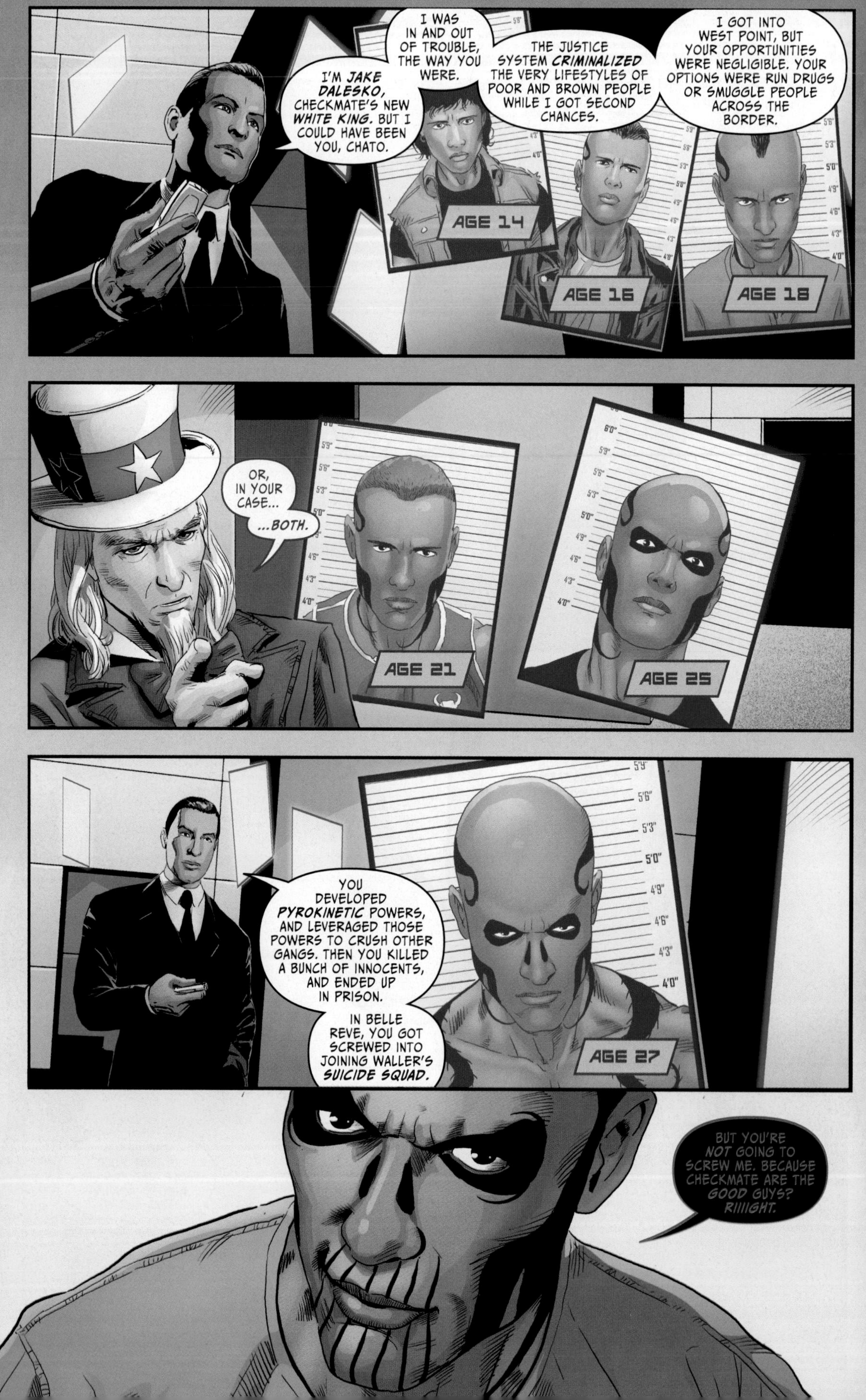
I'M JAKE DALESKO, CHECKMATE'S NEW WHITE KING. BUT I COULD HAVE BEEN YOU, CHATO.
I WAS IN AND OUT OF TROUBLE, THE WAY YOU WERE.
THE JUSTICE SYSTEM CRIMINALIZED THE VERY LIFESTYLES OF POOR AND BROWN PEOPLE WHILE I GOT SECOND CHANCES.
I GOT INTO WEST POINT, BUT YOUR OPPORTUNITIES WERE NEGLIGIBLE. YOUR OPTIONS WERE RUN DRUGS OR SMUGGLE PEOPLE ACROSS THE BORDER.
AGE 14
AGE 16
AGE 18
OR, IN YOUR CASE...
...BOTH.
AGE 21
AGE 25
YOU DEVELOPED PYROKINETIC POWERS, AND LEVERAGED THOSE POWERS TO CRUSH OTHER GANGS. THEN YOU KILLED A BUNCH OF INNOCENTS, AND ENDED UP IN PRISON.
IN BELLE REVE, YOU GOT SCREWED INTO JOINING WALLER'S SUICIDE SQUAD.
AGE 27
BUT YOU'RE NOT GOING TO SCREW ME. BECAUSE CHECKMATE ARE THE GOOD GUYS? RIIIGHT.

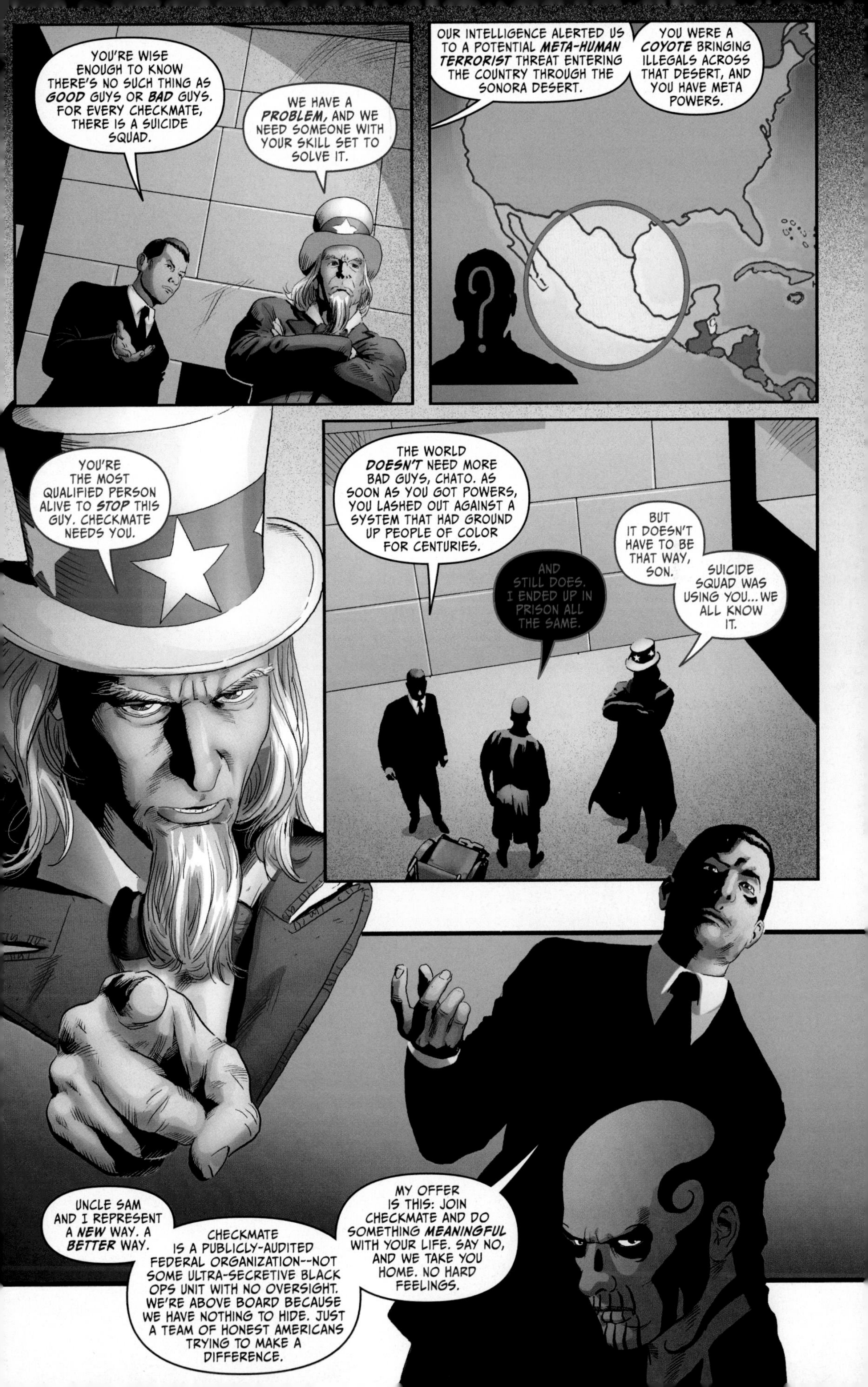
YOU'RE WISE ENOUGH TO KNOW THERE'S NO SUCH THING AS GOOD GUYS OR BAD GUYS. FOR EVERY CHECKMATE, THERE IS A SUICIDE SQUAD.
WE HAVE A PROBLEM, AND WE NEED SOMEONE WITH YOUR SKILL SET TO SOLVE IT.
OUR INTELLIGENCE ALERTED US TO A POTENTIAL META-HUMAN TERRORIST THREAT ENTERING THE COUNTRY THROUGH THE SONORA DESERT.
YOU WERE A COYOTE BRINGING ILLEGALS ACROSS THAT DESERT, AND YOU HAVE META POWERS.
YOU'RE THE MOST QUALIFIED PERSON ALIVE TO STOP THIS GUY. CHECKMATE NEEDS YOU.
THE WORLD DOESN'T NEED MORE BAD GUYS, CHATO. AS SOON AS YOU GOT POWERS, YOU LASHED OUT AGAINST A SYSTEM THAT HAD GROUND UP PEOPLE OF COLOR FOR CENTURIES.
AND STILL DOES. I ENDED UP IN PRISON ALL THE SAME.
BUT IT DOESN'T HAVE TO BE THAT WAY, SON.
SUICIDE SQUAD WAS USING YOU...WE ALL KNOW IT.
UNCLE SAM AND I REPRESENT A NEW WAY. A BETTER WAY.
CHECKMATE IS A PUBLICLY-AUDITED FEDERAL ORGANIZATION--NOT SOME ULTRA-SECRETIVE BLACK OPS UNIT WITH NO OVERSIGHT. WE'RE ABOVE BOARD BECAUSE WE HAVE NOTHING TO HIDE. JUST A TEAM OF HONEST AMERICANS TRYING TO MAKE A DIFFERENCE.
MY OFFER IS THIS: JOIN CHECKMATE AND DO SOMETHING MEANINGFUL WITH YOUR LIFE. SAY NO, AND WE TAKE YOU HOME. NO HARD FEELINGS.

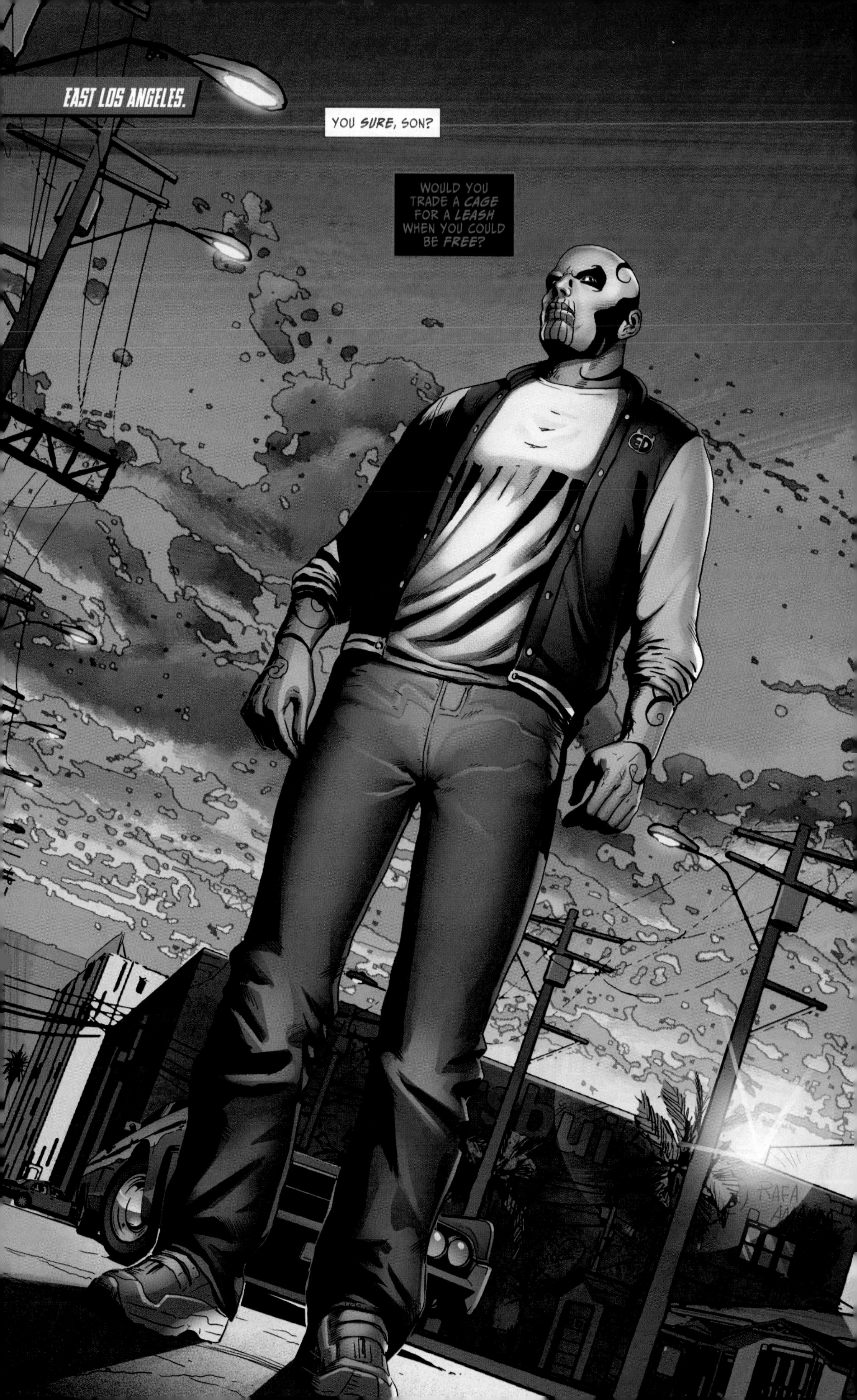
EAST LOS ANGELES.
YOU SURE, SON?
WOULD YOU TRADE A CAGE FOR A LEASH WHEN YOU COULD BE FREE?

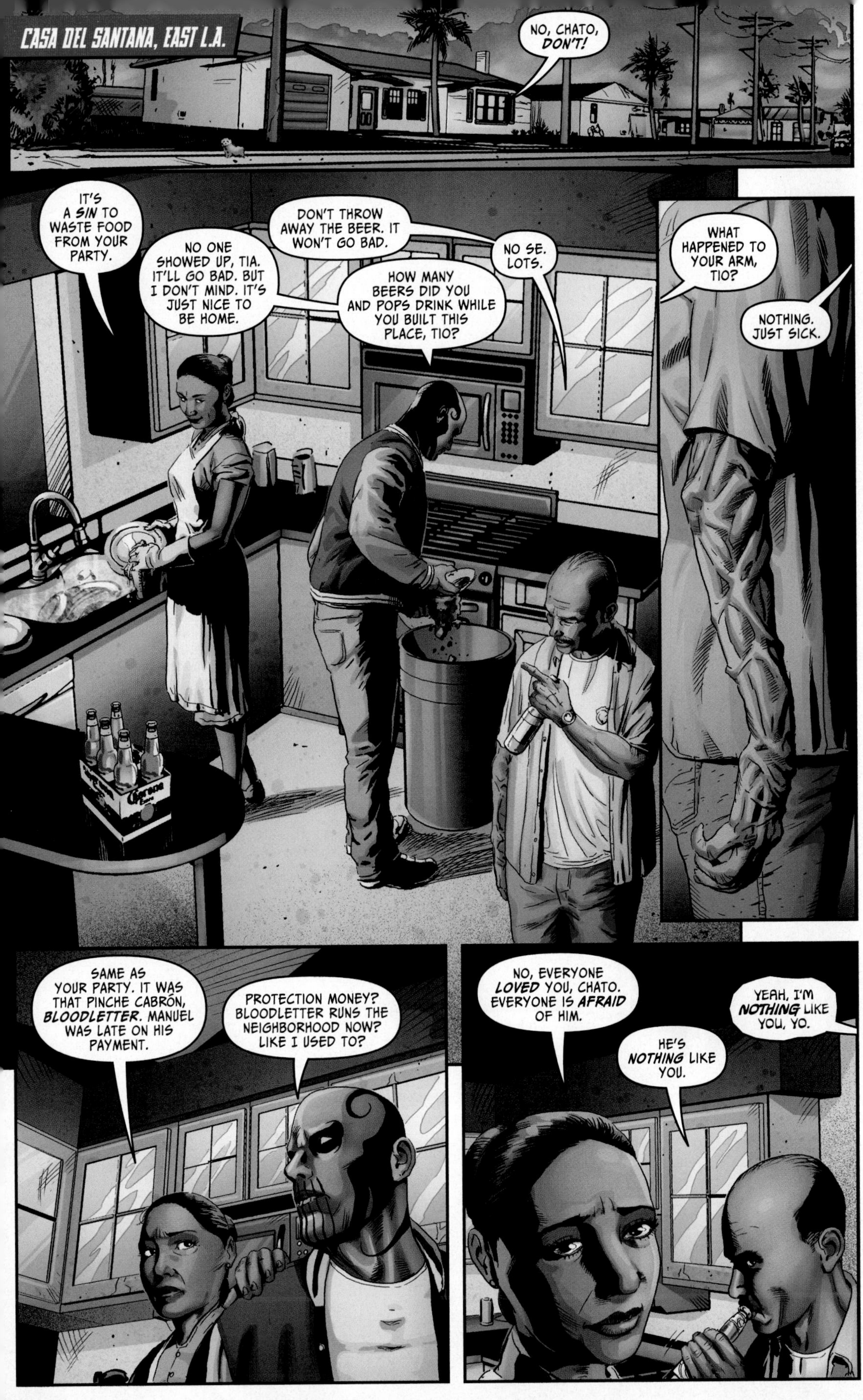
CASA DEL SANTANA, EAST L.A.
NO, CHATO, DON'T!
IT'S A SIN TO WASTE FOOD FROM YOUR PARTY.
NO ONE SHOWED UP, TIA. IT'LL GO BAD. BUT I DON'T MIND. IT'S JUST NICE TO BE HOME.
DON'T THROW AWAY THE BEER. IT WON'T GO BAD.
HOW MANY BEERS DID YOU AND POPS DRINK WHILE YOU BUILT THIS PLACE, TIO?
NO SE. LOTS.
WHAT HAPPENED TO YOUR ARM, TIO?
NOTHING. JUST SICK.
SAME AS YOUR PARTY. IT WAS THAT PINCHE CABRÓN, BLOODLETTER. MANUEL WAS LATE ON HIS PAYMENT.
PROTECTION MONEY? BLOODLETTER RUNS THE NEIGHBORHOOD NOW? LIKE I USED TO?
NO, EVERYONE LOVED YOU, CHATO. EVERYONE IS AFRAID OF HIM.
HE'S NOTHING LIKE YOU.
YEAH, I'M NOTHING LIKE YOU, YO.

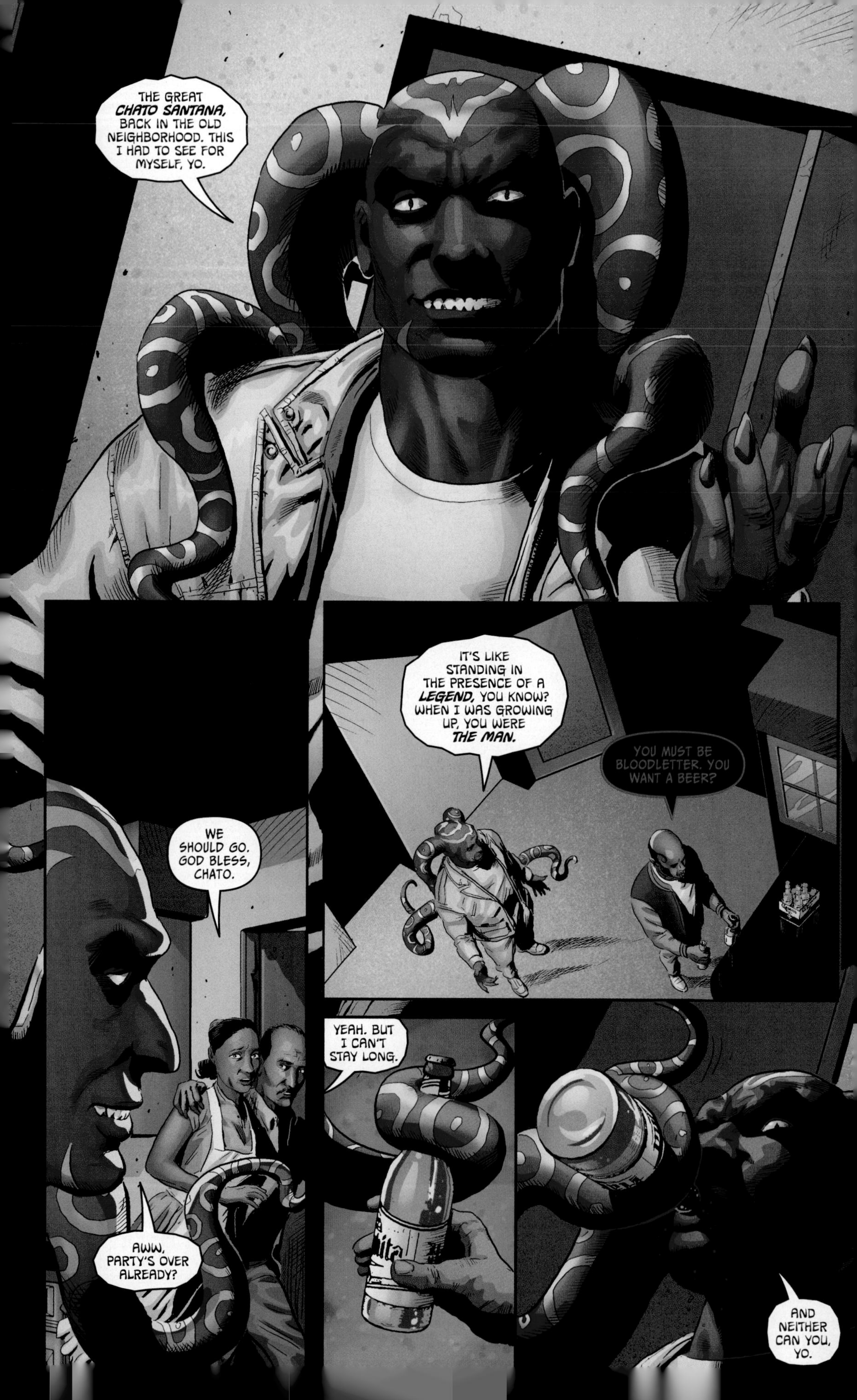
THE GREAT CHATO SANTANA, BACK IN THE OLD NEIGHBORHOOD. THIS I HAD TO SEE FOR MYSELF, YO.
WE SHOULD GO. GOD BLESS, CHATO.
AWW, PARTY'S OVER ALREADY?
IT'S LIKE STANDING IN THE PRESENCE OF A LEGEND, YOU KNOW? WHEN I WAS GROWING UP, YOU WERE THE MAN.
YOU MUST BE BLOODLETTER. YOU WANT A BEER?
YEAH. BUT I CAN'T STAY LONG.
AND NEITHER CAN YOU, YO.

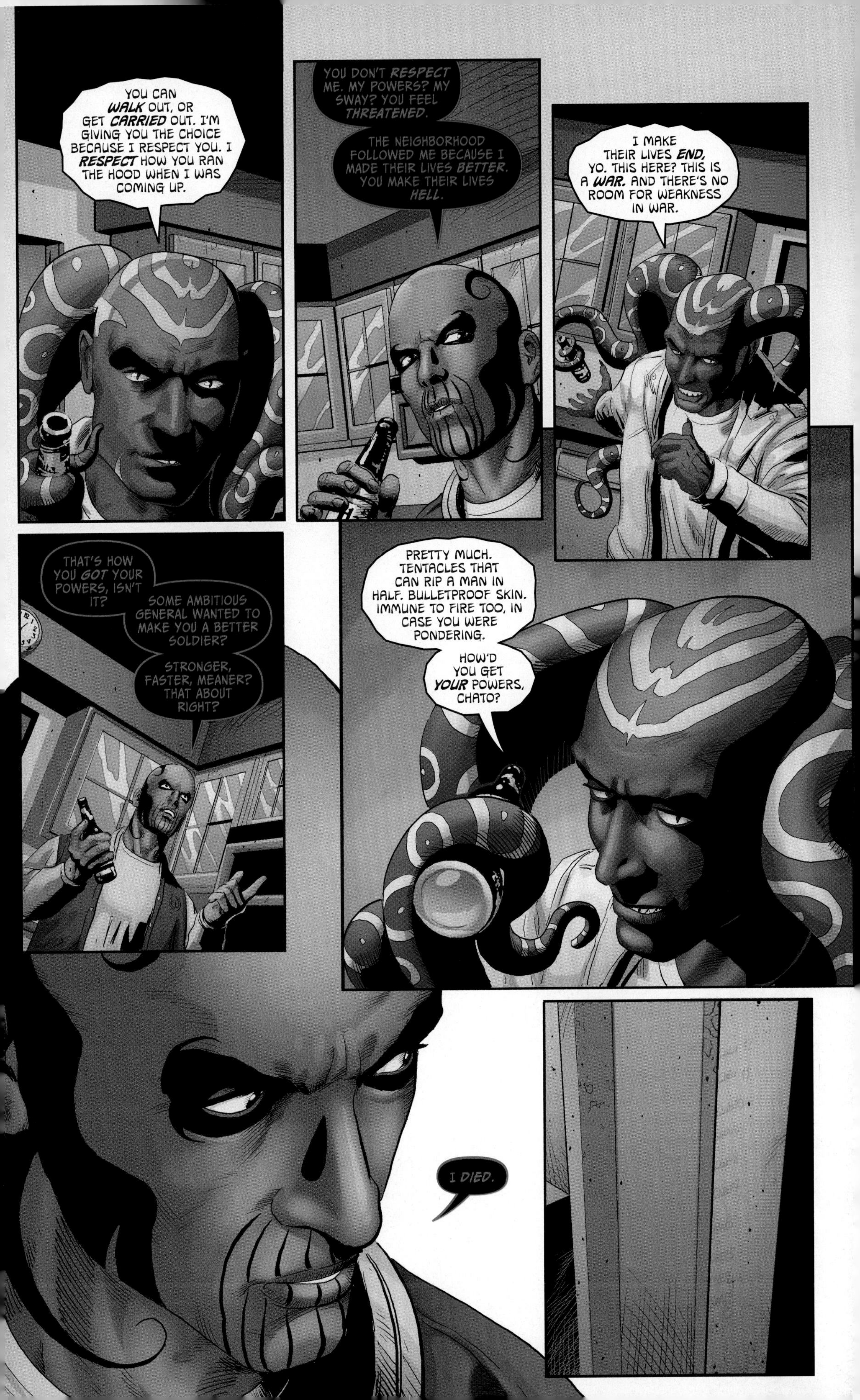
YOU CAN WALK OUT, OR GET CARRIED OUT. I'M GIVING YOU THE CHOICE BECAUSE I RESPECT YOU. I RESPECT HOW YOU RAN THE HOOD WHEN I WAS COMING UP.
YOU DON'T RESPECT ME. MY POWERS? MY SWAY? YOU FEEL THREATENED.
THE NEIGHBORHOOD FOLLOWED ME BECAUSE I MADE THEIR LIVES BETTER. YOU MAKE THEIR LIVES HELL.
I MAKE THEIR LIVES END, YO. THIS HERE? THIS IS A WAR. AND THERE'S NO ROOM FOR WEAKNESS IN WAR.
THAT'S HOW YOU GOT YOUR POWERS, ISN'T IT?
SOME AMBITIOUS GENERAL WANTED TO MAKE YOU A BETTER SOLDIER?
STRONGER, FASTER, MEANER? THAT ABOUT RIGHT?
PRETTY MUCH. TENTACLES THAT CAN RIP A MAN IN HALF. BULLETPROOF SKIN. IMMUNE TO FIRE TOO, IN CASE YOU WERE PONDERING.
HOW'D YOU GET YOUR POWERS, CHATO?
I DIED.

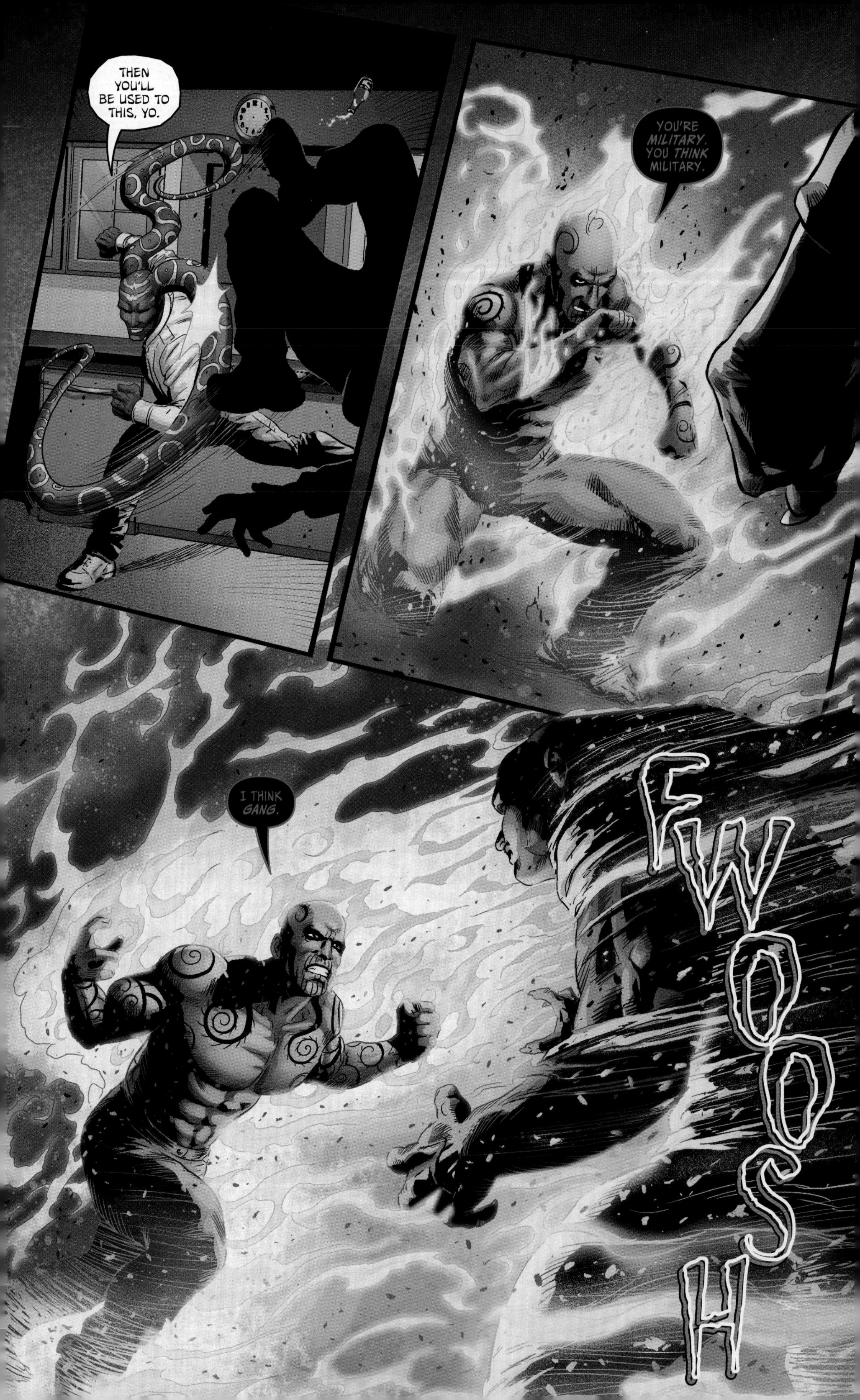
THEN YOU'LL BE USED TO THIS, YO.
YOU'RE *MILITARY*. YOU *THINK* MILITARY.
I THINK *GANG*.
FWOOSH

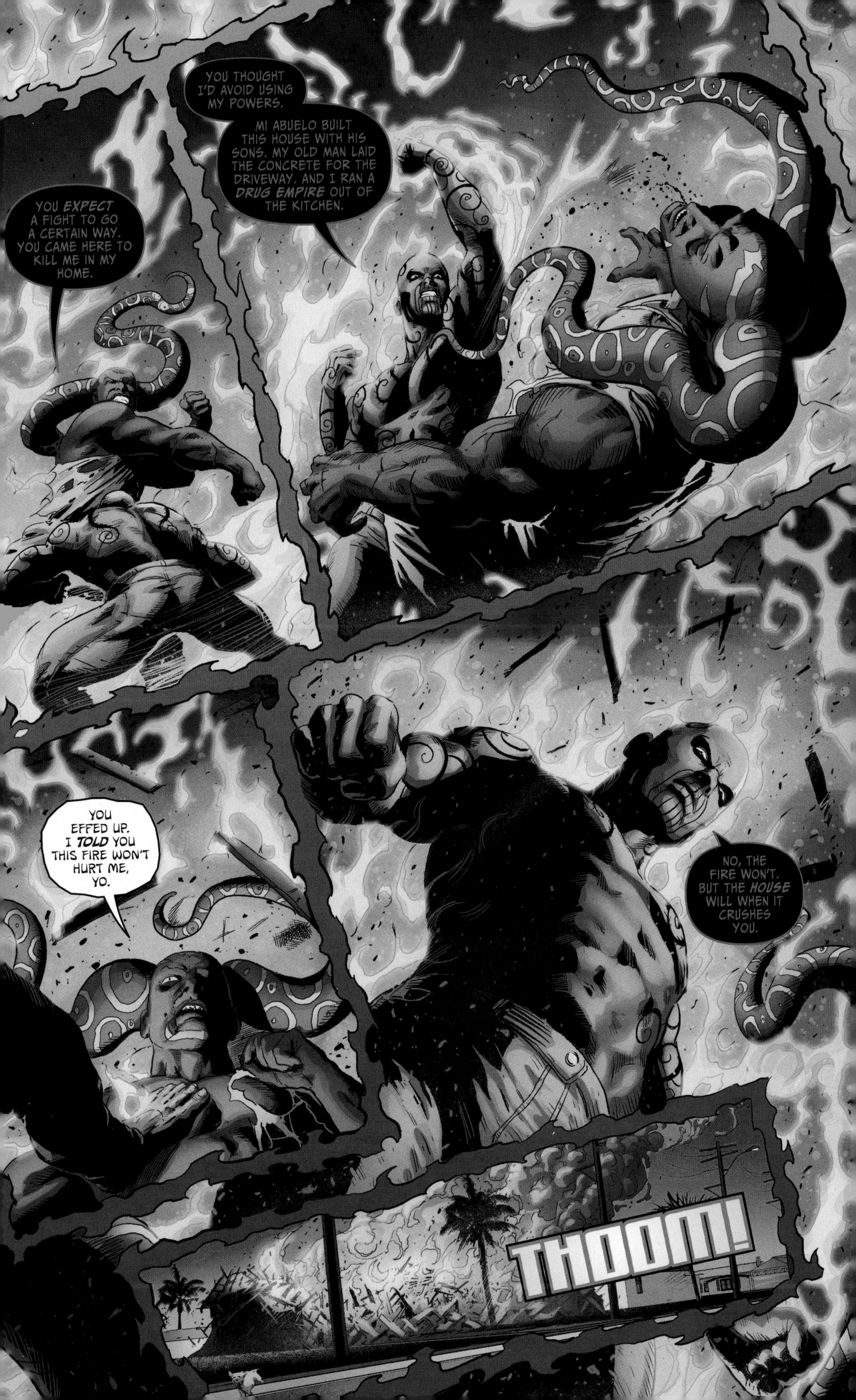
YOU EXPECT A FIGHT TO GO A CERTAIN WAY. YOU CAME HERE TO KILL ME IN MY HOME.
YOU THOUGHT I'D AVOID USING MY POWERS.
MI ABUELO BUILT THIS HOUSE WITH HIS SONS. MY OLD MAN LAID THE CONCRETE FOR THE DRIVEWAY. AND I RAN A DRUG EMPIRE OUT OF THE KITCHEN.
YOU EFFED UP. I TOLD YOU THIS FIRE WON'T HURT ME, YO.
NO, THE FIRE WON'T. BUT THE HOUSE WILL WHEN IT CRUSHES YOU.
THOOM!

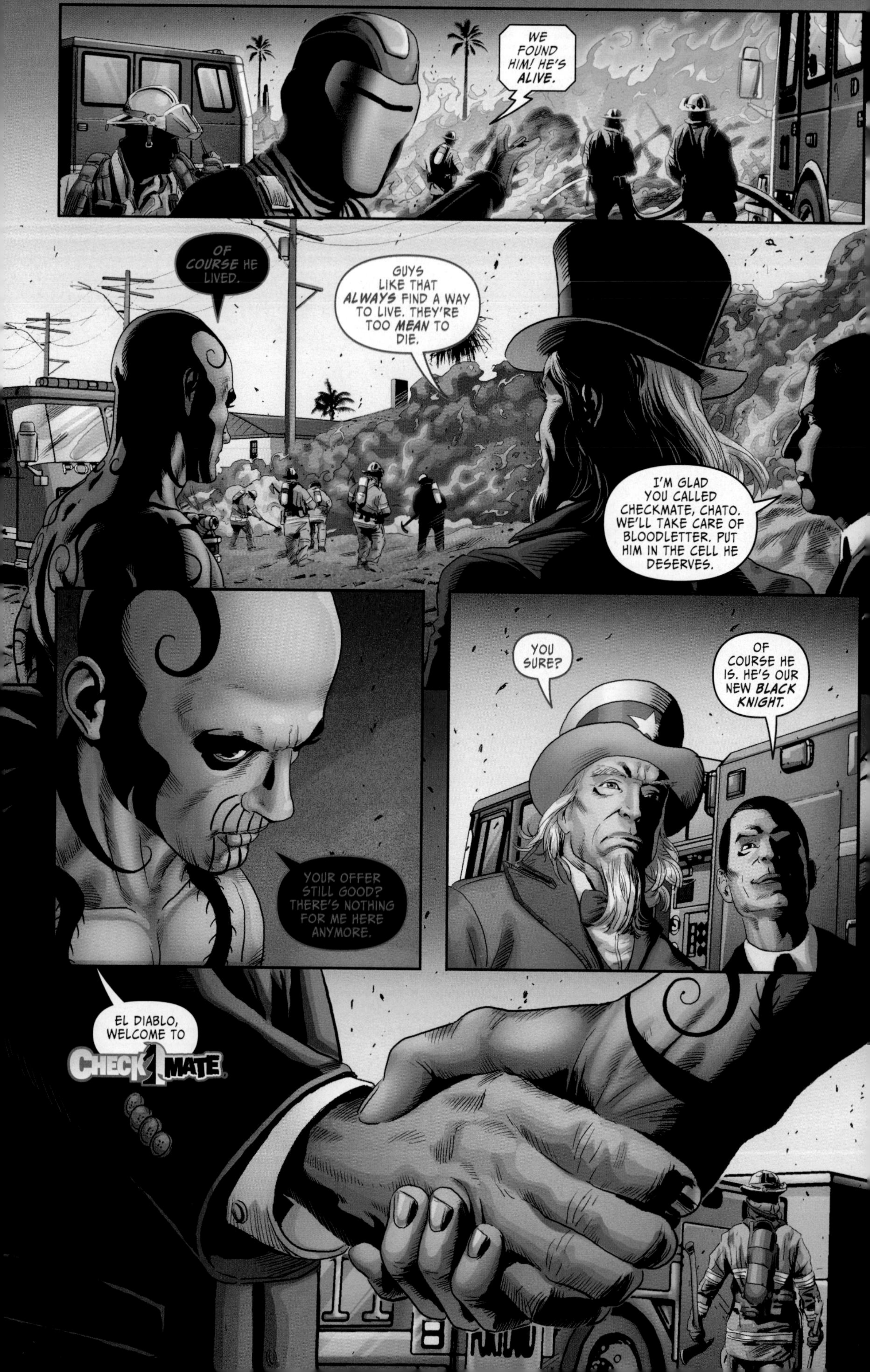
WE FOUND HIM! HE'S ALIVE.
OF COURSE HE LIVED.
GUYS LIKE THAT ALWAYS FIND A WAY TO LIVE. THEY'RE TOO MEAN TO DIE.
I'M GLAD YOU CALLED CHECKMATE, CHATO. WE'LL TAKE CARE OF BLOODLETTER. PUT HIM IN THE CELL HE DESERVES.
YOUR OFFER STILL GOOD? THERE'S NOTHING FOR ME HERE ANYMORE.
YOU SURE?
OF COURSE HE IS. HE'S OUR NEW BLACK KNIGHT.
EL DIABLO, WELCOME TO
CHECKMATE

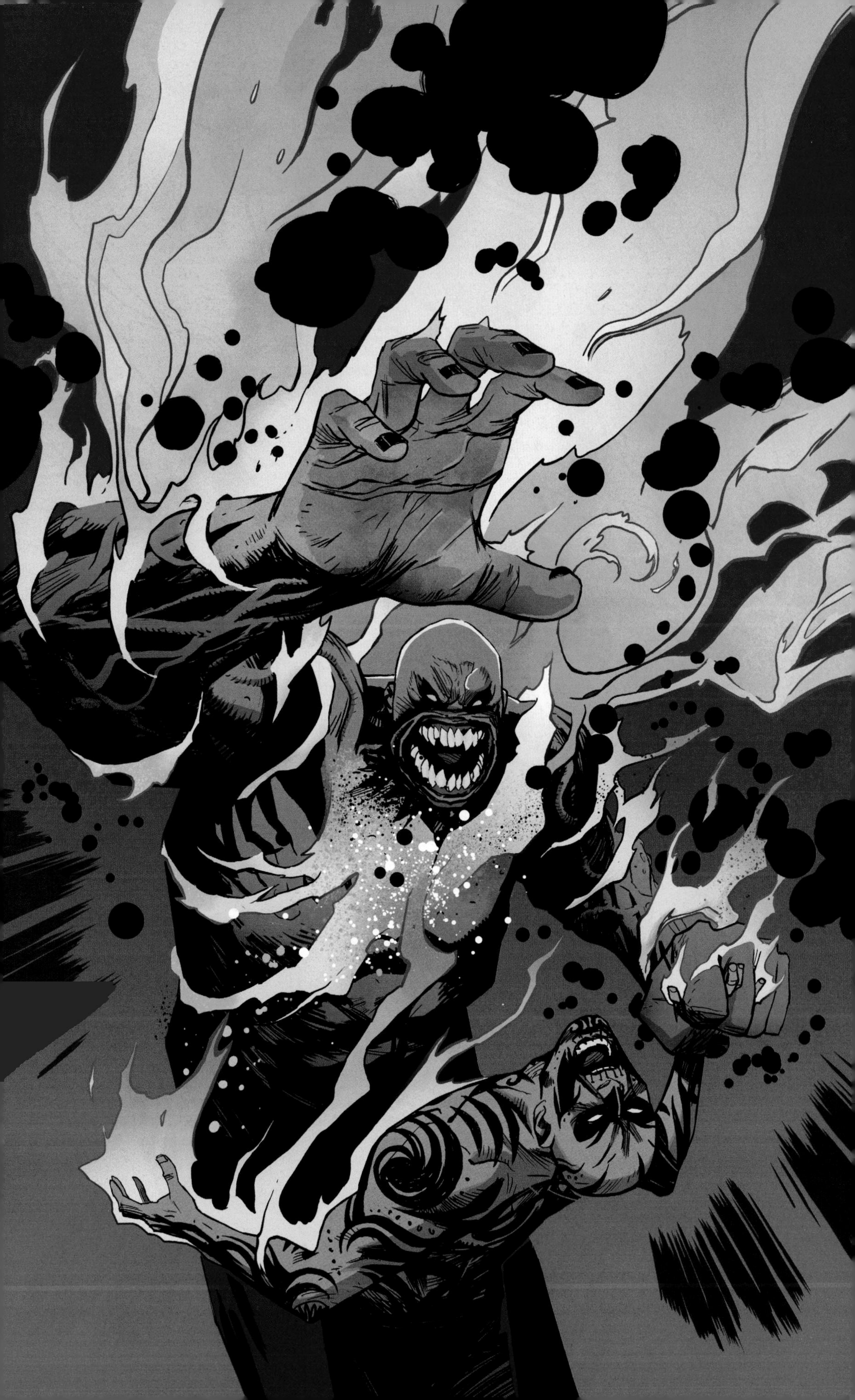

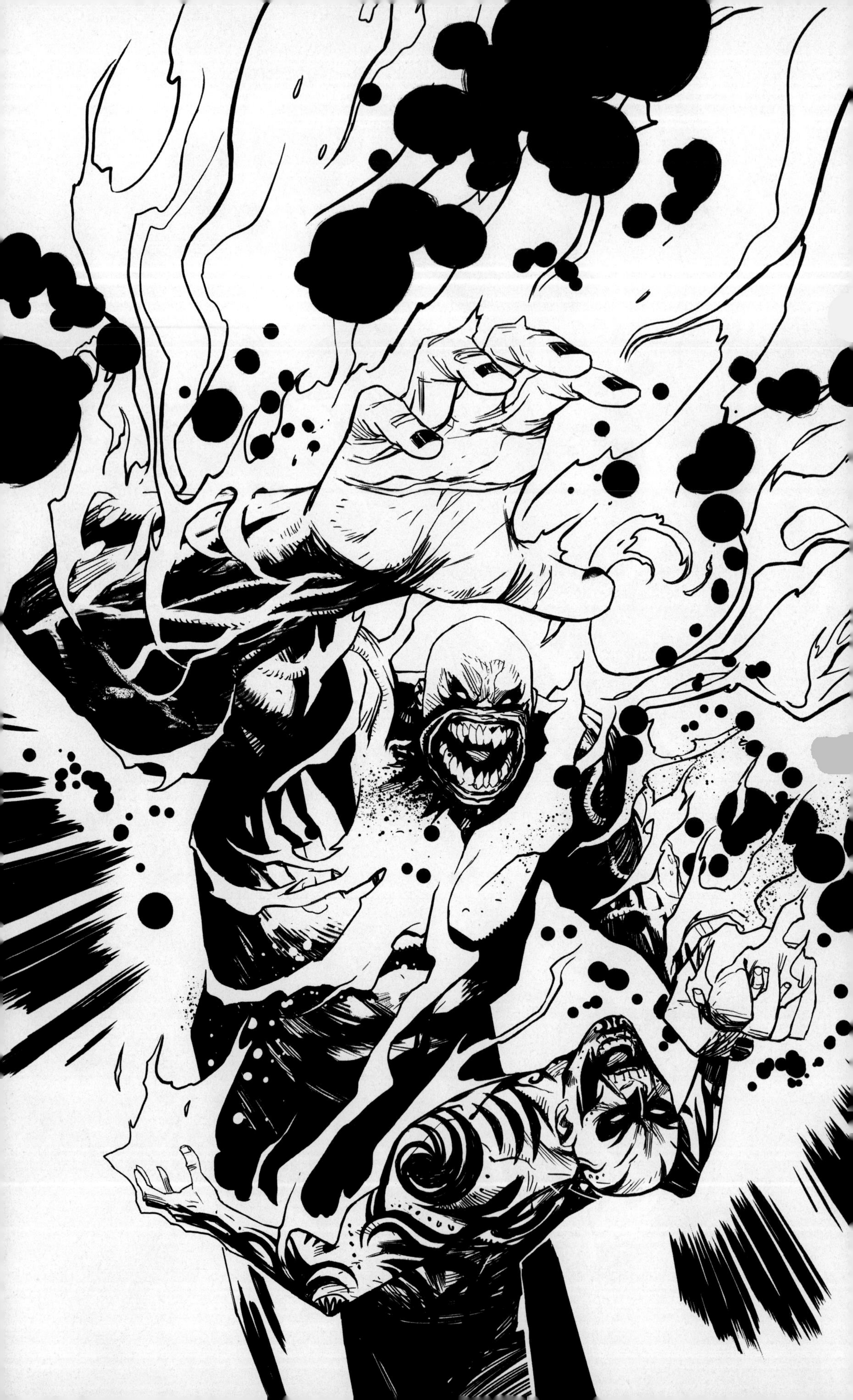

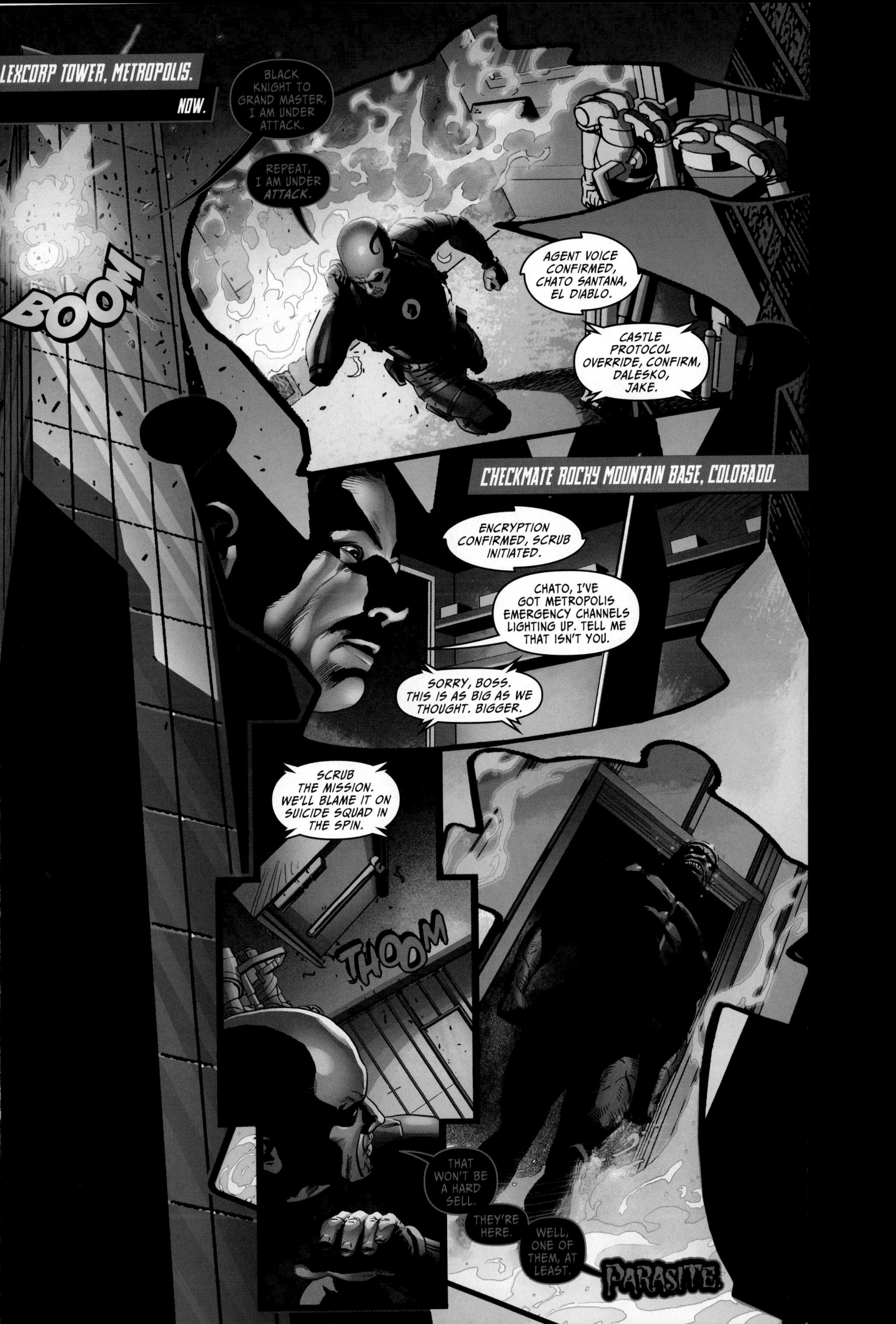
LEXCORP TOWER, METROPOLIS.
NOW.
BLACK KNIGHT TO GRAND MASTER, I AM UNDER ATTACK.
REPEAT, I AM UNDER ATTACK.
BOOM
AGENT VOICE CONFIRMED, CHATO SANTANA, EL DIABLO.
CASTLE PROTOCOL OVERRIDE, CONFIRM, DALESKO, JAKE.
CHECKMATE ROCKY MOUNTAIN BASE, COLORADO.
ENCRYPTION CONFIRMED, SCRUB INITIATED.
CHATO, I'VE GOT METROPOLIS EMERGENCY CHANNELS LIGHTING UP. TELL ME THAT ISN'T YOU.
SORRY, BOSS. THIS IS AS BIG AS WE THOUGHT. BIGGER.
SCRUB THE MISSION. WE'LL BLAME IT ON SUICIDE SQUAD IN THE SPIN.
THOOM
THAT WON'T BE A HARD SELL.
THEY'RE HERE.
WELL, ONE OF THEM, AT LEAST.
PARASITE.

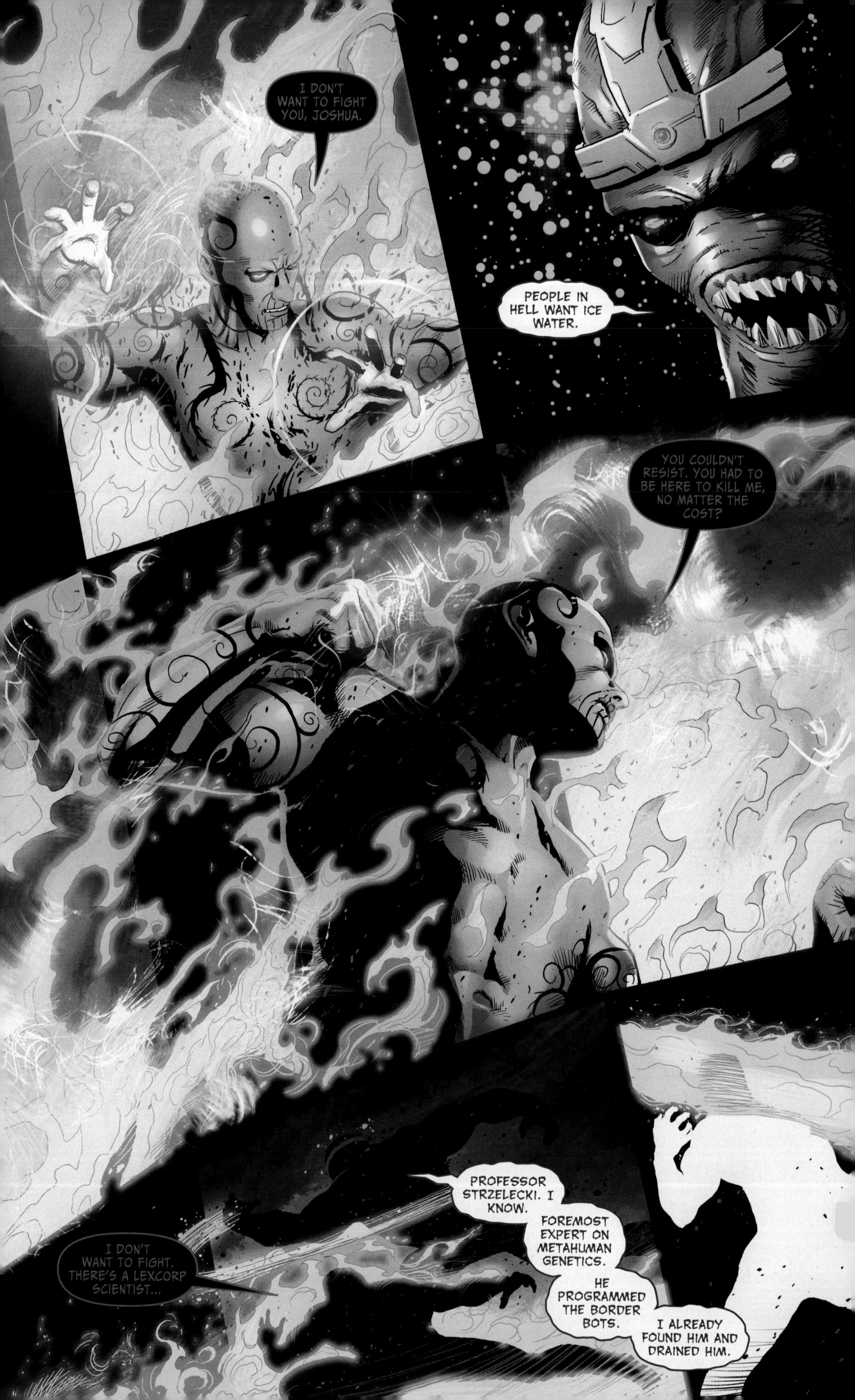
I DON'T WANT TO FIGHT YOU, JOSHUA.
PEOPLE IN HELL WANT ICE WATER.
YOU COULDN'T RESIST. YOU HAD TO BE HERE TO KILL ME, NO MATTER THE COST?
I DON'T WANT TO FIGHT. THERE'S A LEXCORP SCIENTIST...
PROFESSOR STRZELECKI. I KNOW.
FOREMOST EXPERT ON METAHUMAN GENETICS.
HE PROGRAMMED THE BORDER BOTS.
I ALREADY FOUND HIM AND DRAINED HIM.

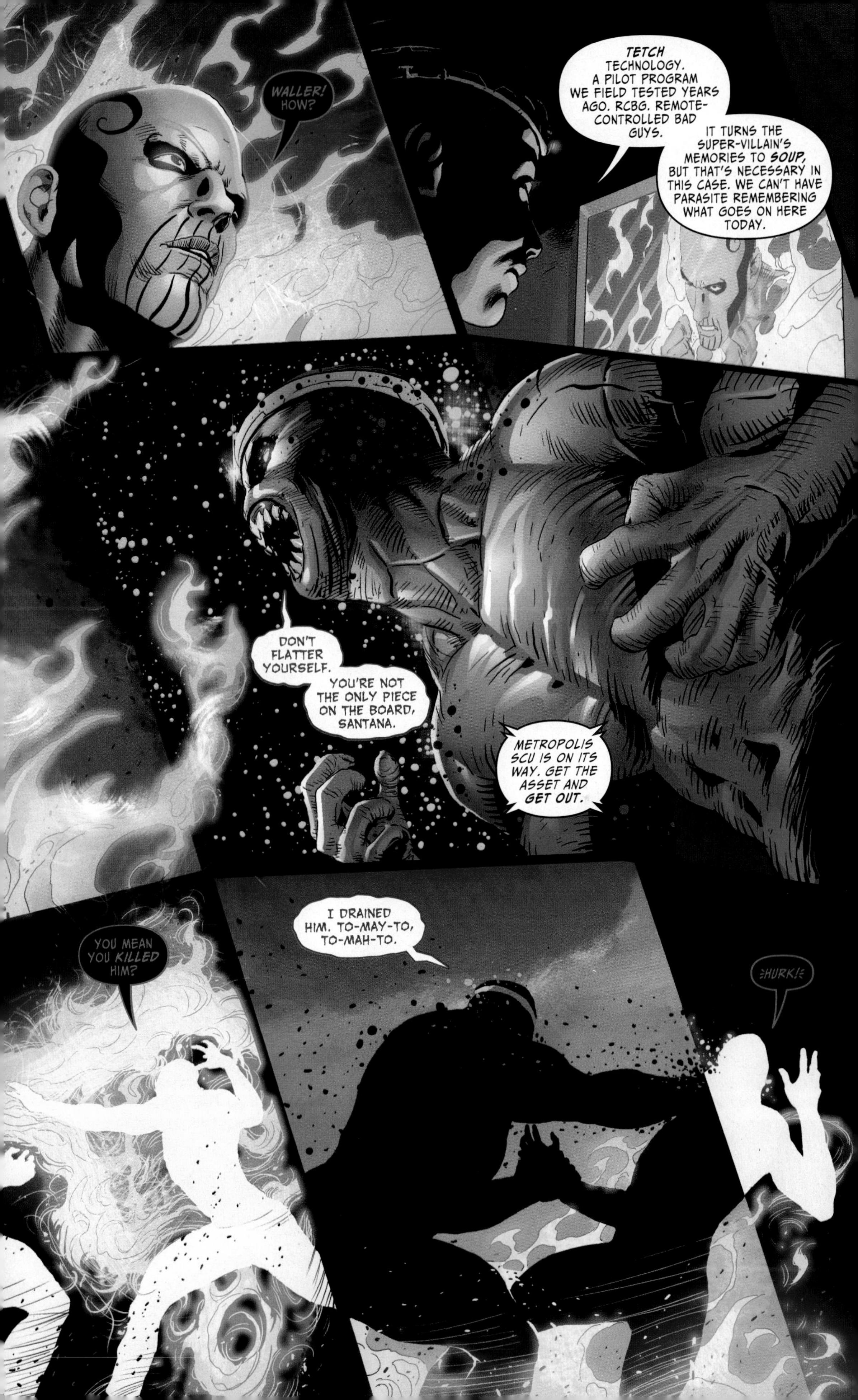
WALLER! HOW?
TETCH TECHNOLOGY. A PILOT PROGRAM WE FIELD TESTED YEARS AGO. RCBG. REMOTE-CONTROLLED BAD GUYS.
IT TURNS THE SUPER-VILLAIN'S MEMORIES TO SOUP, BUT THAT'S NECESSARY IN THIS CASE. WE CAN'T HAVE PARASITE REMEMBERING WHAT GOES ON HERE TODAY.
DON'T FLATTER YOURSELF.
YOU'RE NOT THE ONLY PIECE ON THE BOARD, SANTANA.
METROPOLIS SCU IS ON ITS WAY. GET THE ASSET AND GET OUT.
YOU MEAN YOU KILLED HIM?
I DRAINED HIM. TO-MAY-TO, TO-MAH-TO.
HURK!

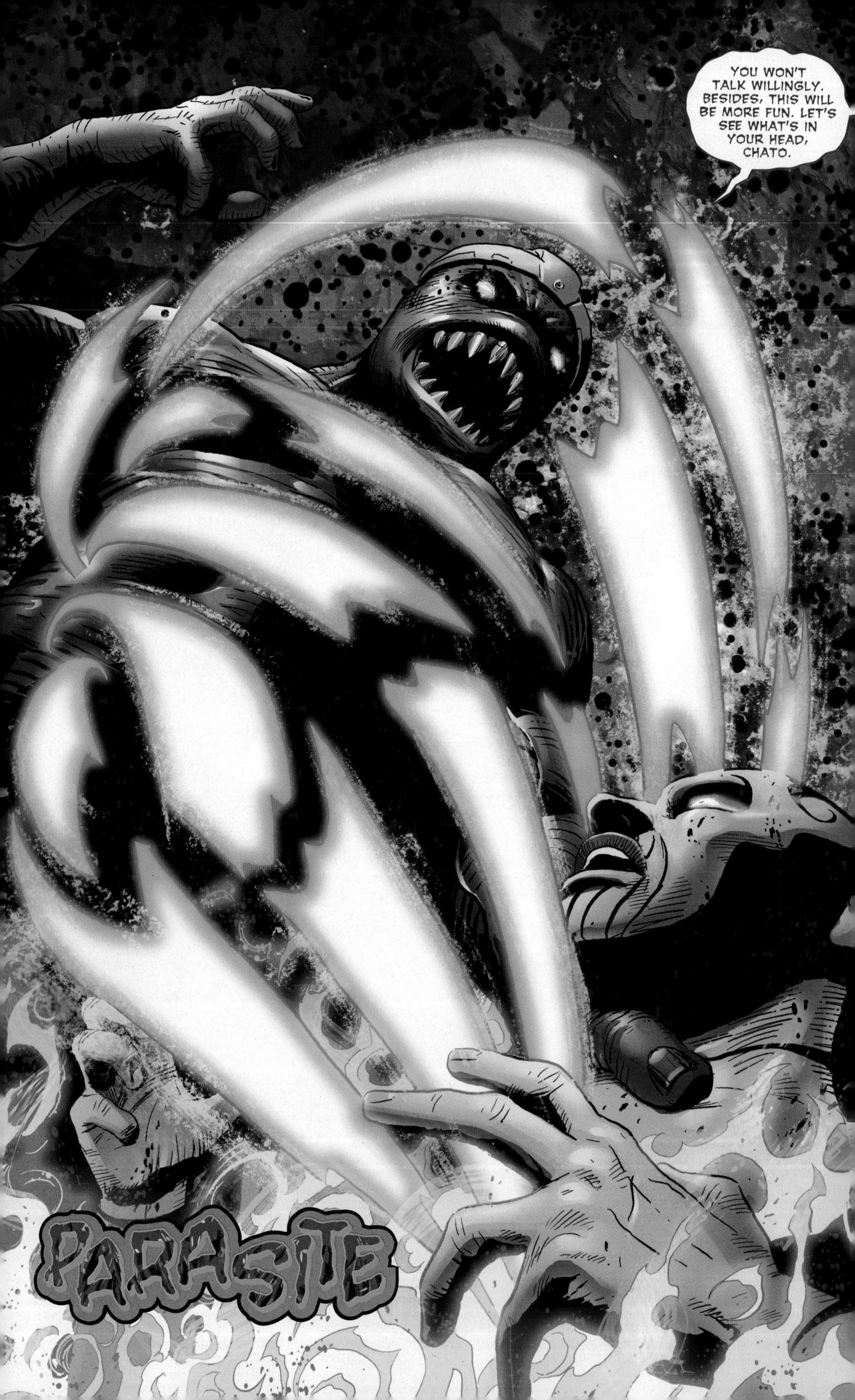
YOU WON'T TALK WILLINGLY. BESIDES, THIS WILL BE MORE FUN. LET'S SEE WHAT'S IN YOUR HEAD, CHATO.
PARASITE

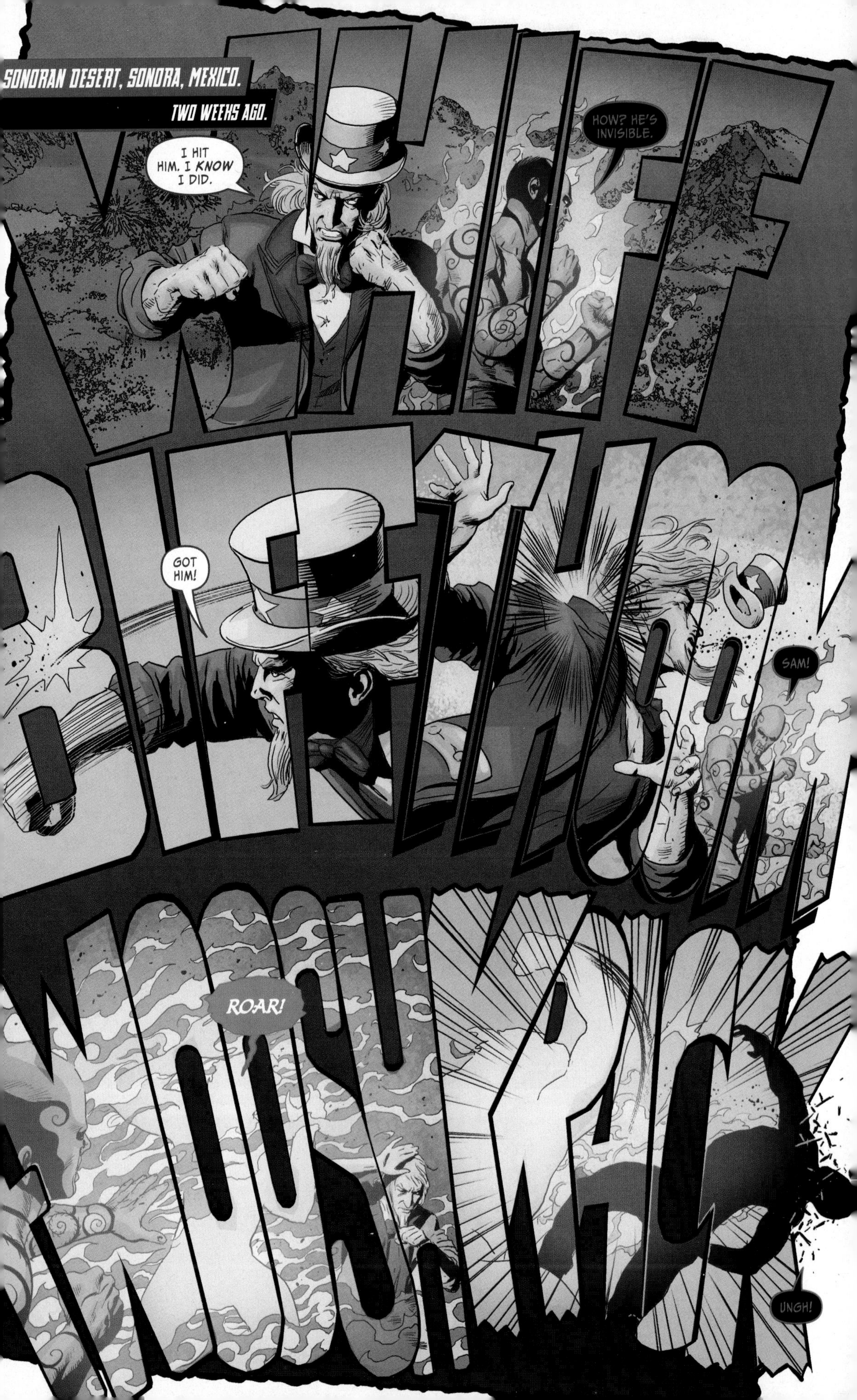
SONORAN DESERT, SONORA, MEXICO.
TWO WEEKS AGO.
I HIT HIM. I KNOW I DID.
HOW? HE'S INVISIBLE.
GOT HIM!
SAM!
ROAR!
UNGH!

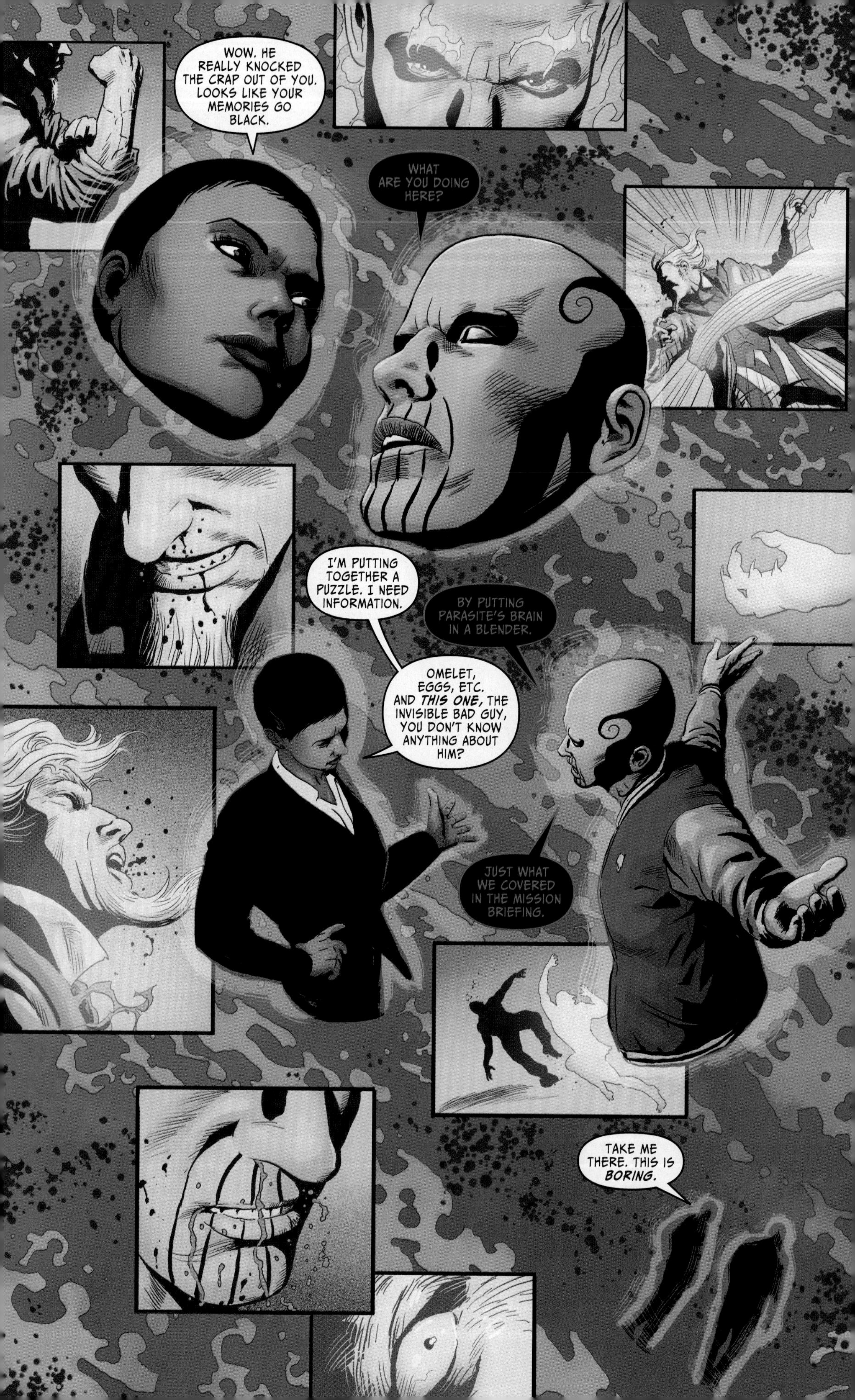
WOW. HE REALLY KNOCKED THE CRAP OUT OF YOU. LOOKS LIKE YOUR MEMORIES GO BLACK.
WHAT ARE YOU DOING HERE?
I'M PUTTING TOGETHER A PUZZLE. I NEED INFORMATION.
BY PUTTING PARASITE'S BRAIN IN A BLENDER.
OMELET, EGGS, ETC. AND *THIS ONE,* THE INVISIBLE BAD GUY, YOU DON'T KNOW ANYTHING ABOUT HIM?
JUST WHAT WE COVERED IN THE MISSION BRIEFING.
TAKE ME THERE. THIS IS *BORING.*

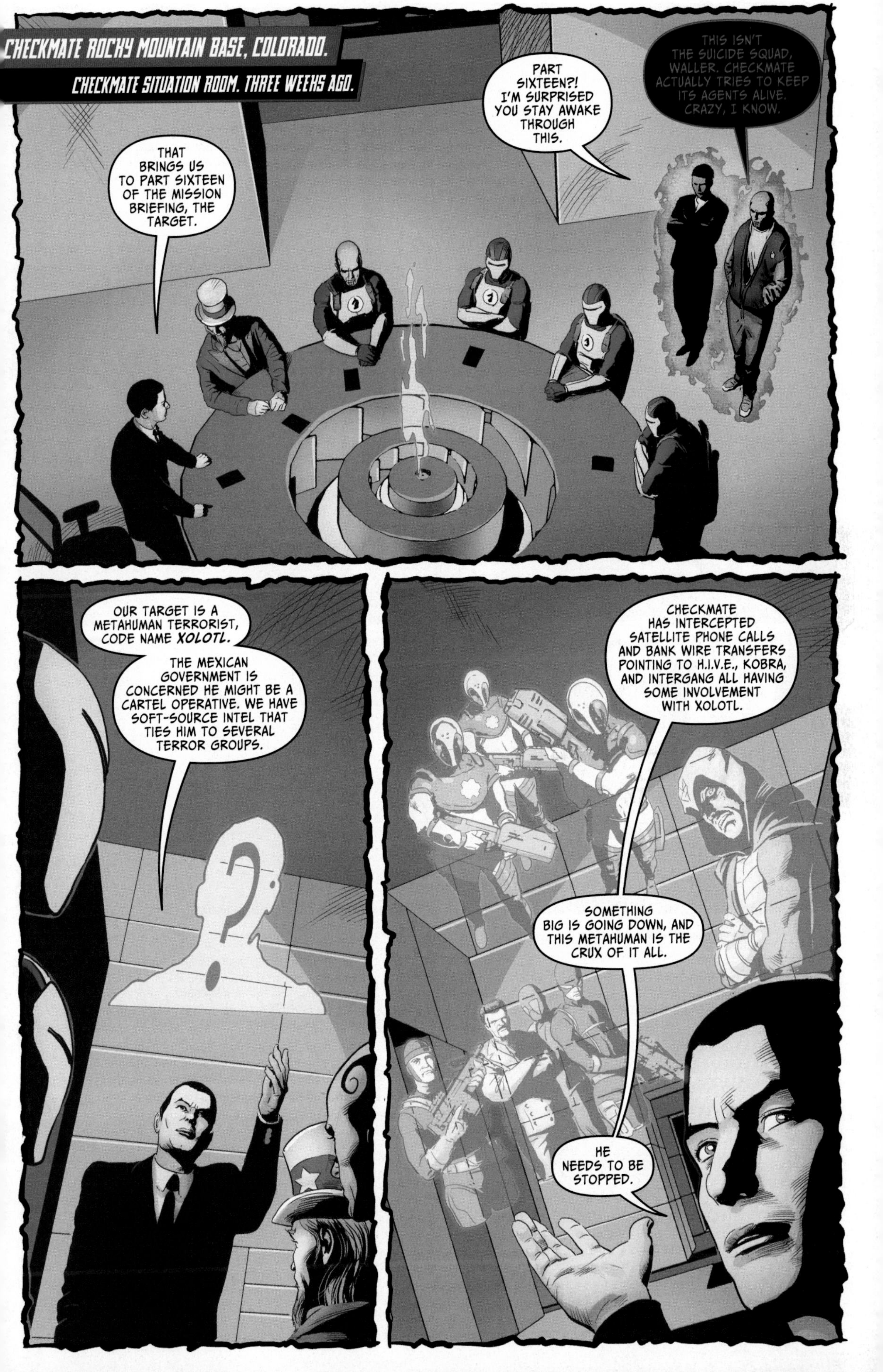
CHECKMATE ROCKY MOUNTAIN BASE, COLORADO.
CHECKMATE SITUATION ROOM. THREE WEEKS AGO.
THAT BRINGS US TO PART SIXTEEN OF THE MISSION BRIEFING, THE TARGET.
PART SIXTEEN?! I'M SURPRISED YOU STAY AWAKE THROUGH THIS.
THIS ISN'T THE SUICIDE SQUAD, WALLER. CHECKMATE ACTUALLY TRIES TO KEEP ITS AGENTS ALIVE. CRAZY, I KNOW.
OUR TARGET IS A METAHUMAN TERRORIST, CODE NAME *XOLOTL*.
THE MEXICAN GOVERNMENT IS CONCERNED HE MIGHT BE A CARTEL OPERATIVE. WE HAVE SOFT-SOURCE INTEL THAT TIES HIM TO SEVERAL TERROR GROUPS.
CHECKMATE HAS INTERCEPTED SATELLITE PHONE CALLS AND BANK WIRE TRANSFERS POINTING TO H.I.V.E., KOBRA, AND INTERGANG ALL HAVING SOME INVOLVEMENT WITH XOLOTL.
SOMETHING BIG IS GOING DOWN, AND THIS METAHUMAN IS THE CRUX OF IT ALL.
HE NEEDS TO BE STOPPED.

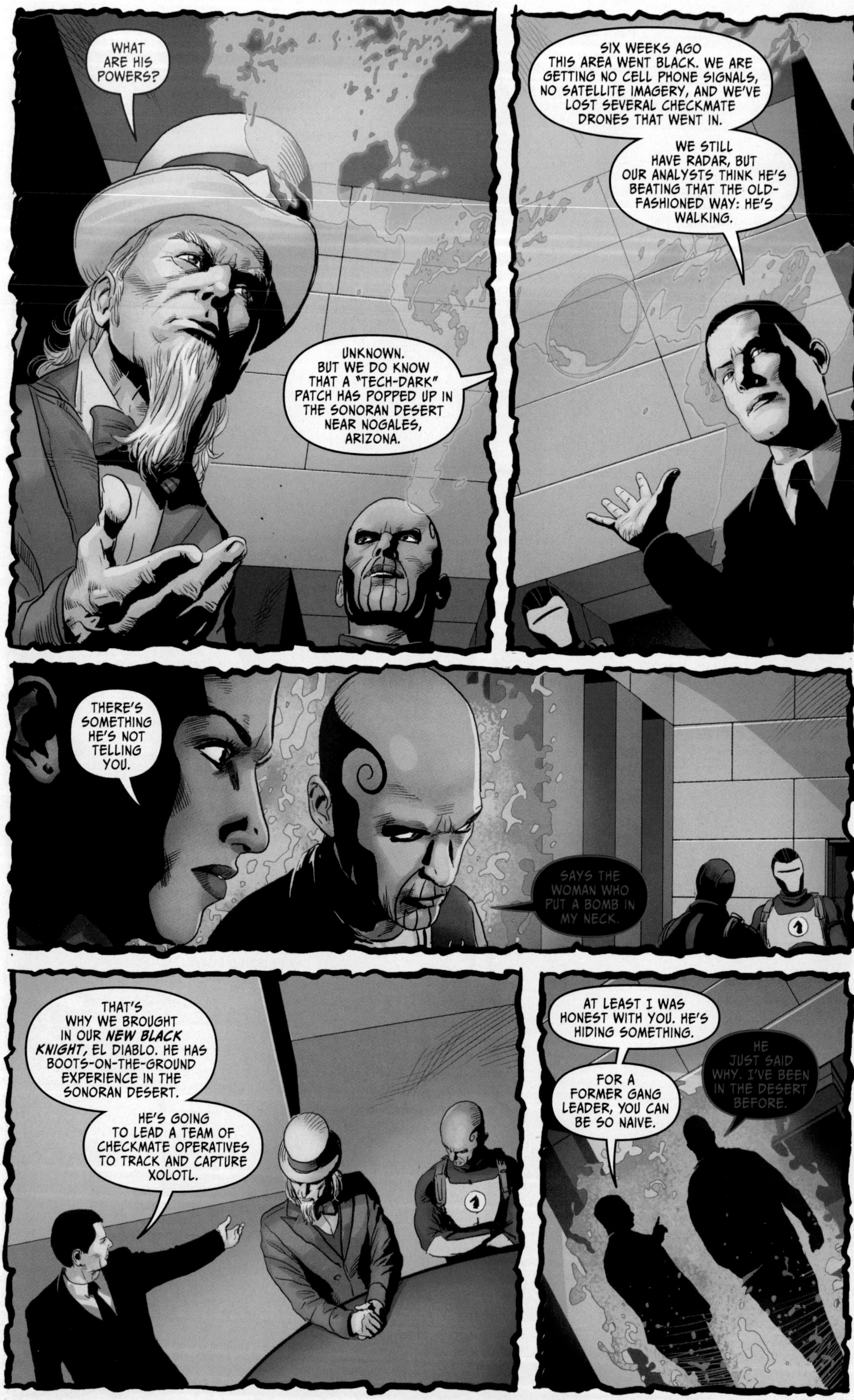
WHAT ARE HIS POWERS?
UNKNOWN. BUT WE DO KNOW THAT A "TECH-DARK" PATCH HAS POPPED UP IN THE SONORAN DESERT NEAR NOGALES, ARIZONA.
SIX WEEKS AGO THIS AREA WENT BLACK. WE ARE GETTING NO CELL PHONE SIGNALS, NO SATELLITE IMAGERY, AND WE'VE LOST SEVERAL CHECKMATE DRONES THAT WENT IN.
WE STILL HAVE RADAR, BUT OUR ANALYSTS THINK HE'S BEATING THAT THE OLD-FASHIONED WAY: HE'S WALKING.
THERE'S SOMETHING HE'S NOT TELLING YOU.
SAYS THE WOMAN WHO PUT A BOMB IN MY NECK.
THAT'S WHY WE BROUGHT IN OUR *NEW BLACK KNIGHT,* EL DIABLO. HE HAS BOOTS-ON-THE-GROUND EXPERIENCE IN THE SONORAN DESERT.
HE'S GOING TO LEAD A TEAM OF CHECKMATE OPERATIVES TO TRACK AND CAPTURE XOLOTL.
AT LEAST I WAS HONEST WITH YOU. HE'S HIDING SOMETHING.
HE JUST SAID WHY. I'VE BEEN IN THE DESERT BEFORE.
FOR A FORMER GANG LEADER, YOU CAN BE SO NAIVE.

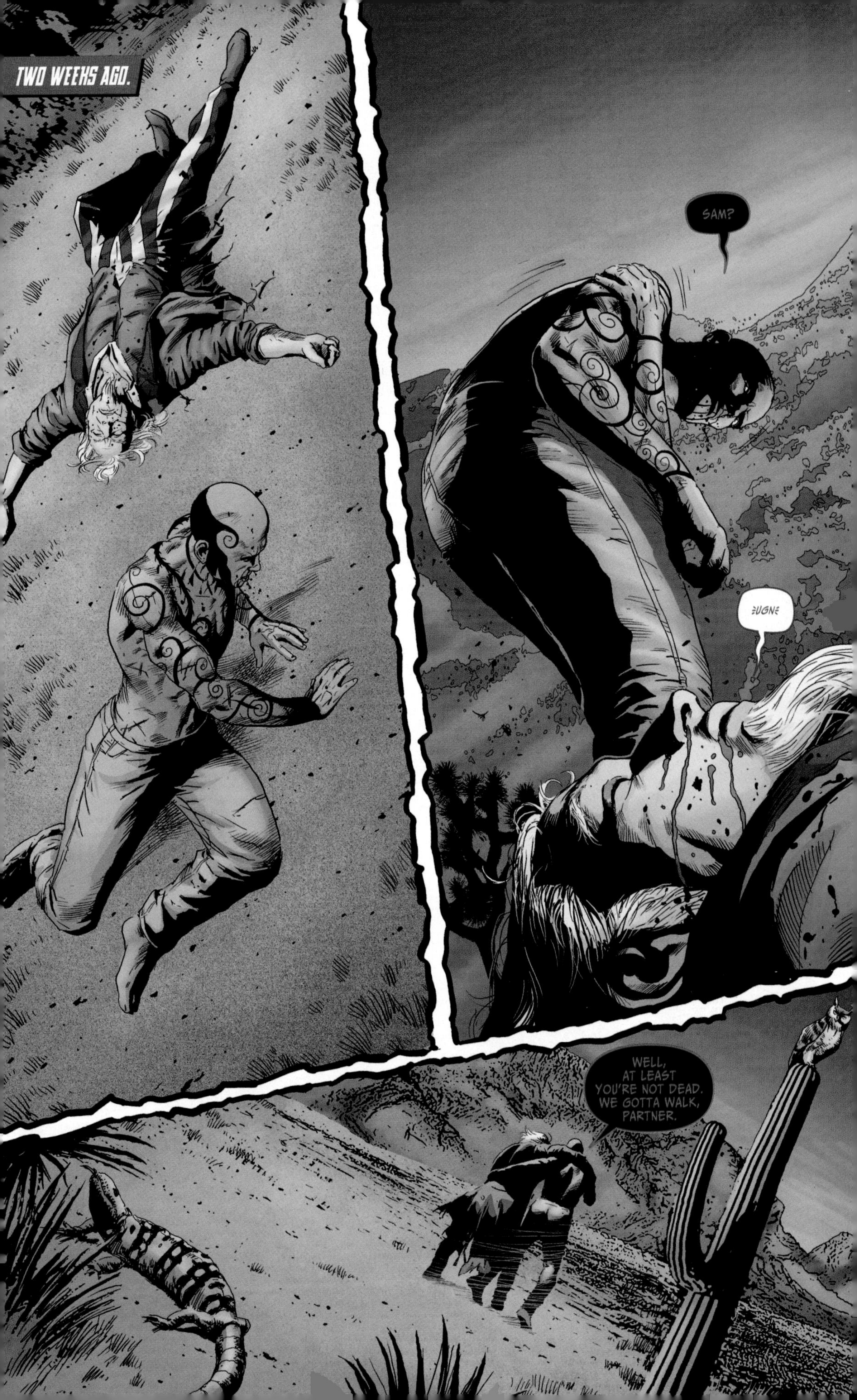
TWO WEEKS AGO.
SAM?
UGN
WELL, AT LEAST YOU'RE NOT DEAD. WE GOTTA WALK, PARTNER.

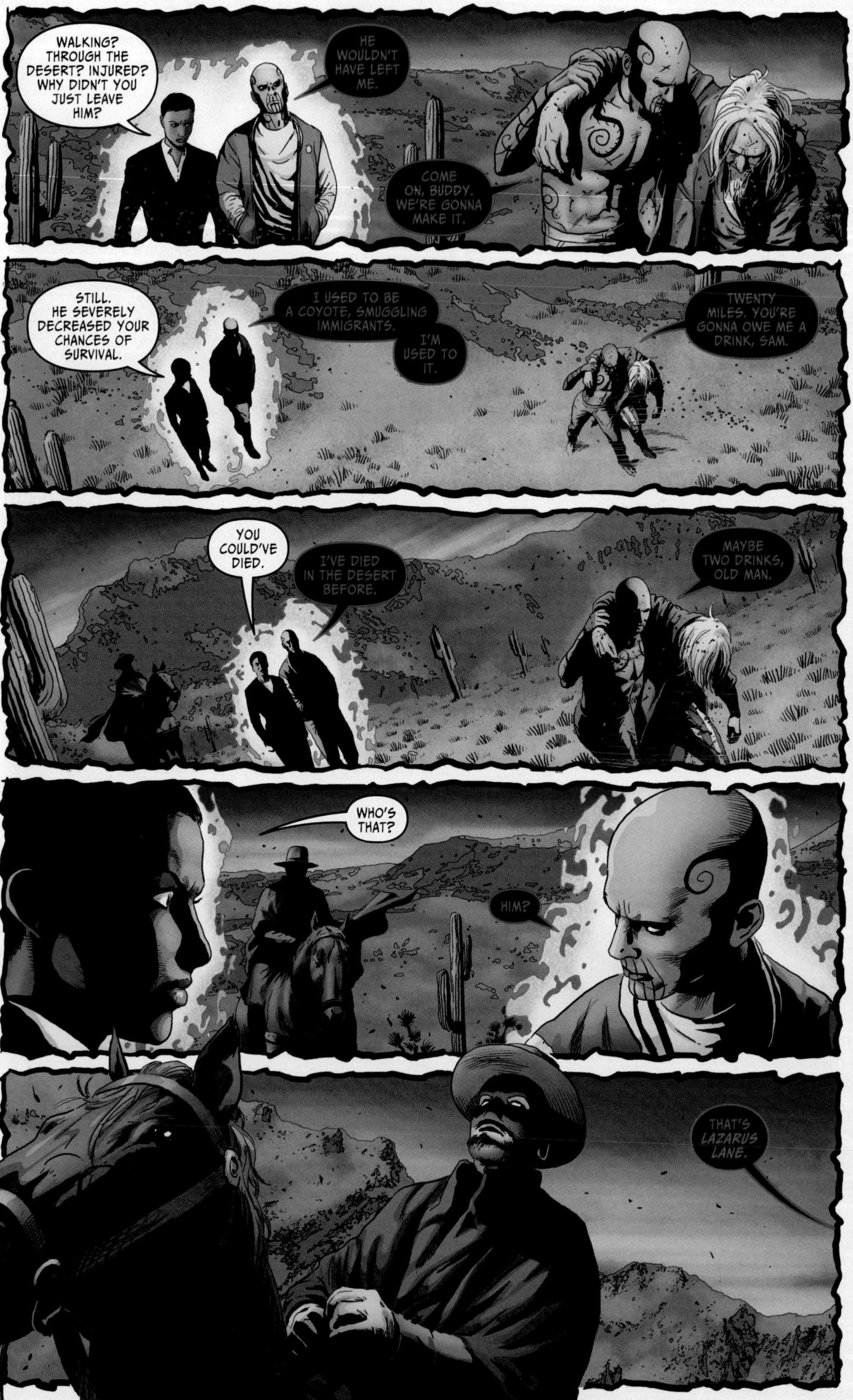
WALKING? THROUGH THE DESERT? INJURED? WHY DIDN'T YOU JUST LEAVE HIM?
HE WOULDN'T HAVE LEFT ME.
COME ON, BUDDY. WE'RE GONNA MAKE IT.
STILL. HE SEVERELY DECREASED YOUR CHANCES OF SURVIVAL.
I USED TO BE A COYOTE, SMUGGLING IMMIGRANTS.
I'M USED TO IT.
TWENTY MILES. YOU'RE GONNA OWE ME A DRINK, SAM.
YOU COULD'VE DIED.
I'VE DIED IN THE DESERT BEFORE.
MAYBE TWO DRINKS, OLD MAN.
WHO'S THAT?
HIM?
THAT'S LAZARUS LANE.

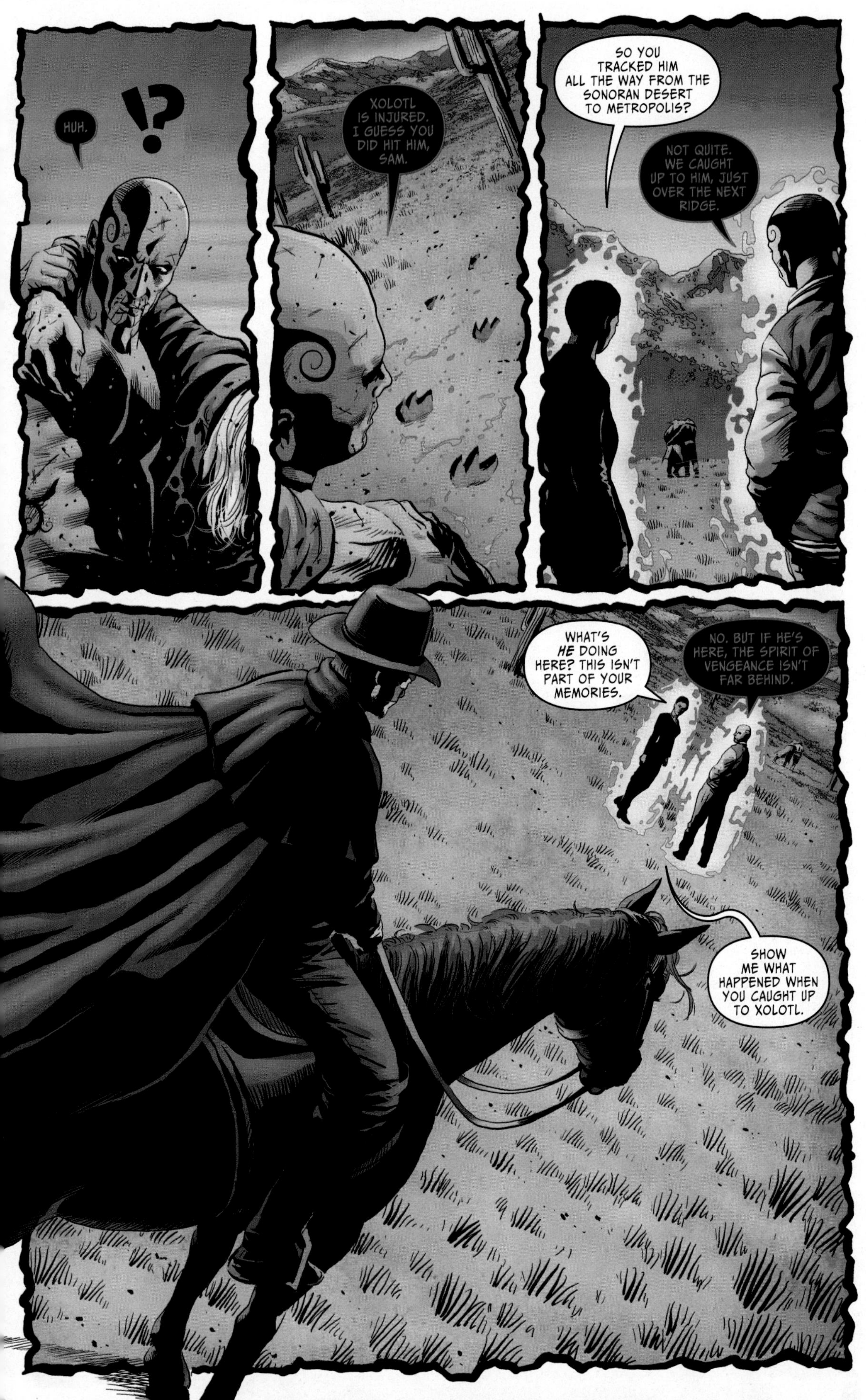
HUH.
!?
XOLOTL IS INJURED. I GUESS YOU DID HIT HIM, SAM.
SO YOU TRACKED HIM ALL THE WAY FROM THE SONORAN DESERT TO METROPOLIS?
NOT QUITE. WE CAUGHT UP TO HIM, JUST OVER THE NEXT RIDGE.
WHAT'S HE DOING HERE? THIS ISN'T PART OF YOUR MEMORIES.
NO. BUT IF HE'S HERE, THE SPIRIT OF VENGEANCE ISN'T FAR BEHIND.
SHOW ME WHAT HAPPENED WHEN YOU CAUGHT UP TO XOLOTL.

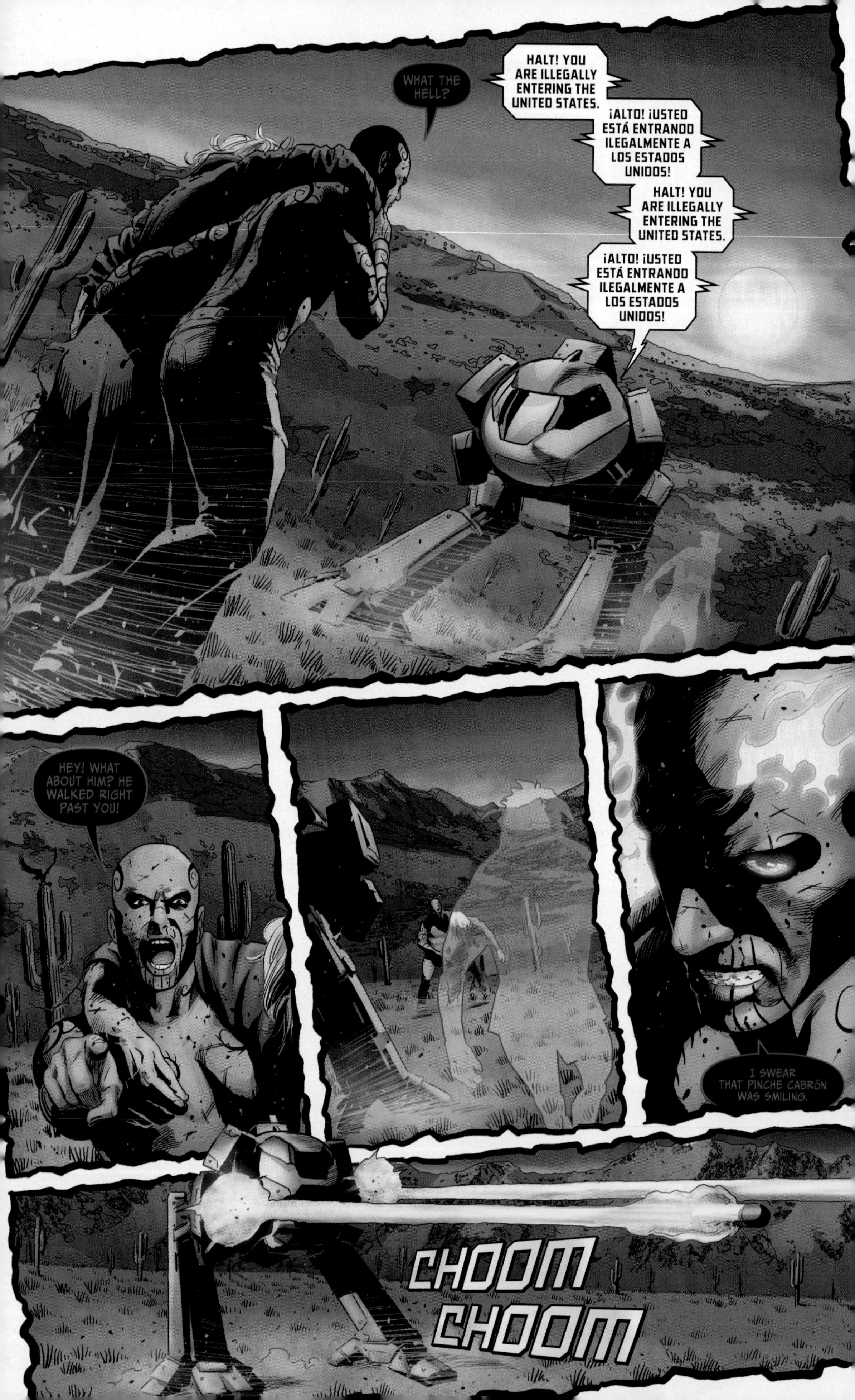

WHAT THE HELL?
HALT! YOU ARE ILLEGALLY ENTERING THE UNITED STATES.
¡ALTO! ¡USTED ESTÁ ENTRANDO ILEGALMENTE A LOS ESTADOS UNIDOS!
HALT! YOU ARE ILLEGALLY ENTERING THE UNITED STATES.
¡ALTO! ¡USTED ESTÁ ENTRANDO ILEGALMENTE A LOS ESTADOS UNIDOS!
HEY! WHAT ABOUT HIM? HE WALKED RIGHT PAST YOU!
I SWEAR THAT PINCHE CABRÓN WAS SMILING.
CHOOM
CHOOM

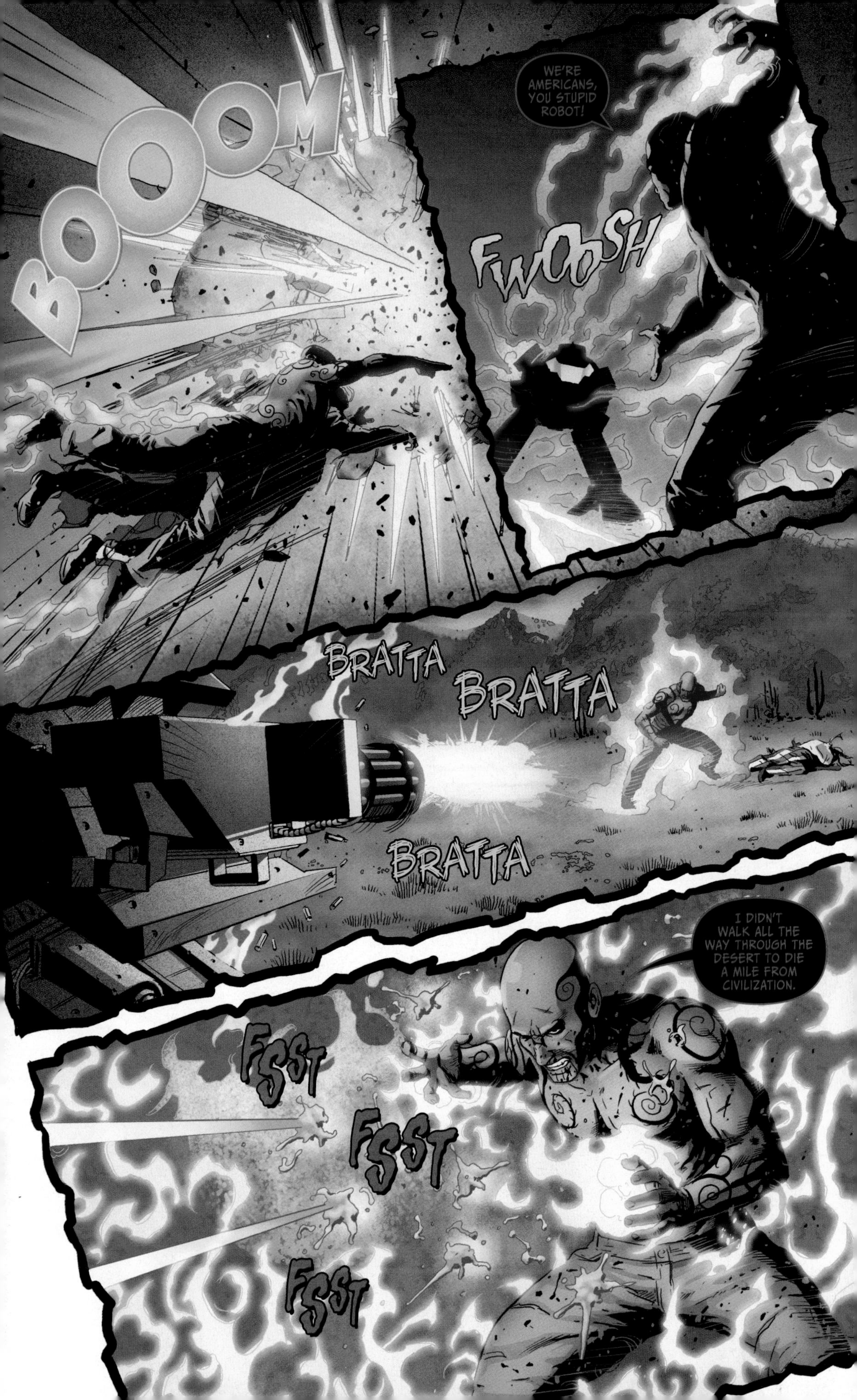
BOOOOM
WE'RE AMERICANS, YOU STUPID ROBOT!
FWOOSH
BRATTA
BRATTA
BRATTA
I DIDN'T WALK ALL THE WAY THROUGH THE DESERT TO DIE A MILE FROM CIVILIZATION.
FSST
FSST
FSST

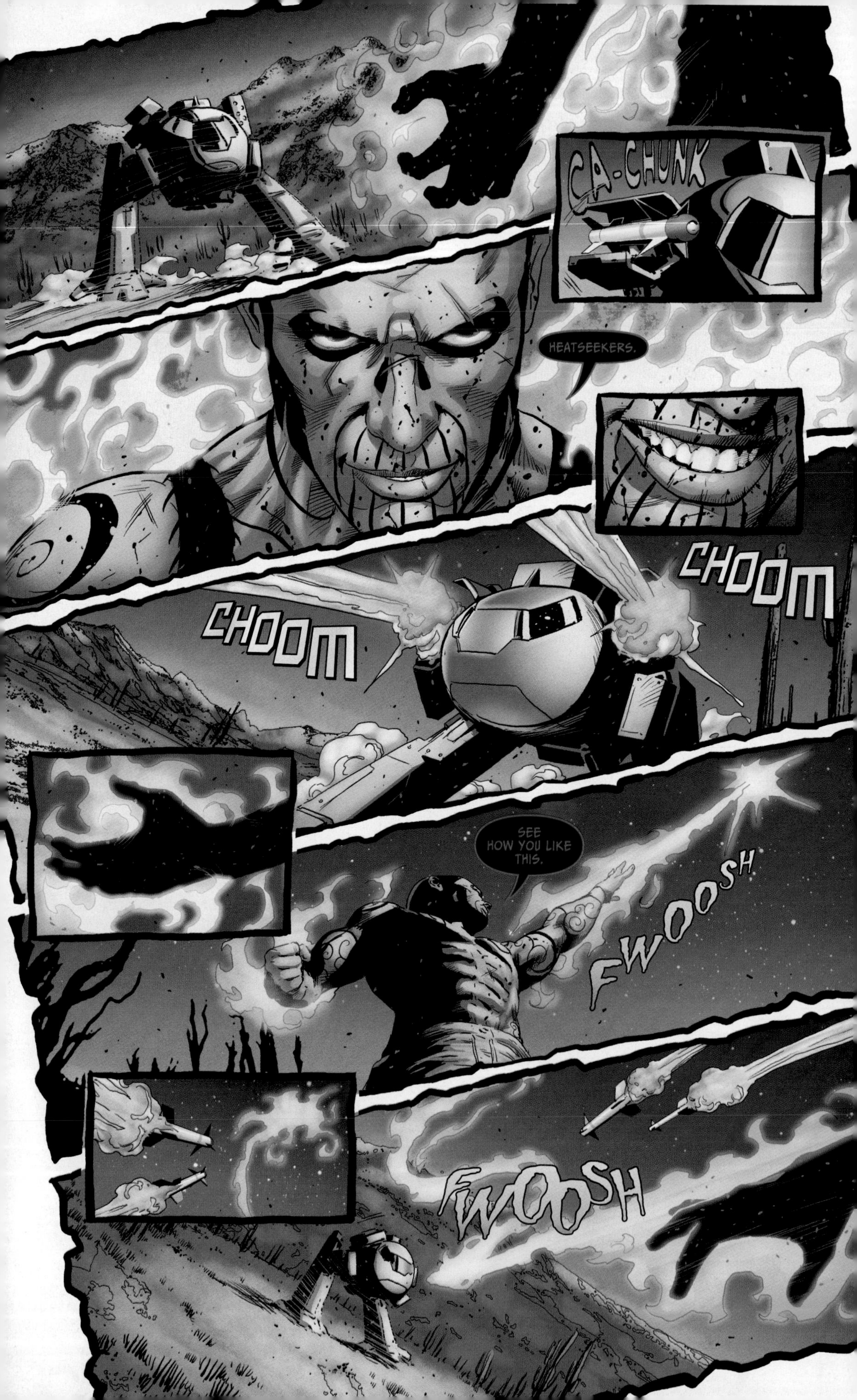
CA-CHUNK
HEATSEEKERS.
CHOOM
CHOOM
SEE HOW YOU LIKE THIS.
FWOOSH
FWOOSH

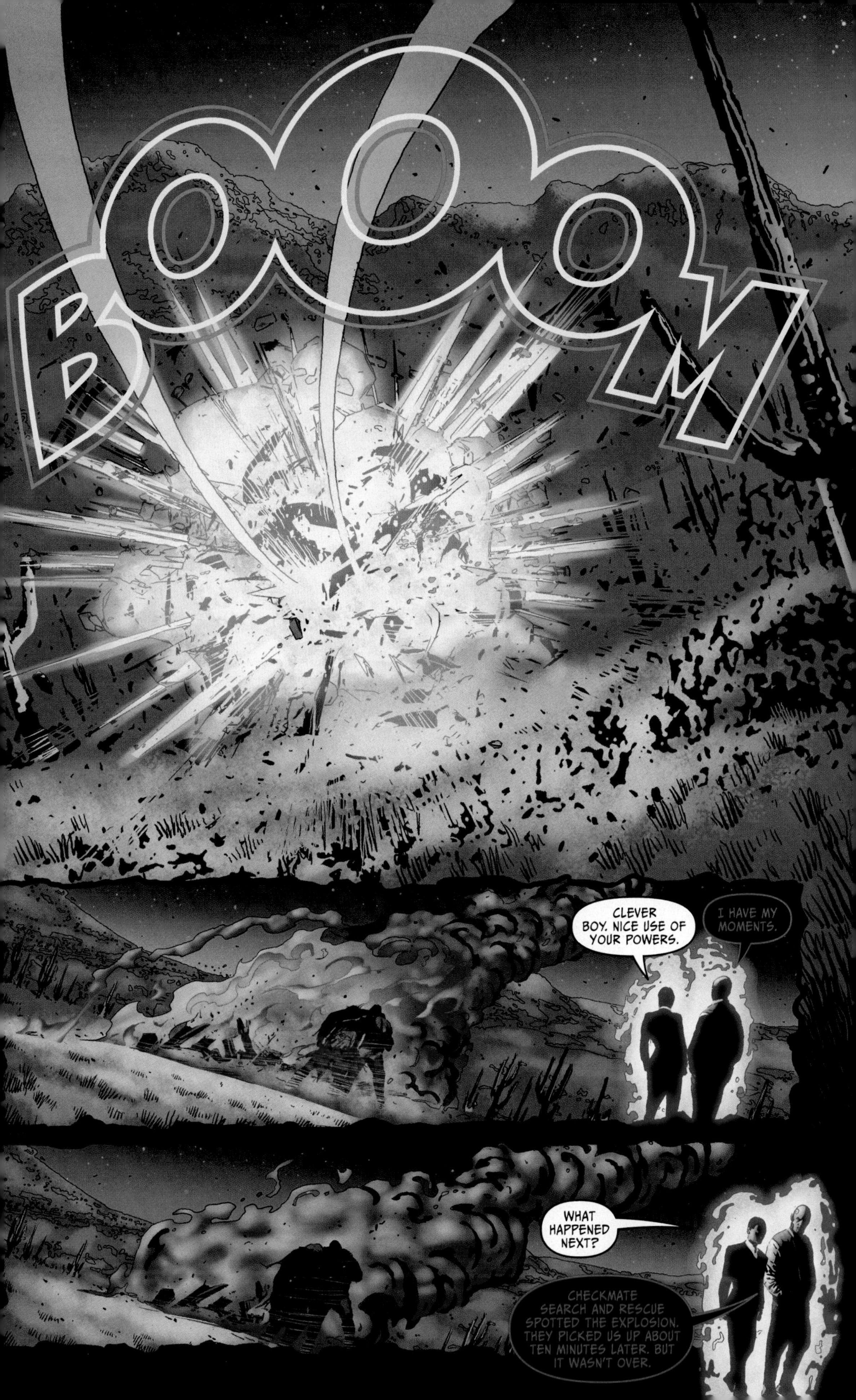
BOOOM
CLEVER BOY. NICE USE OF YOUR POWERS.
I HAVE MY MOMENTS.
WHAT HAPPENED NEXT?
CHECKMATE SEARCH AND RESCUE SPOTTED THE EXPLOSION. THEY PICKED US UP ABOUT TEN MINUTES LATER. BUT IT WASN'T OVER.

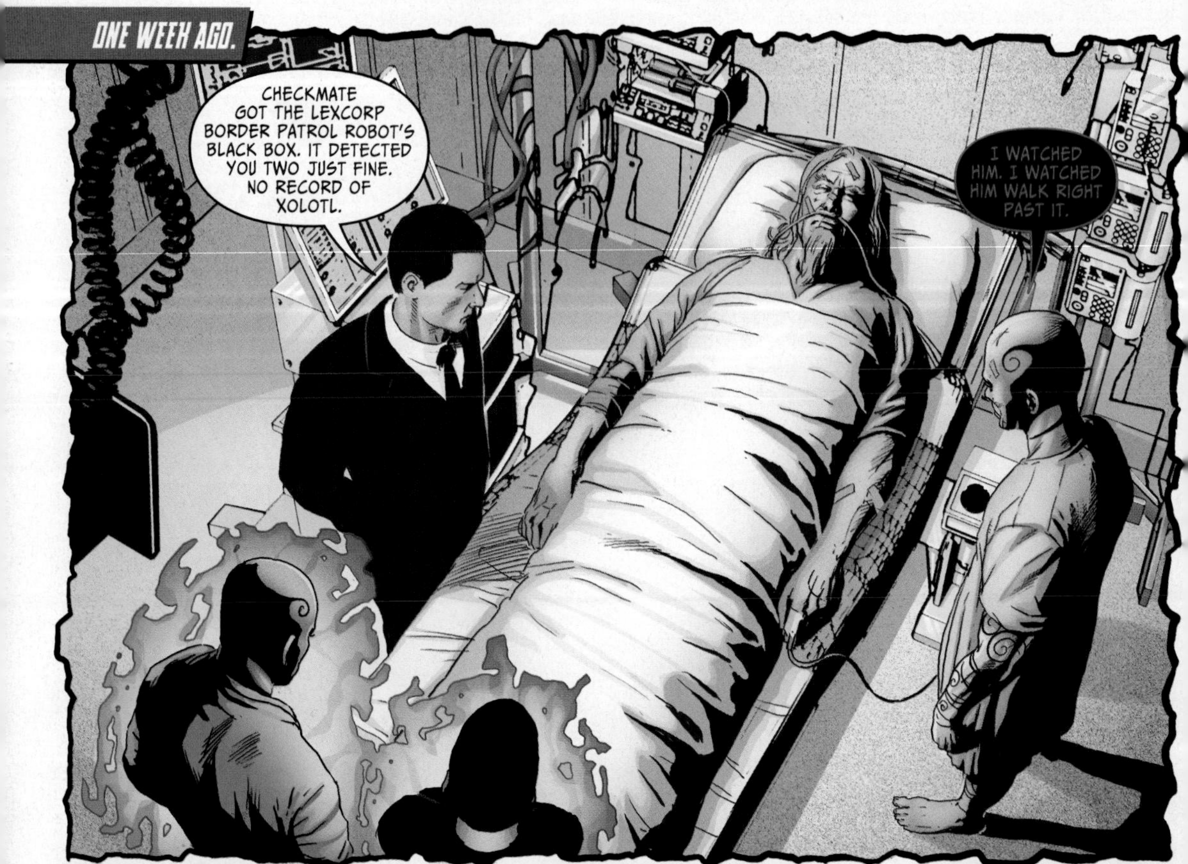
ONE WEEK AGO.
CHECKMATE GOT THE LEXCORP BORDER PATROL ROBOT'S BLACK BOX. IT DETECTED YOU TWO JUST FINE. NO RECORD OF XOLOTL.
I WATCHED HIM. I WATCHED HIM WALK RIGHT PAST IT.

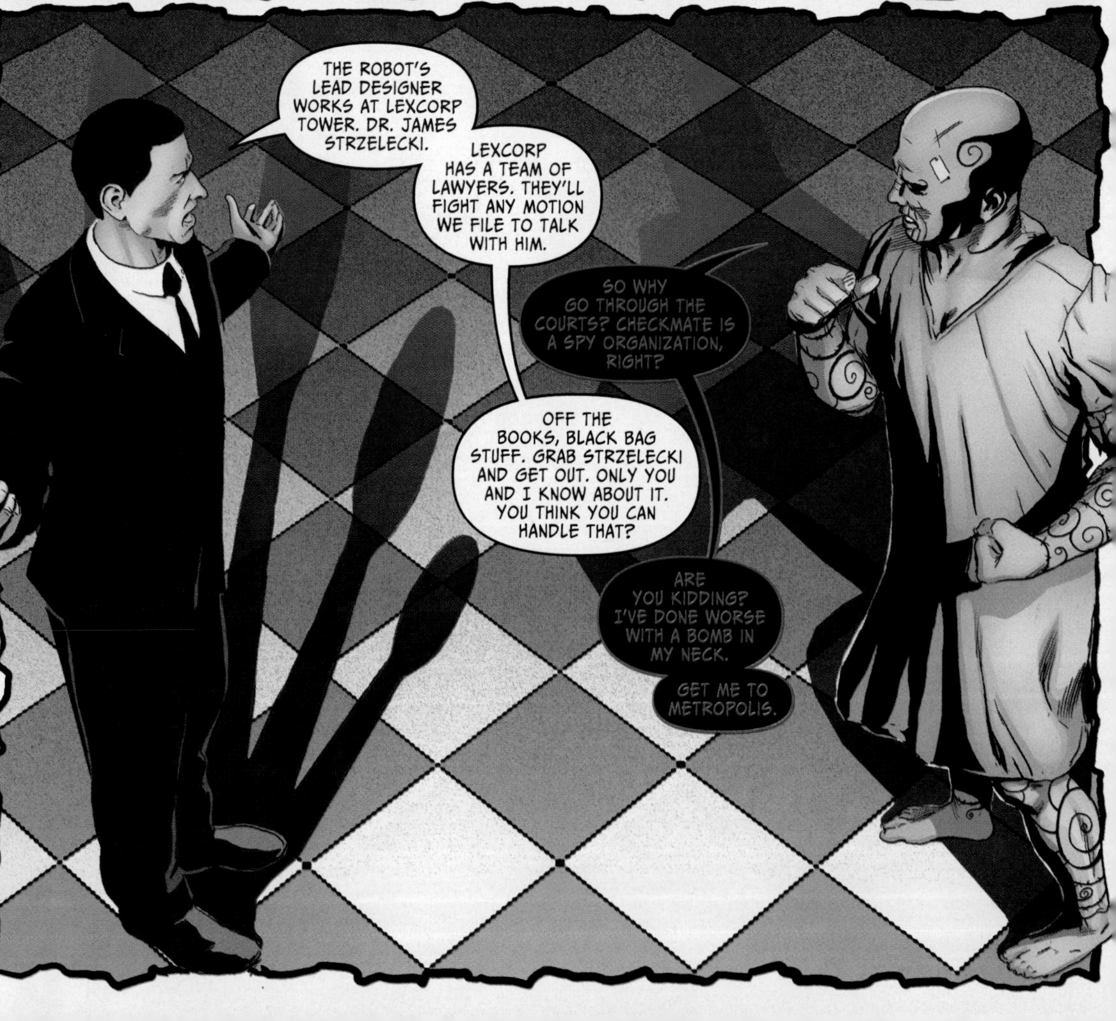
THE ROBOT'S LEAD DESIGNER WORKS AT LEXCORP TOWER. DR. JAMES STRZELECKI.
LEXCORP HAS A TEAM OF LAWYERS. THEY'LL FIGHT ANY MOTION WE FILE TO TALK WITH HIM.
SO WHY GO THROUGH THE COURTS? CHECKMATE IS A SPY ORGANIZATION, RIGHT?
OFF THE BOOKS, BLACK BAG STUFF. GRAB STRZELECKI AND GET OUT. ONLY YOU AND I KNOW ABOUT IT. YOU THINK YOU CAN HANDLE THAT?
ARE YOU KIDDING? I'VE DONE WORSE WITH A BOMB IN MY NECK.
GET ME TO METROPOLIS.

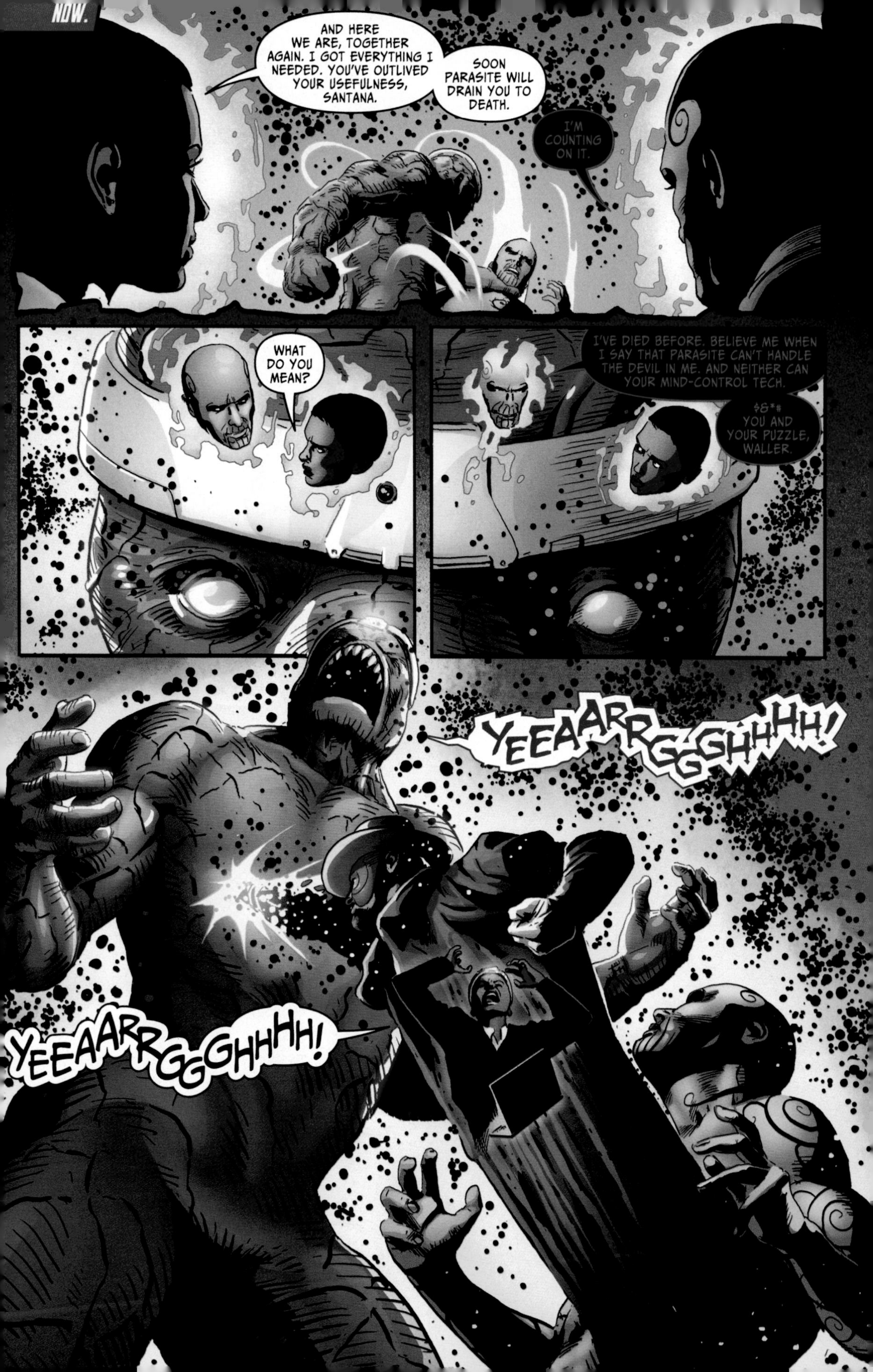
NOW.
AND HERE WE ARE, TOGETHER AGAIN. I GOT EVERYTHING I NEEDED. YOU'VE OUTLIVED YOUR USEFULNESS, SANTANA.
SOON PARASITE WILL DRAIN YOU TO DEATH.
I'M COUNTING ON IT.
WHAT DO YOU MEAN?
I'VE DIED BEFORE. BELIEVE ME WHEN I SAY THAT PARASITE CAN'T HANDLE THE DEVIL IN ME. AND NEITHER CAN YOUR MIND-CONTROL TECH.
$&*# YOU AND YOUR PUZZLE, WALLER.
YEEAARRGGGHHHH!
YEEAARRGGGHHHH!

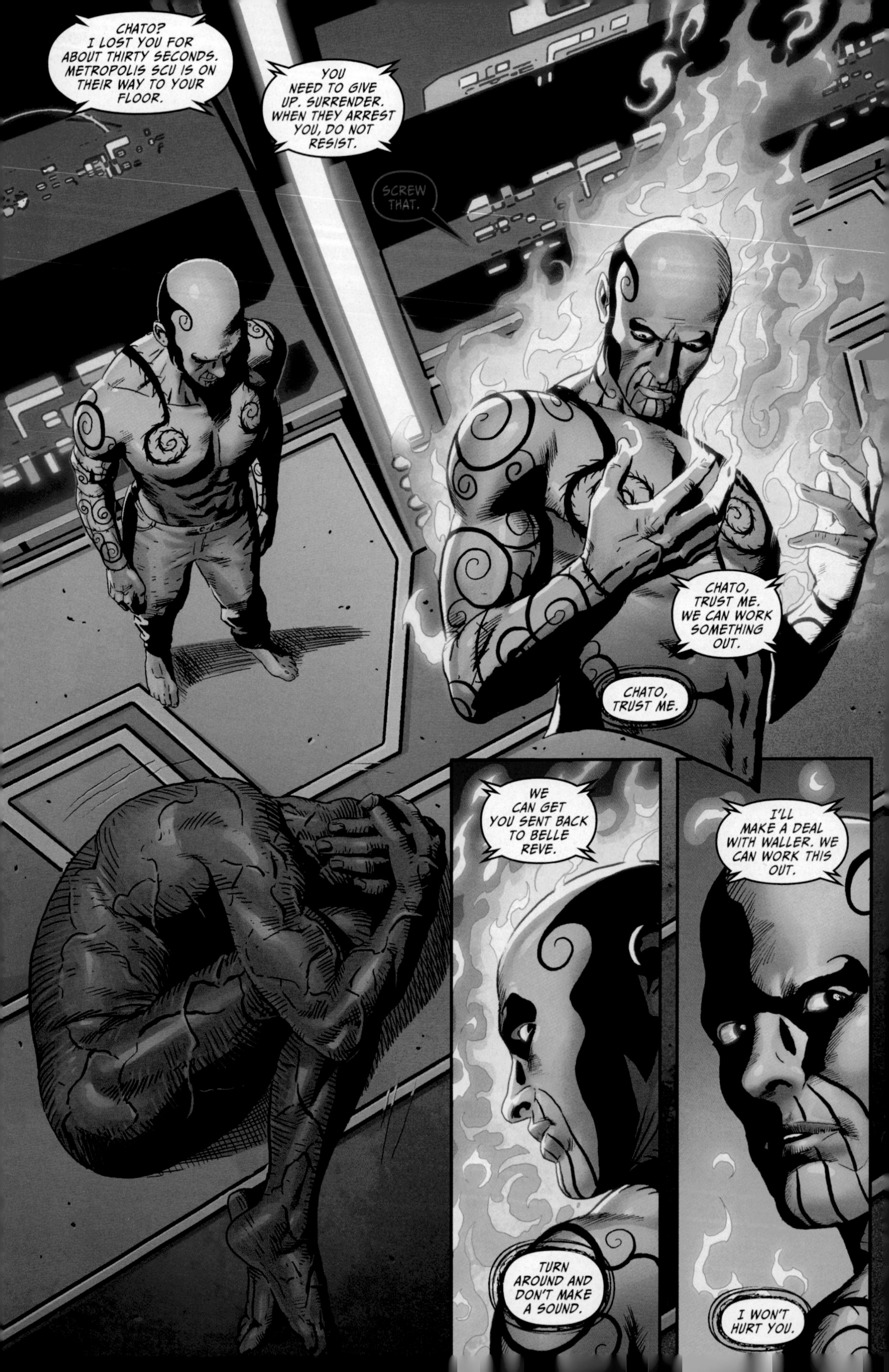

CHATO? I LOST YOU FOR ABOUT THIRTY SECONDS. METROPOLIS SCU IS ON THEIR WAY TO YOUR FLOOR.
YOU NEED TO GIVE UP. SURRENDER. WHEN THEY ARREST YOU, DO NOT RESIST.
SCREW THAT.
CHATO, TRUST ME. WE CAN WORK SOMETHING OUT.
CHATO, TRUST ME.
WE CAN GET YOU SENT BACK TO BELLE REVE.
TURN AROUND AND DON'T MAKE A SOUND.
I'LL MAKE A DEAL WITH WALLER. WE CAN WORK THIS OUT.
I WON'T HURT YOU.

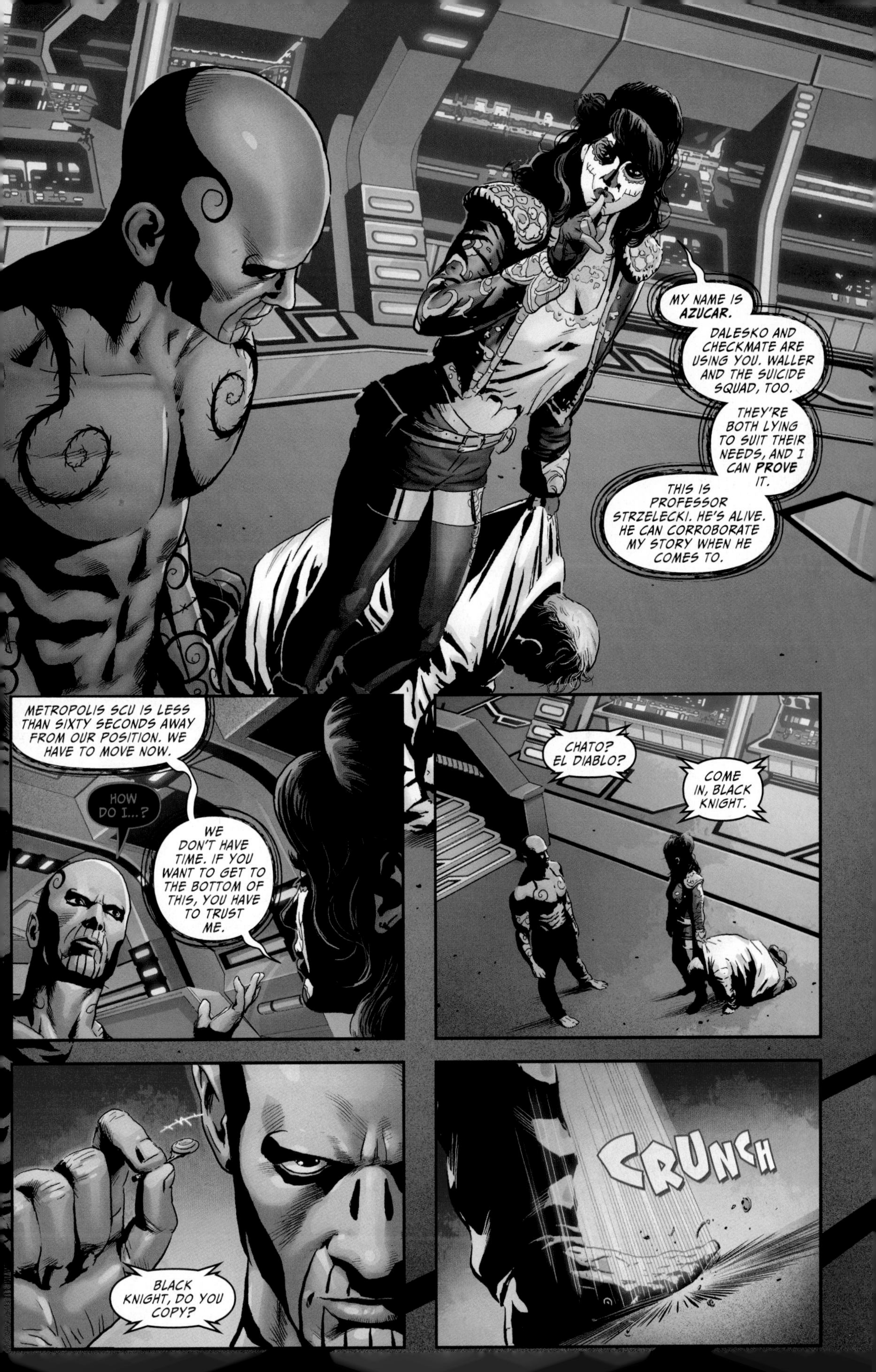
MY NAME IS AZUCAR.
DALESKO AND CHECKMATE ARE USING YOU. WALLER AND THE SUICIDE SQUAD, TOO.
THEY'RE BOTH LYING TO SUIT THEIR NEEDS, AND I CAN PROVE IT.
THIS IS PROFESSOR STRZELECKI. HE'S ALIVE. HE CAN CORROBORATE MY STORY WHEN HE COMES TO.
METROPOLIS SCU IS LESS THAN SIXTY SECONDS AWAY FROM OUR POSITION. WE HAVE TO MOVE NOW.
HOW DO I...?
WE DON'T HAVE TIME. IF YOU WANT TO GET TO THE BOTTOM OF THIS, YOU HAVE TO TRUST ME.
CHATO? EL DIABLO?
COME IN, BLACK KNIGHT.
BLACK KNIGHT, DO YOU COPY?
CRUNCH

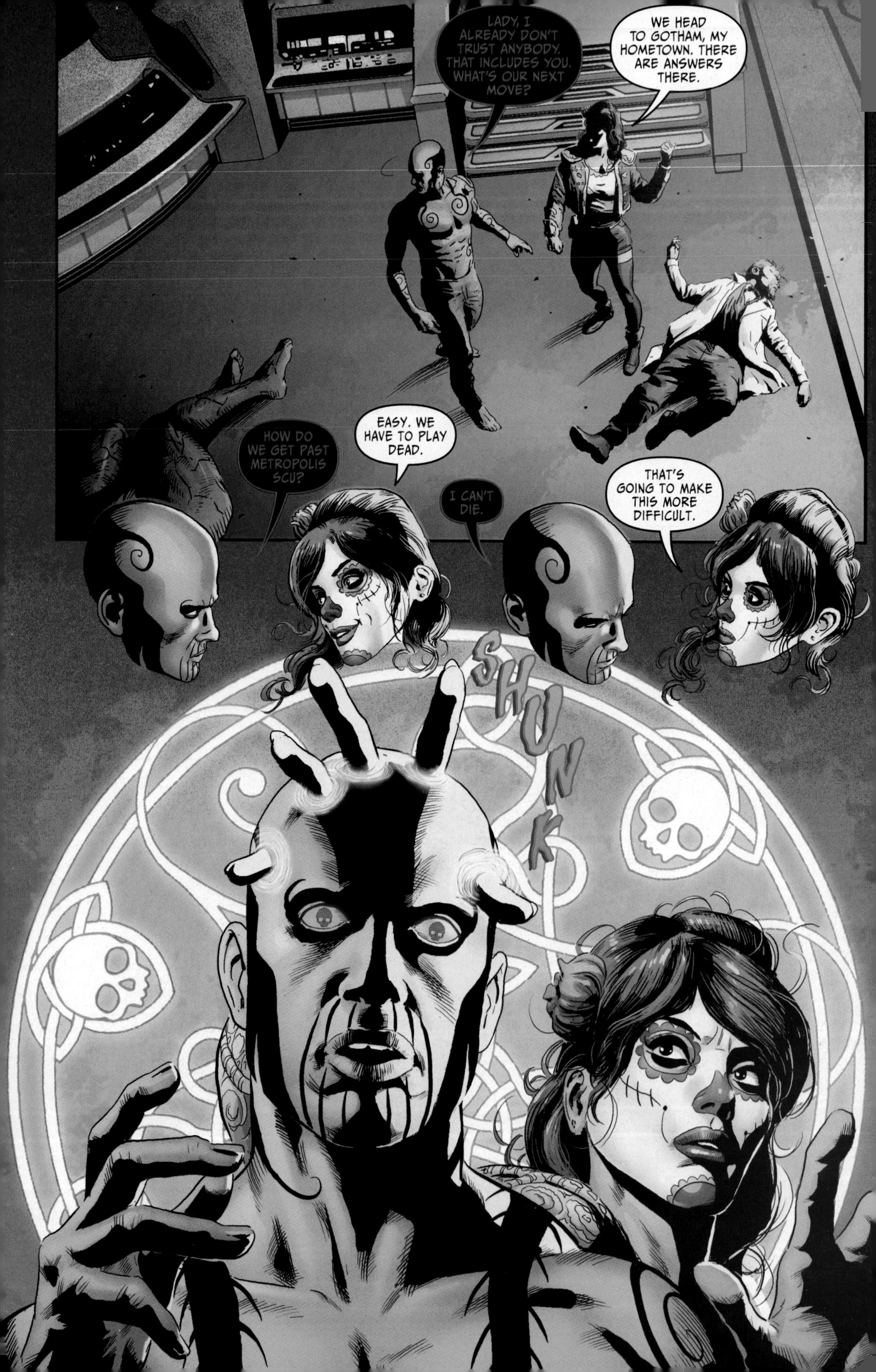
LADY, I ALREADY DON'T TRUST ANYBODY. THAT INCLUDES YOU. WHAT'S OUR NEXT MOVE?
WE HEAD TO GOTHAM, MY HOMETOWN. THERE ARE ANSWERS THERE.
HOW DO WE GET PAST METROPOLIS SCU?
EASY. WE HAVE TO PLAY DEAD.
I CAN'T DIE.
THAT'S GOING TO MAKE THIS MORE DIFFICULT.
SHUNK

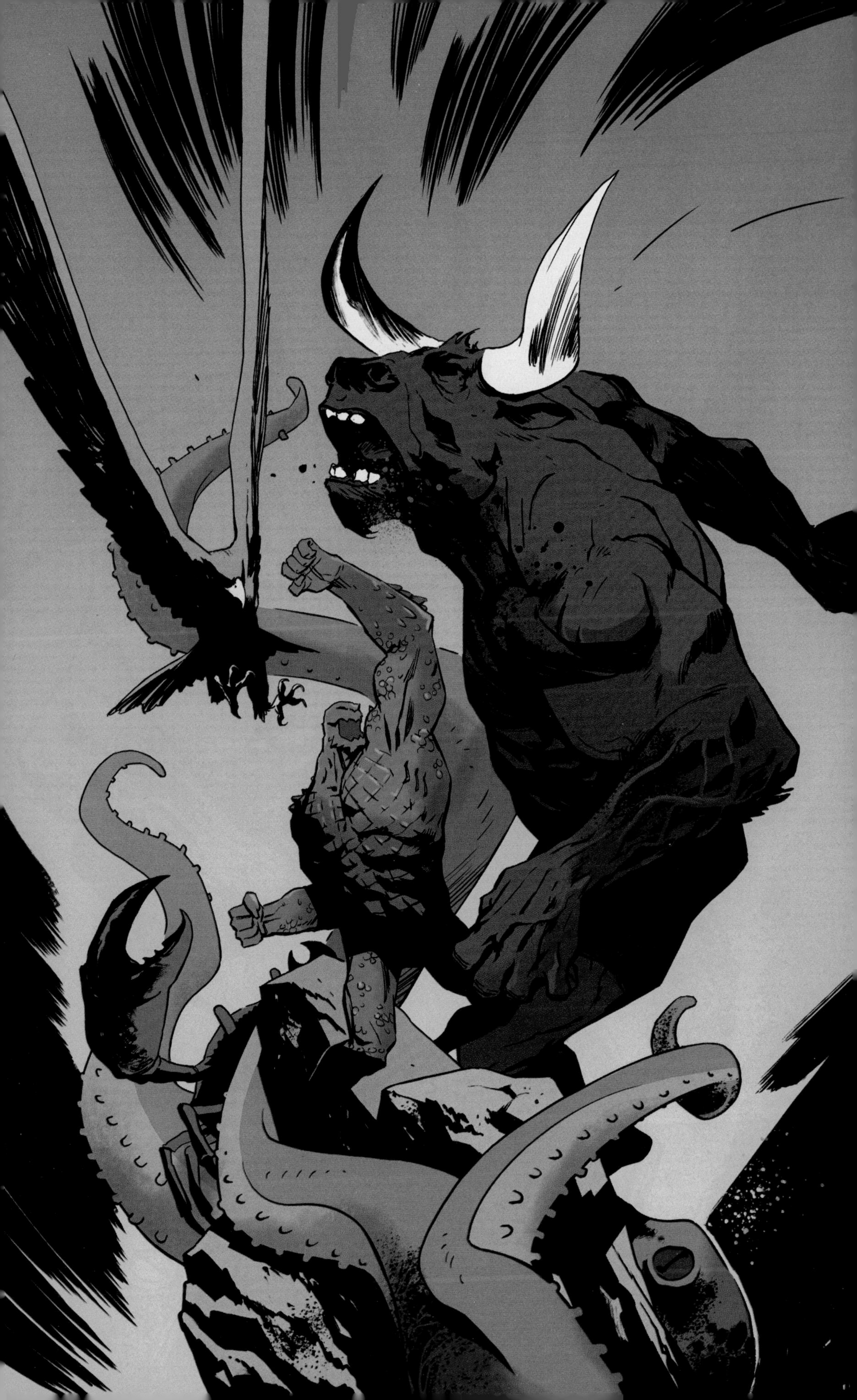

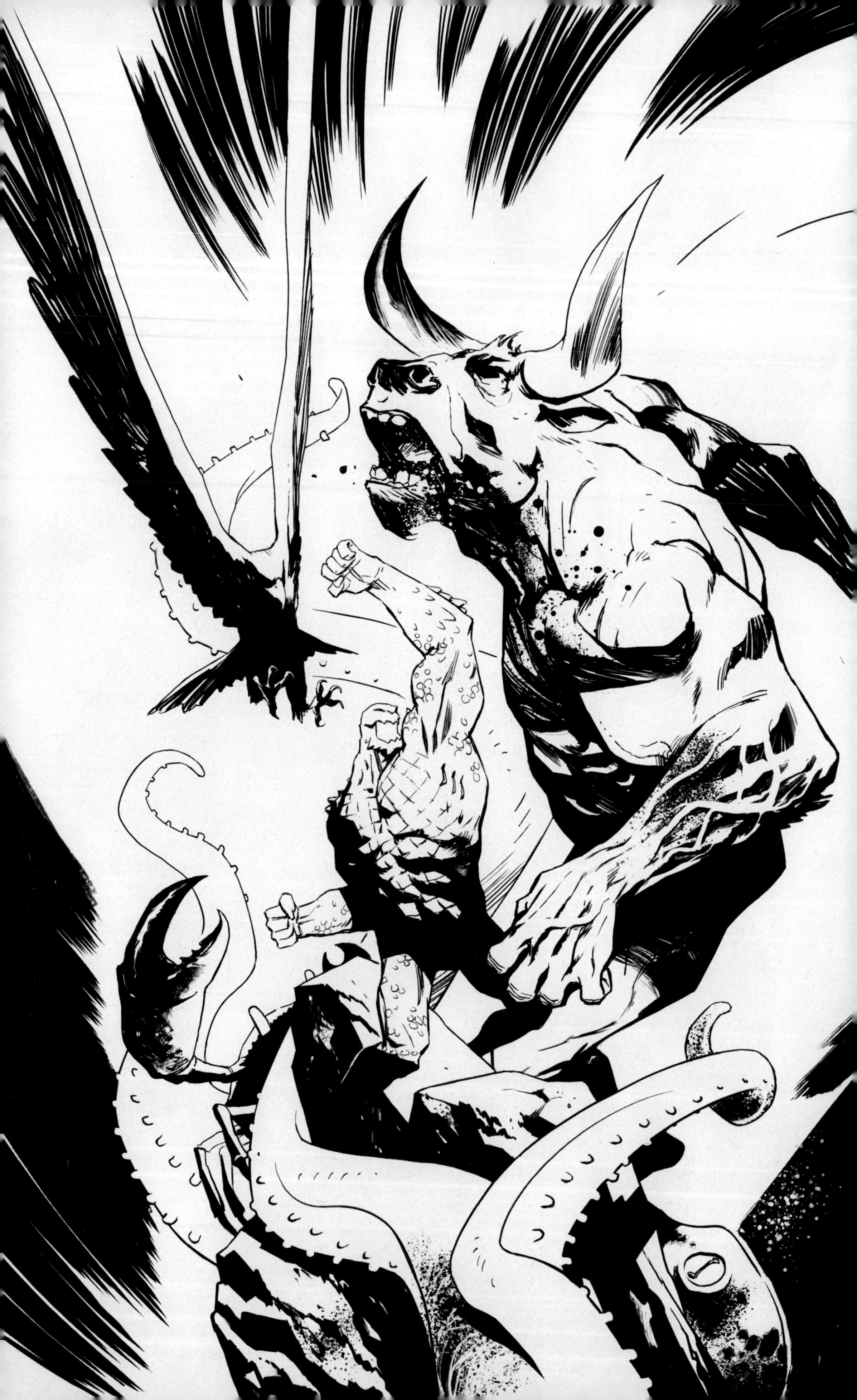

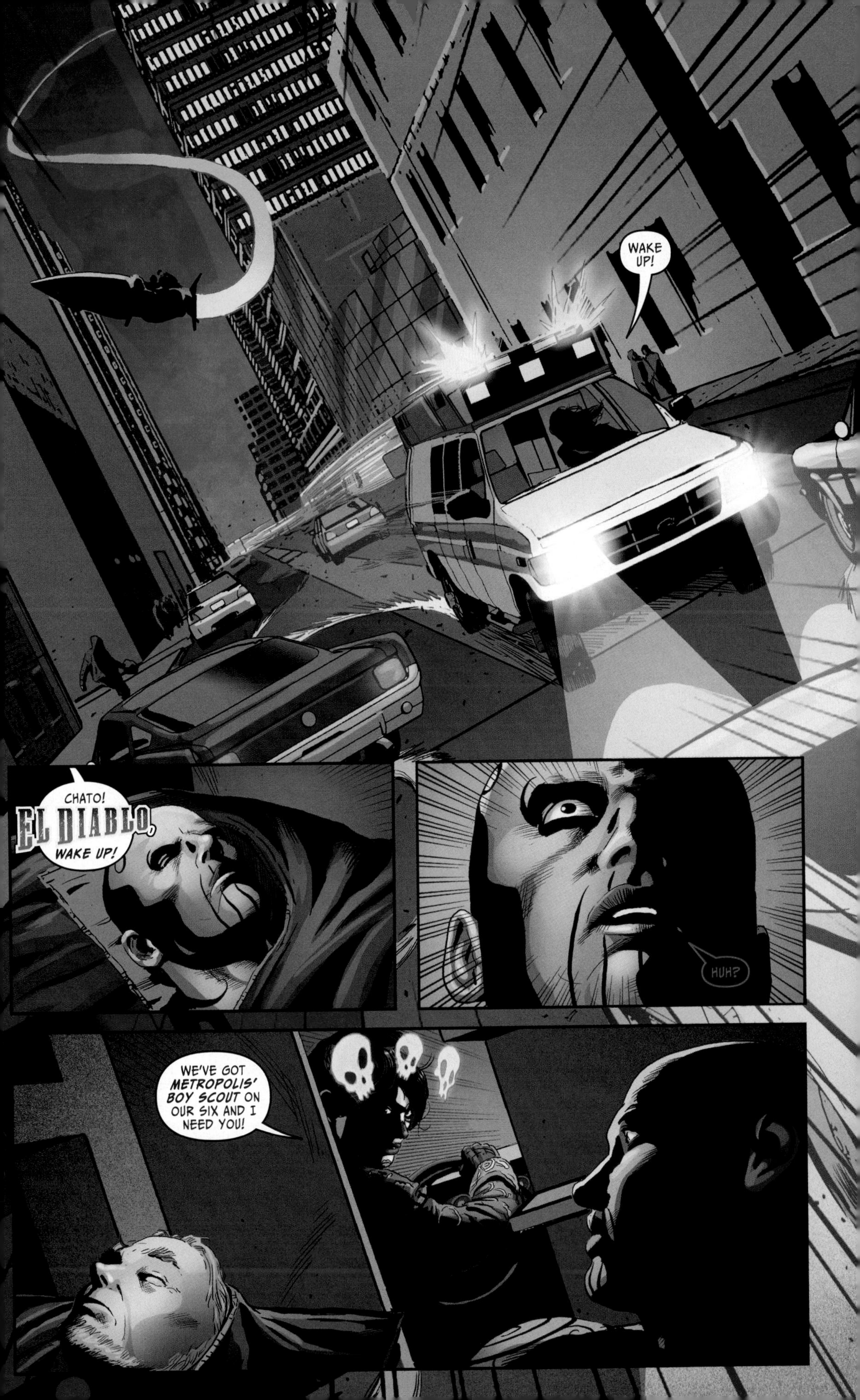
WAKE UP!
CHATO! EL DIABLO, WAKE UP!
HUH?
WE'VE GOT *METROPOLIS' BOY SCOUT* ON OUR SIX AND I NEED YOU!

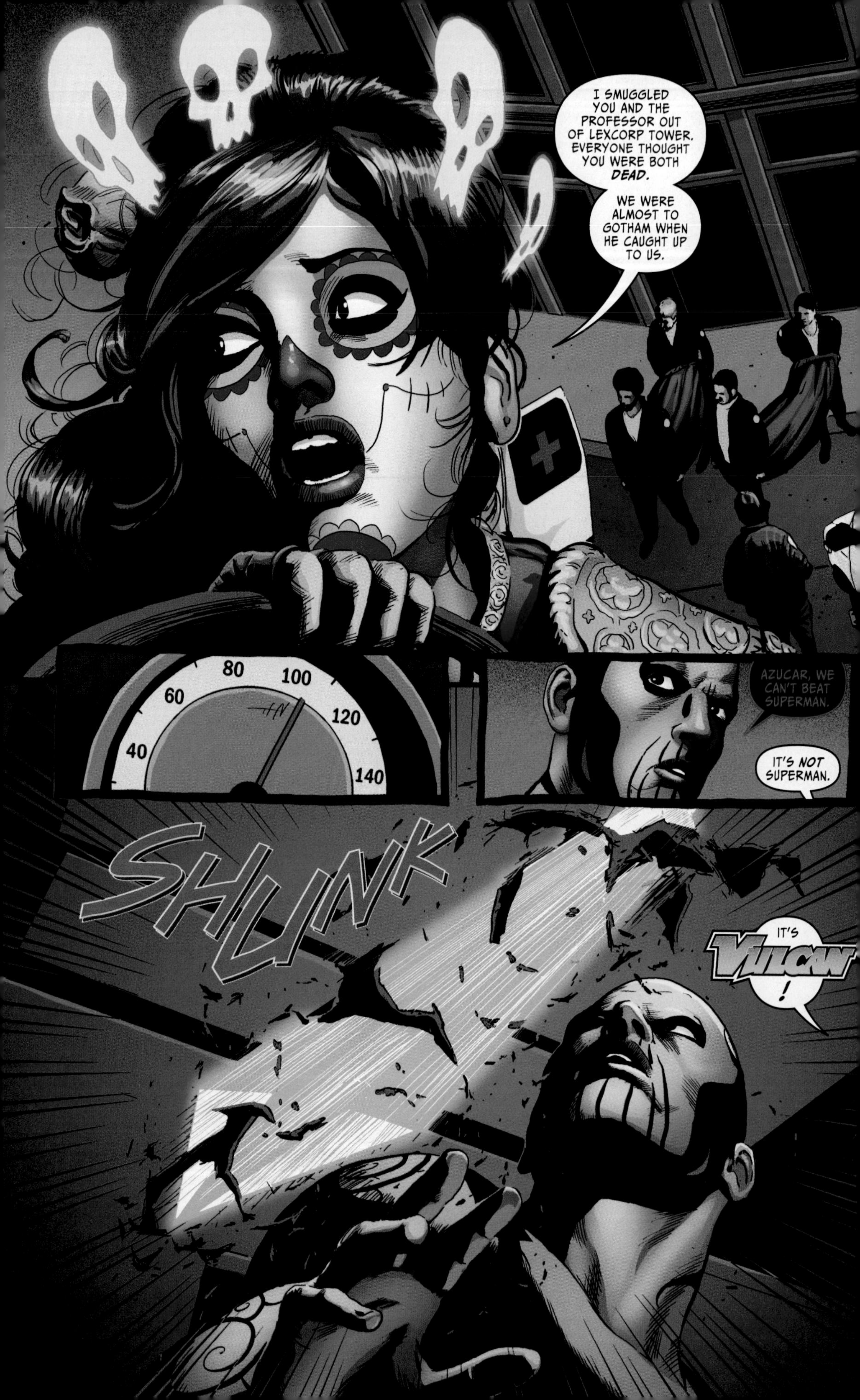
I SMUGGLED YOU AND THE PROFESSOR OUT OF LEXCORP TOWER. EVERYONE THOUGHT YOU WERE BOTH *DEAD.*
WE WERE ALMOST TO GOTHAM WHEN HE CAUGHT UP TO US.
40
60
80
100
120
140
AZUCAR, WE CAN'T BEAT SUPERMAN.
IT'S *NOT* SUPERMAN.
SHUNK
IT'S VULCAN!

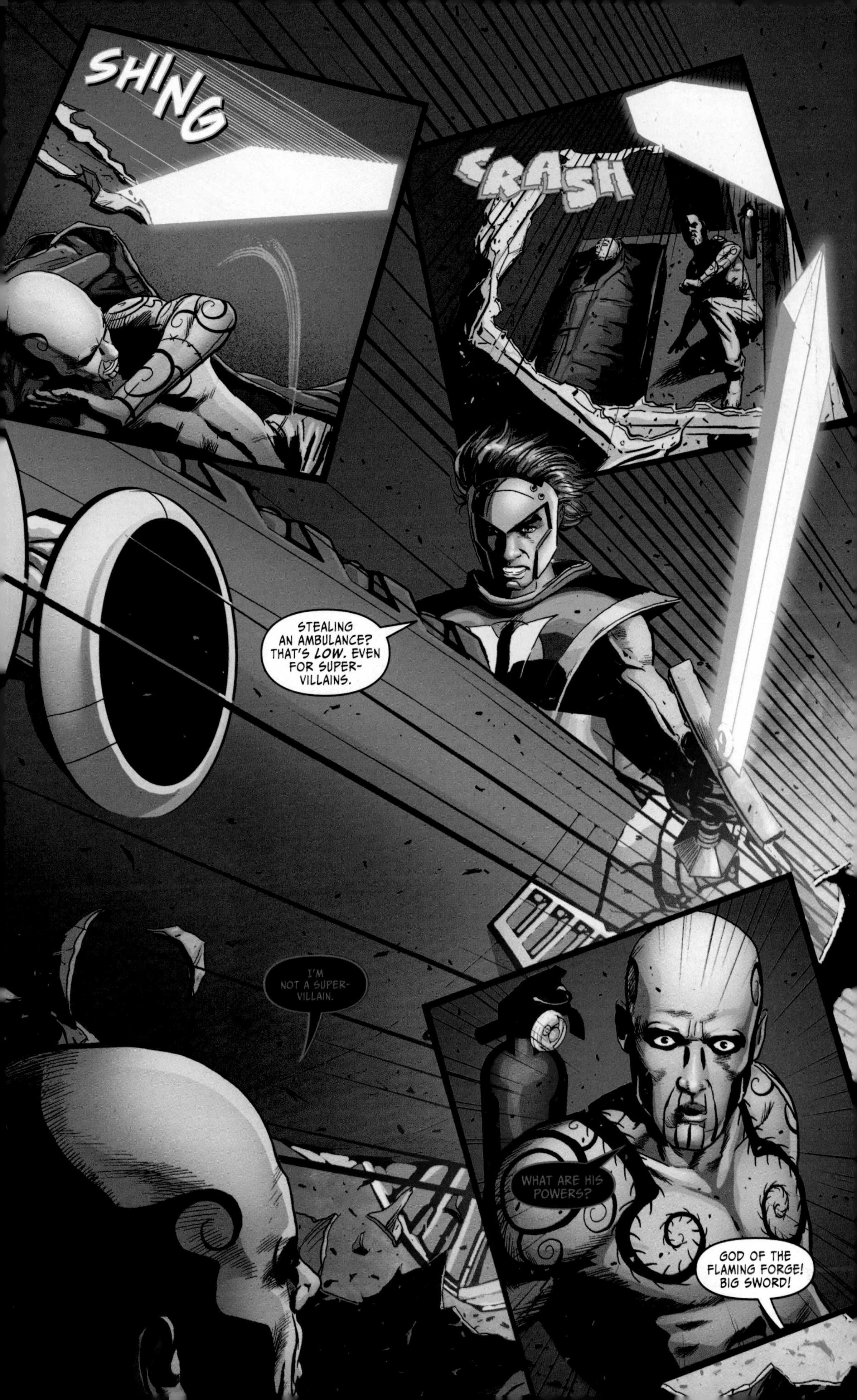
SHING
CRASH
STEALING AN AMBULANCE? THAT'S LOW. EVEN FOR SUPER-VILLAINS.
I'M NOT A SUPER-VILLAIN.
WHAT ARE HIS POWERS?
GOD OF THE FLAMING FORGE! BIG SWORD!

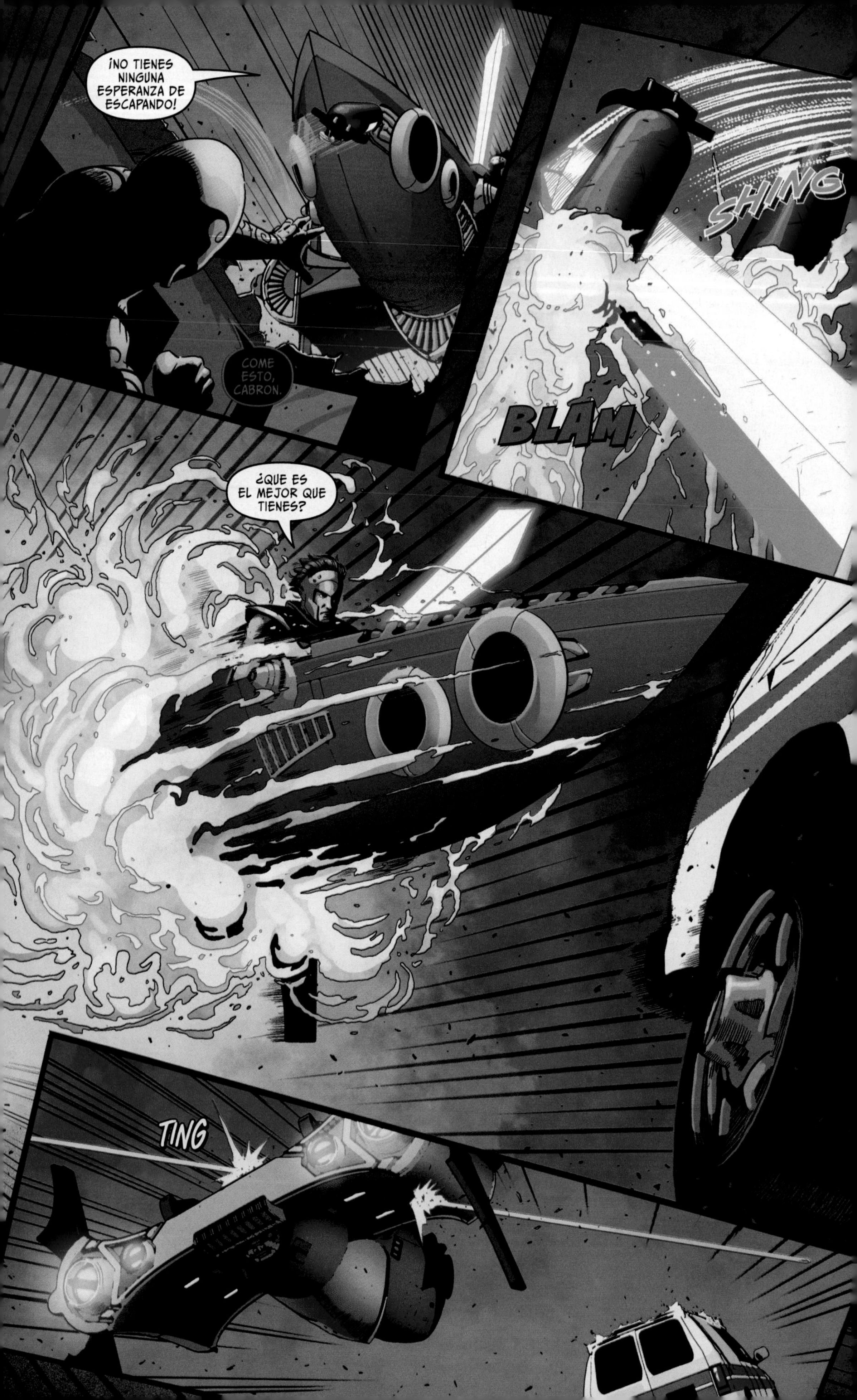
¡NO TIENES NINGUNA ESPERANZA DE ESCAPANDO!
SHING
COME ESTO, CABRON.
BLAM
¿QUE ES EL MEJOR QUE TIENES?
TING

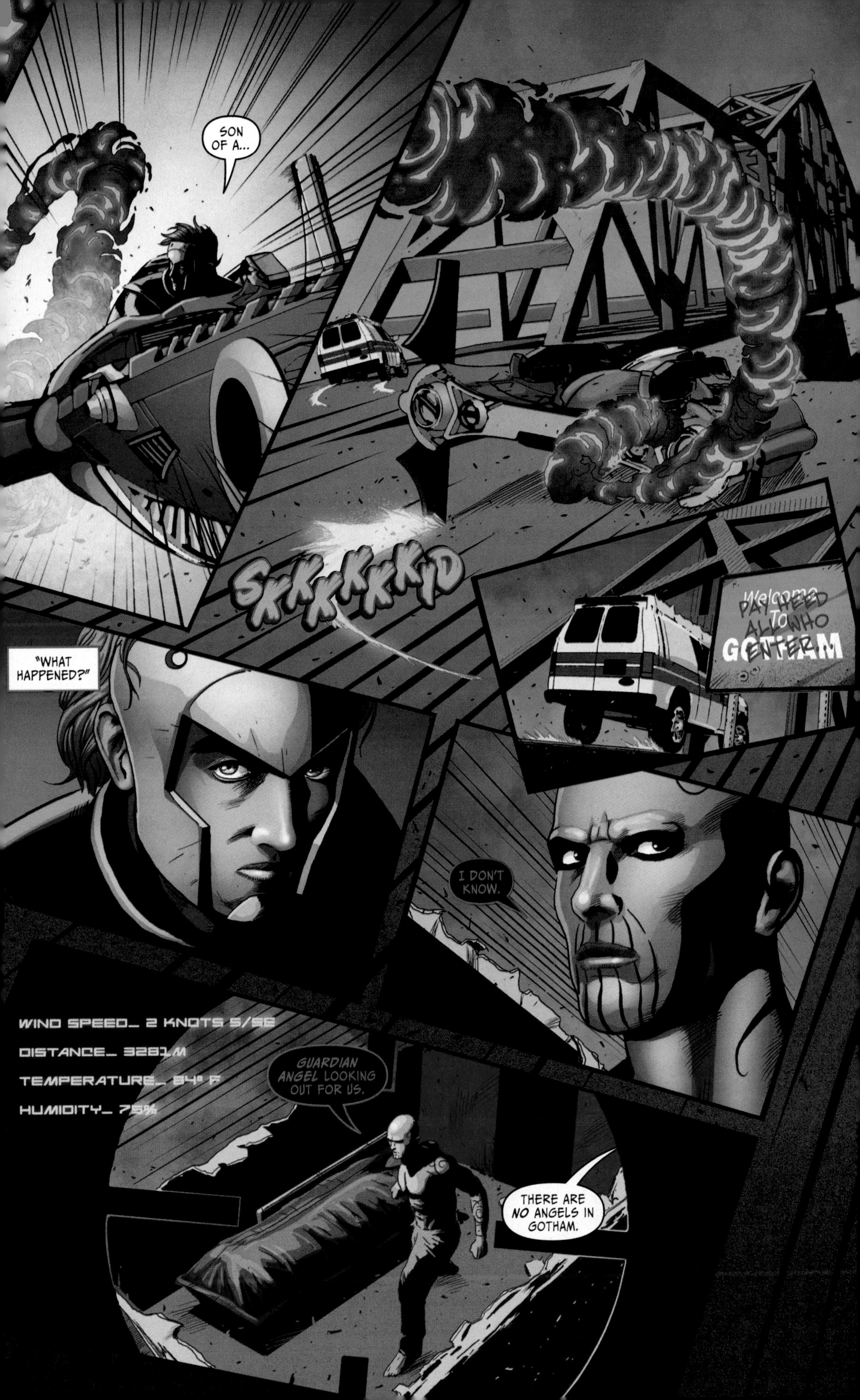
SON OF A...
SKKKKKKID
PAY HEED TO ALL WHO ENTER
Welcome To GOTHAM
"WHAT HAPPENED?"
I DON'T KNOW.
WIND SPEED_ 2 KNOTS S/SE
DISTANCE_ 3281M
TEMPERATURE_ 84° F
HUMIDITY_ 75%
GUARDIAN ANGEL LOOKING OUT FOR US.
THERE ARE NO ANGELS IN GOTHAM.

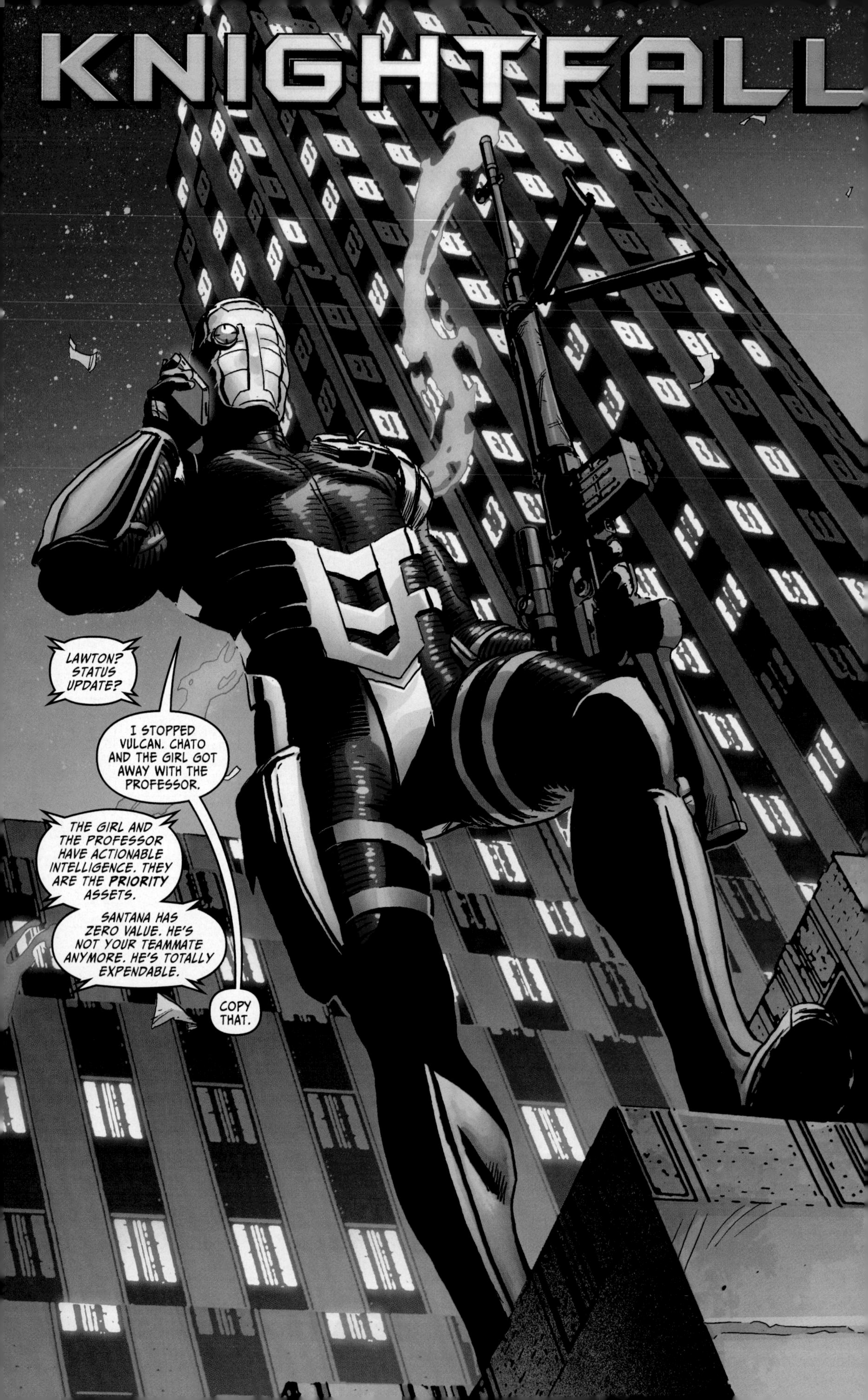
KNIGHTFALL
LAWTON? STATUS UPDATE?
I STOPPED VULCAN. CHATO AND THE GIRL GOT AWAY WITH THE PROFESSOR.
THE GIRL AND THE PROFESSOR HAVE ACTIONABLE INTELLIGENCE. THEY ARE THE PRIORITY ASSETS.
SANTANA HAS ZERO VALUE. HE'S NOT YOUR TEAMMATE ANYMORE. HE'S TOTALLY EXPENDABLE.
COPY THAT.

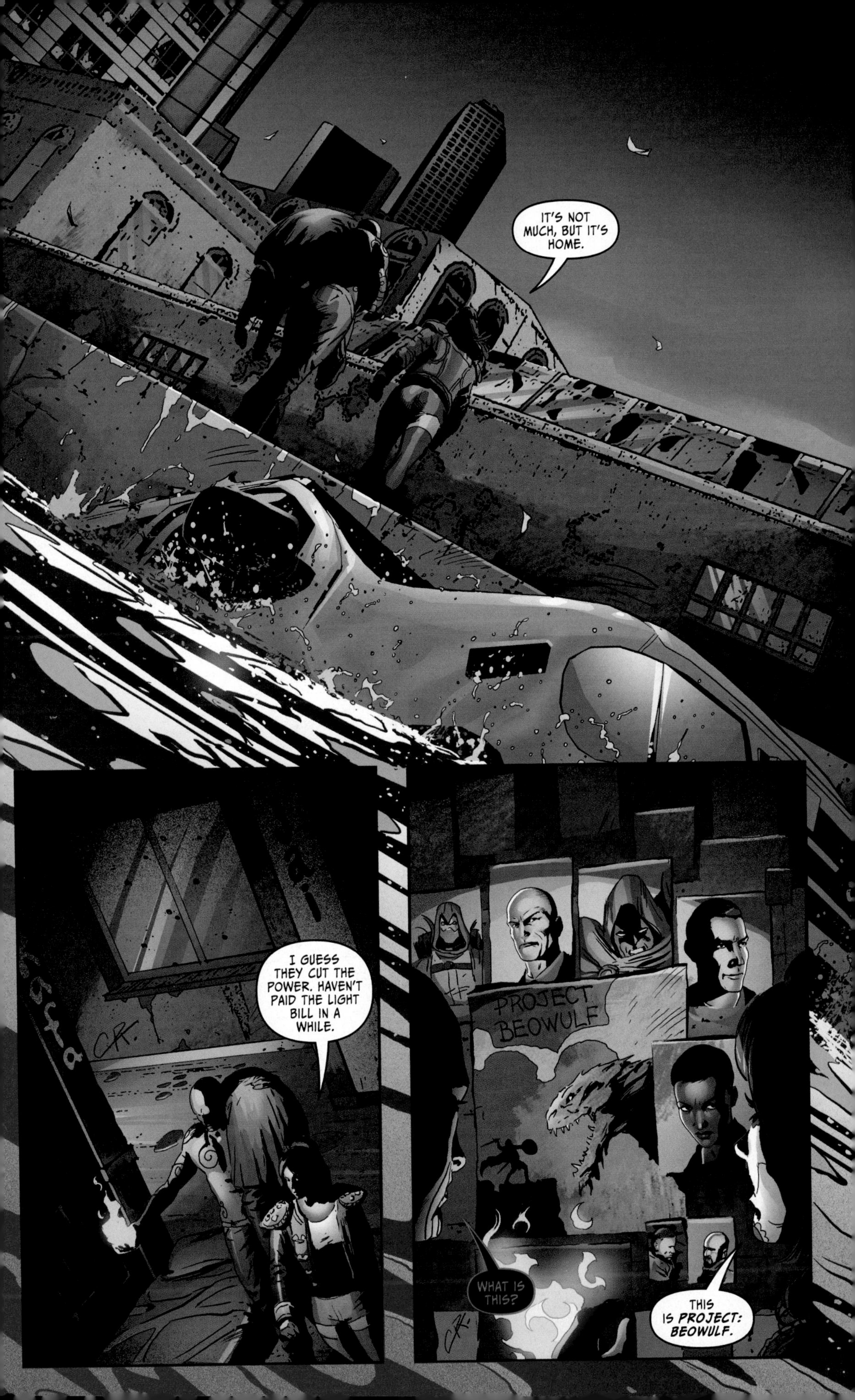
IT'S NOT MUCH, BUT IT'S HOME.
I GUESS THEY CUT THE POWER. HAVEN'T PAID THE LIGHT BILL IN A WHILE.
PROJECT BEOWULF
WHAT IS THIS?
THIS IS PROJECT: BEOWULF.

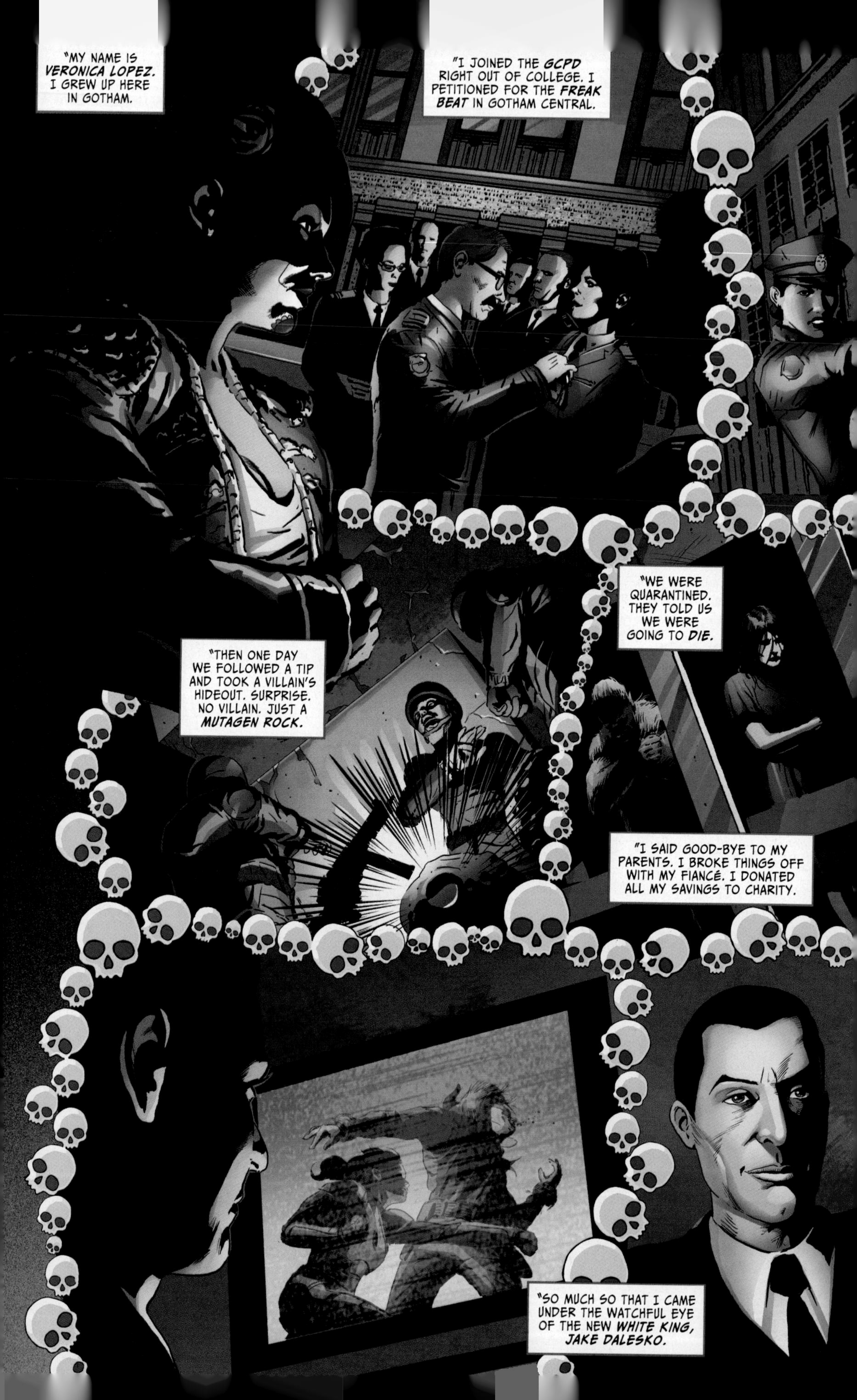
"MY NAME IS VERONICA LOPEZ. I GREW UP HERE IN GOTHAM.
"I JOINED THE GCPD RIGHT OUT OF COLLEGE. I PETITIONED FOR THE FREAK BEAT IN GOTHAM CENTRAL.
"THEN ONE DAY WE FOLLOWED A TIP AND TOOK A VILLAIN'S HIDEOUT. SURPRISE. NO VILLAIN. JUST A MUTAGEN ROCK.
"WE WERE QUARANTINED. THEY TOLD US WE WERE GOING TO DIE.
"I SAID GOOD-BYE TO MY PARENTS. I BROKE THINGS OFF WITH MY FIANCÉ. I DONATED ALL MY SAVINGS TO CHARITY.
"SO MUCH SO THAT I CAME UNDER THE WATCHFUL EYE OF THE NEW WHITE KING, JAKE DALESKO.

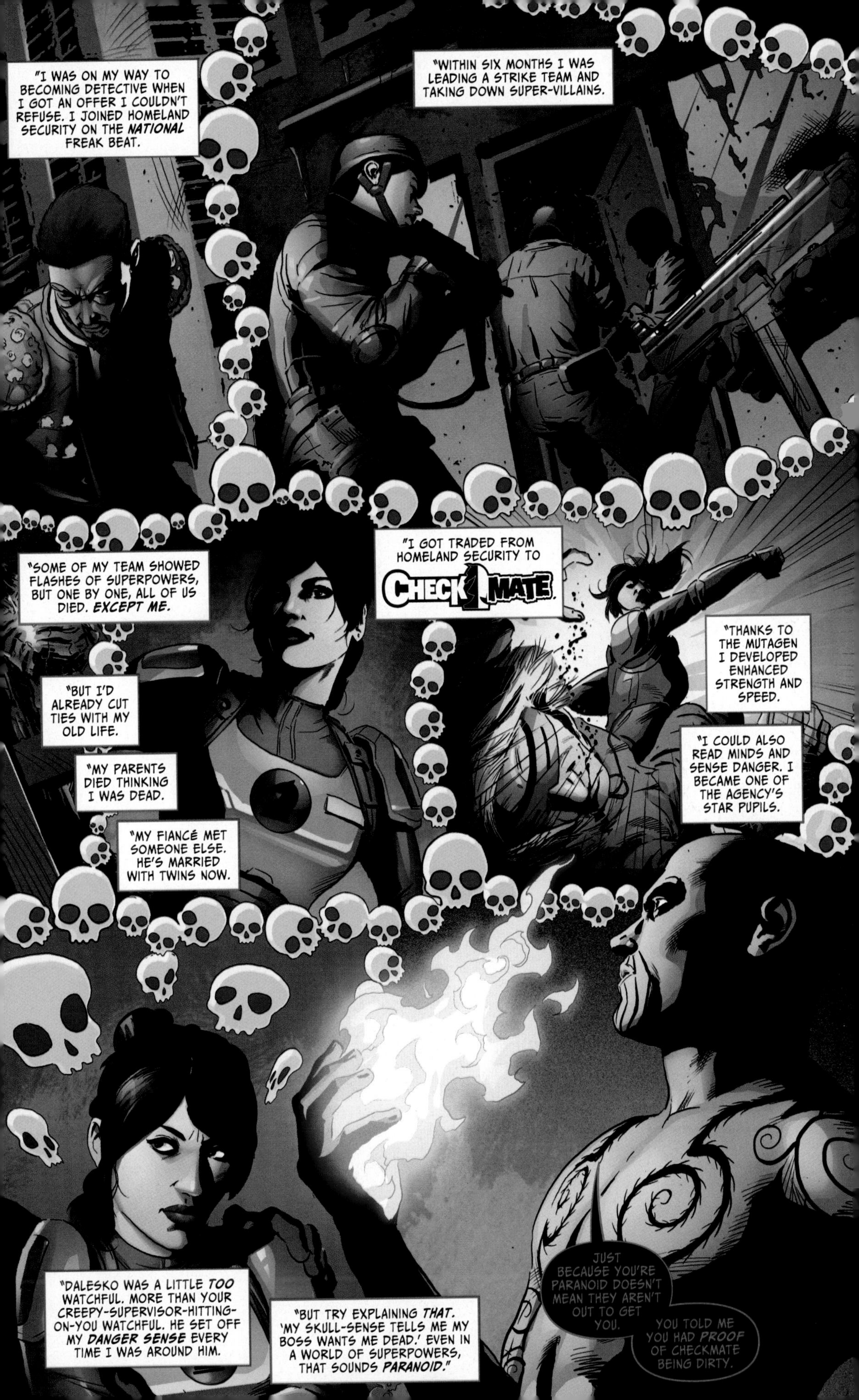
"I WAS ON MY WAY TO BECOMING DETECTIVE WHEN I GOT AN OFFER I COULDN'T REFUSE. I JOINED HOMELAND SECURITY ON THE *NATIONAL* FREAK BEAT.
"WITHIN SIX MONTHS I WAS LEADING A STRIKE TEAM AND TAKING DOWN SUPER-VILLAINS.
"SOME OF MY TEAM SHOWED FLASHES OF SUPERPOWERS, BUT ONE BY ONE, ALL OF US DIED. *EXCEPT ME.*
"BUT I'D ALREADY CUT TIES WITH MY OLD LIFE.
"MY PARENTS DIED THINKING I WAS DEAD.
"MY FIANCÉ MET SOMEONE ELSE. HE'S MARRIED WITH TWINS NOW.
"I GOT TRADED FROM HOMELAND SECURITY TO CHECKMATE.
"THANKS TO THE MUTAGEN I DEVELOPED ENHANCED STRENGTH AND SPEED.
"I COULD ALSO READ MINDS AND SENSE DANGER. I BECAME ONE OF THE AGENCY'S STAR PUPILS.
"DALESKO WAS A LITTLE *TOO* WATCHFUL. MORE THAN YOUR CREEPY-SUPERVISOR-HITTING-ON-YOU WATCHFUL. HE SET OFF MY *DANGER SENSE* EVERY TIME I WAS AROUND HIM.
"BUT TRY EXPLAINING *THAT.* 'MY SKULL-SENSE TELLS ME MY BOSS WANTS ME DEAD.' EVEN IN A WORLD OF SUPERPOWERS, THAT SOUNDS *PARANOID.*"
JUST BECAUSE YOU'RE PARANOID DOESN'T MEAN THEY AREN'T OUT TO GET YOU.
YOU TOLD ME YOU HAD *PROOF* OF CHECKMATE BEING DIRTY.

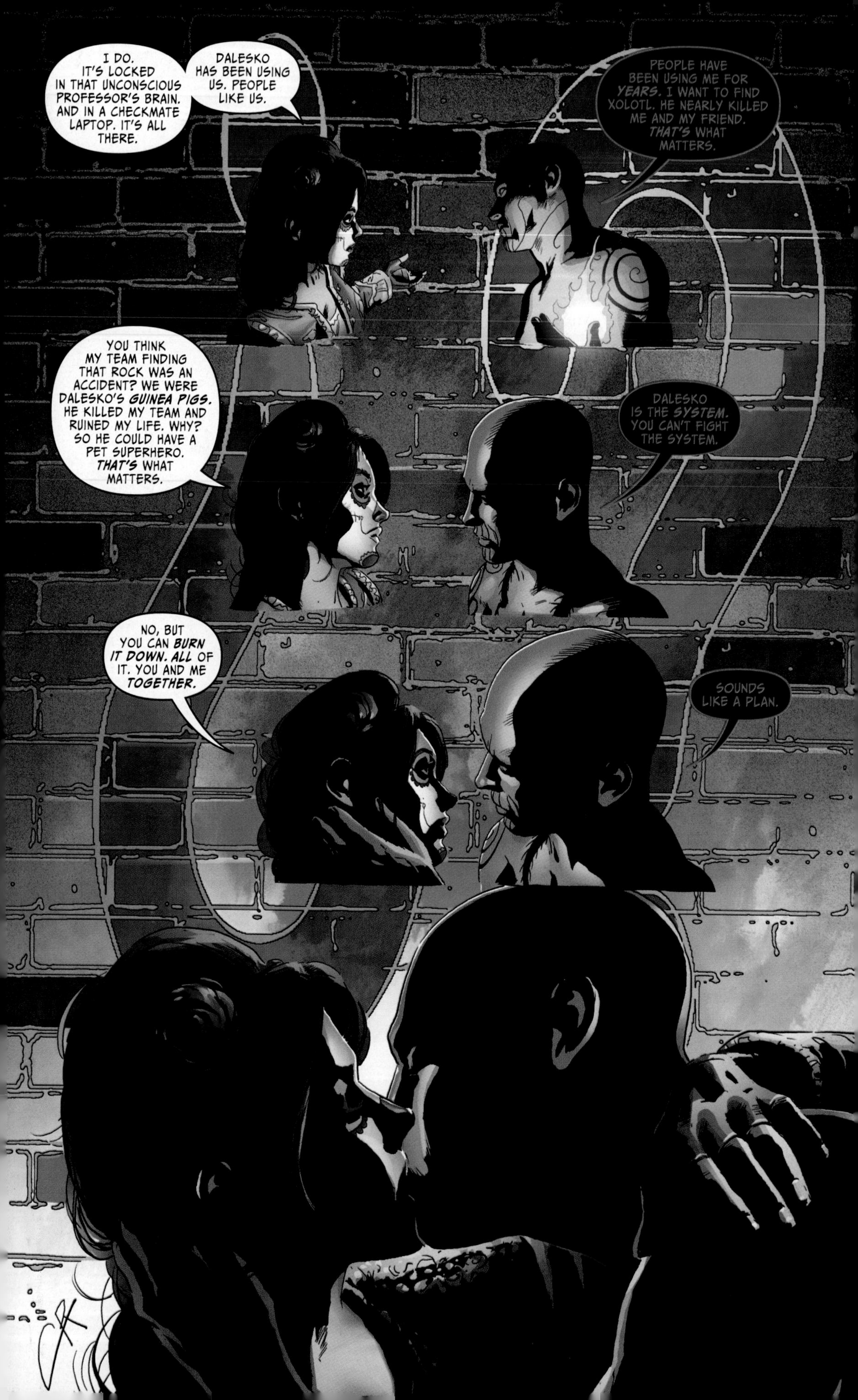
DALESKO HAS BEEN USING US. PEOPLE LIKE US.
I DO. IT'S LOCKED IN THAT UNCONSCIOUS PROFESSOR'S BRAIN. AND IN A CHECKMATE LAPTOP. IT'S ALL THERE.
PEOPLE HAVE BEEN USING ME FOR YEARS. I WANT TO FIND XOLOTL. HE NEARLY KILLED ME AND MY FRIEND. THAT'S WHAT MATTERS.
YOU THINK MY TEAM FINDING THAT ROCK WAS AN ACCIDENT? WE WERE DALESKO'S GUINEA PIGS. HE KILLED MY TEAM AND RUINED MY LIFE. WHY? SO HE COULD HAVE A PET SUPERHERO. THAT'S WHAT MATTERS.
DALESKO IS THE SYSTEM. YOU CAN'T FIGHT THE SYSTEM.
NO, BUT YOU CAN BURN IT DOWN. ALL OF IT. YOU AND ME TOGETHER.
SOUNDS LIKE A PLAN.

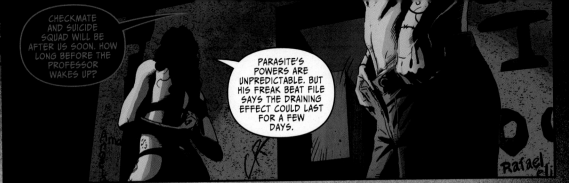

CHECKMATE AND SUICIDE SQUAD WILL BE AFTER US SOON. HOW LONG BEFORE THE PROFESSOR WAKES UP?

PARASITE'S POWERS ARE UNPREDICTABLE. BUT HIS FREAK BEAT FILE SAYS THE DRAINING EFFECT COULD LAST FOR A FEW DAYS.

Rafael
Eli

WHAT ABOUT THE CHECKMATE LAPTOP FULL OF EVIDENCE?

ABOUT THAT.

I DON'T EXACTLY HAVE IT.

CLUEMASTER DOES.

NO PROBLEM.

NO PROBLEM? ONCE THE WORD HITS THE STREETS THAT CHECKMATE AND SUICIDE SQUAD ARE AFTER US, THAT LAPTOP WILL BECOME THE MOST VALUABLE THING IN GOTHAM.

YOU STAY HERE WITH THE PROFESSOR. I'LL TAKE CARE OF THE LAPTOP.

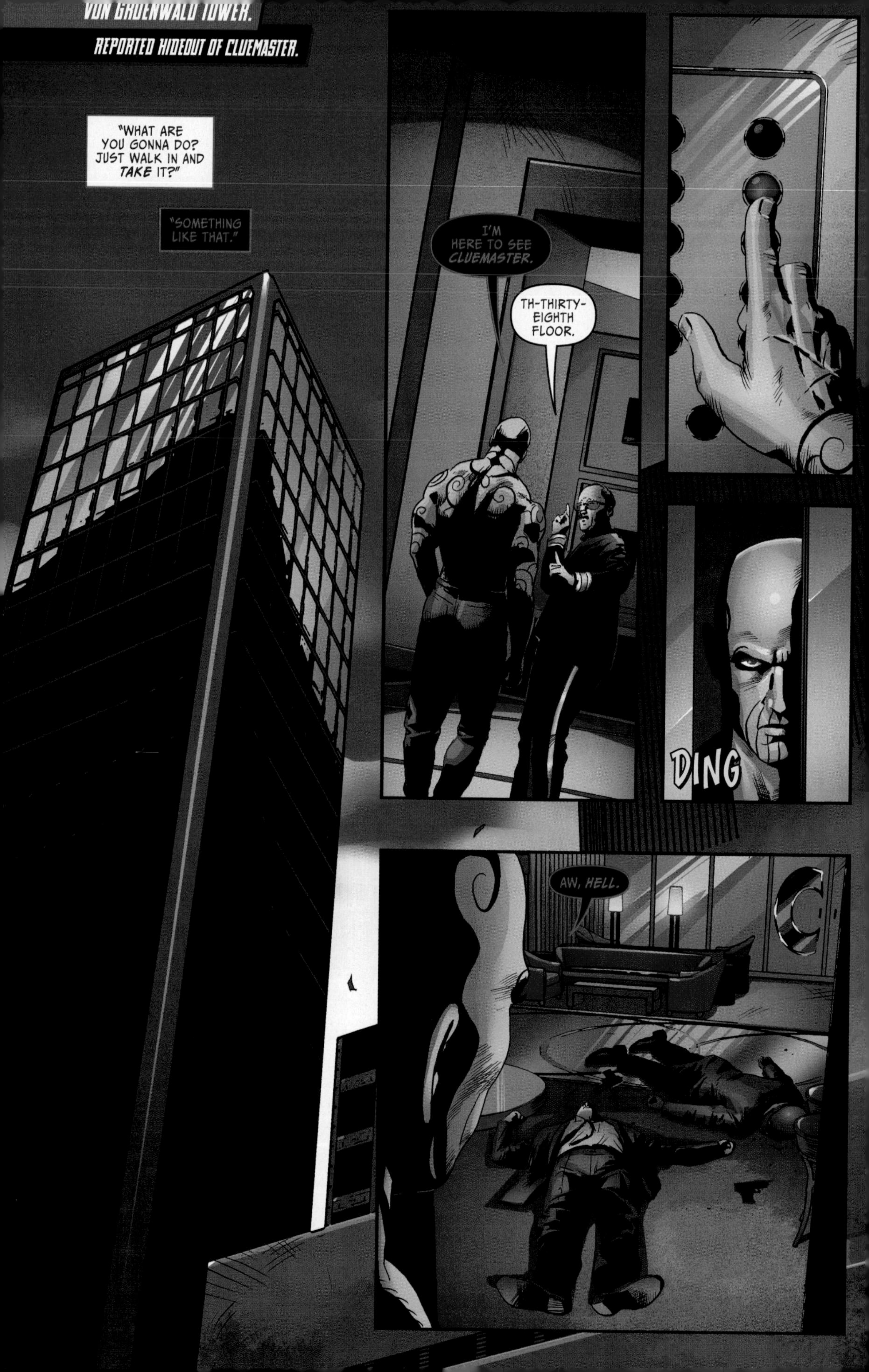
VON GRUENWALD TOWER.
REPORTED HIDEOUT OF CLUEMASTER.
"WHAT ARE YOU GONNA DO? JUST WALK IN AND TAKE IT?"
"SOMETHING LIKE THAT."
I'M HERE TO SEE CLUEMASTER.
TH-THIRTY-EIGHTH FLOOR.
DING
AW, HELL.

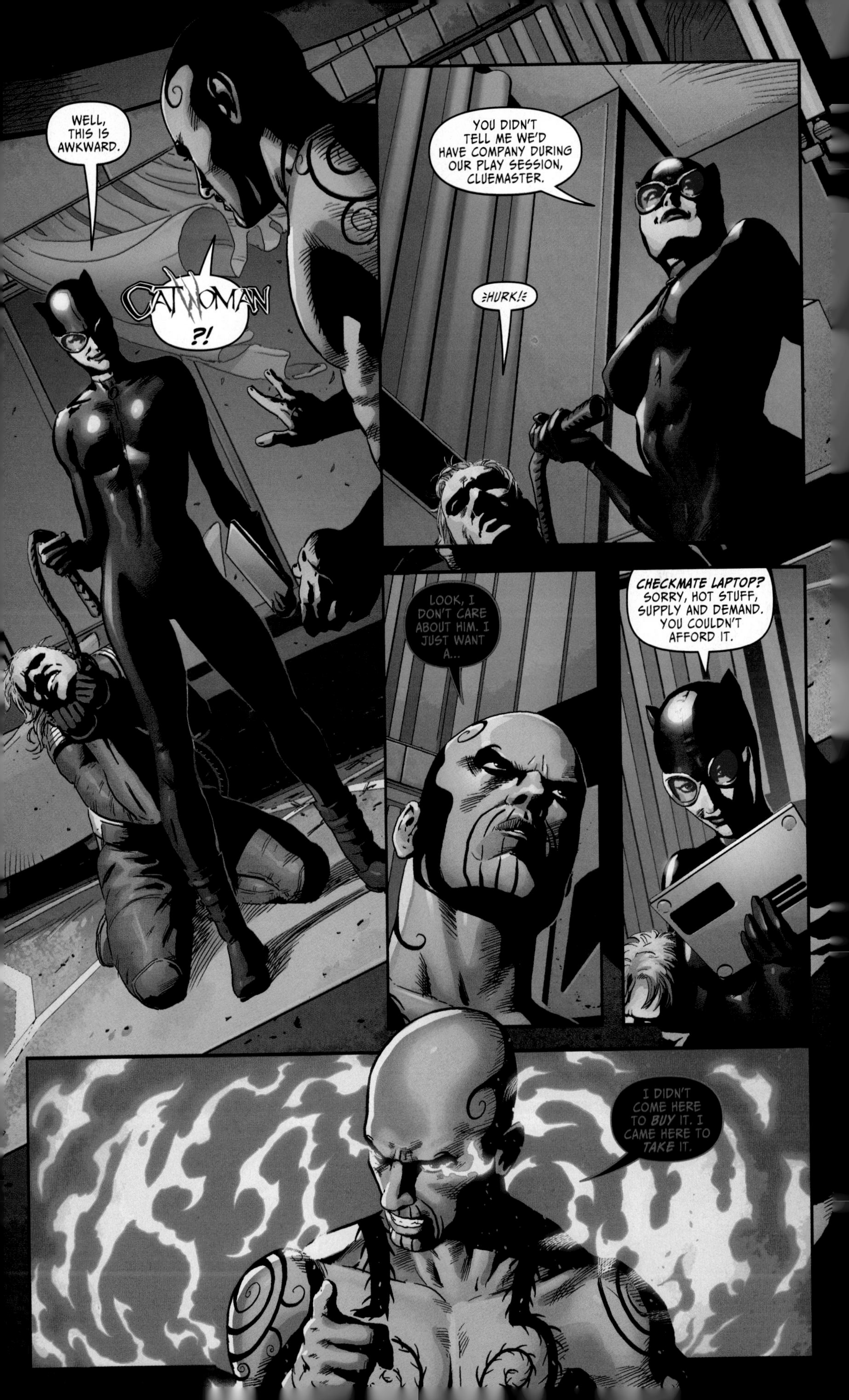

WELL, THIS IS AWKWARD.
CATWOMAN ?!
YOU DIDN'T TELL ME WE'D HAVE COMPANY DURING OUR PLAY SESSION, CLUEMASTER.
HURK!
LOOK, I DON'T CARE ABOUT HIM. I JUST WANT A...
CHECKMATE LAPTOP? SORRY, HOT STUFF, SUPPLY AND DEMAND. YOU COULDN'T AFFORD IT.
I DIDN'T COME HERE TO BUY IT. I CAME HERE TO TAKE IT.

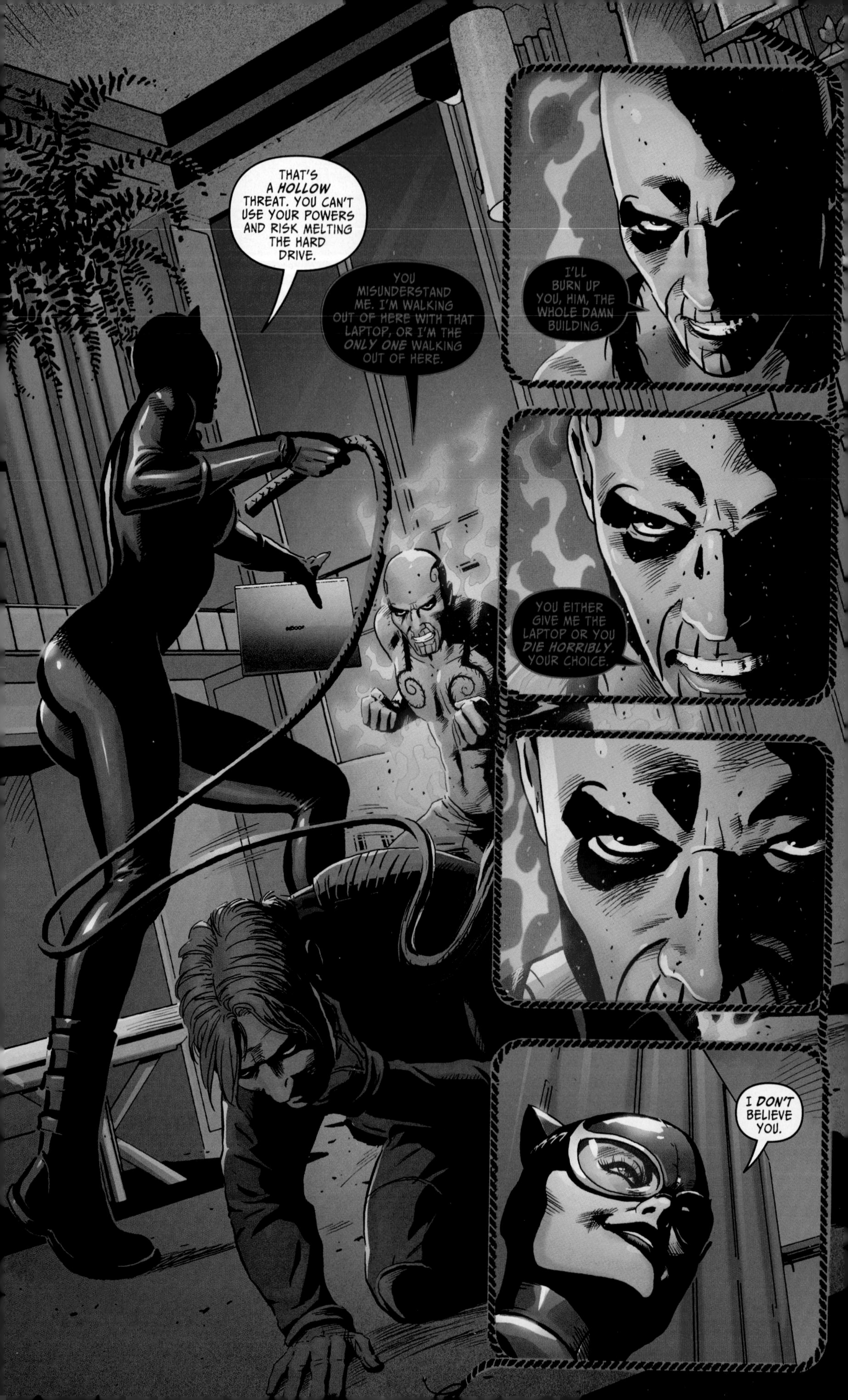
THAT'S A HOLLOW THREAT. YOU CAN'T USE YOUR POWERS AND RISK MELTING THE HARD DRIVE.
YOU MISUNDERSTAND ME. I'M WALKING OUT OF HERE WITH THAT LAPTOP, OR I'M THE ONLY ONE WALKING OUT OF HERE.
I'LL BURN UP YOU, HIM, THE WHOLE DAMN BUILDING.
YOU EITHER GIVE ME THE LAPTOP OR YOU DIE HORRIBLY. YOUR CHOICE.
I DON'T BELIEVE YOU.

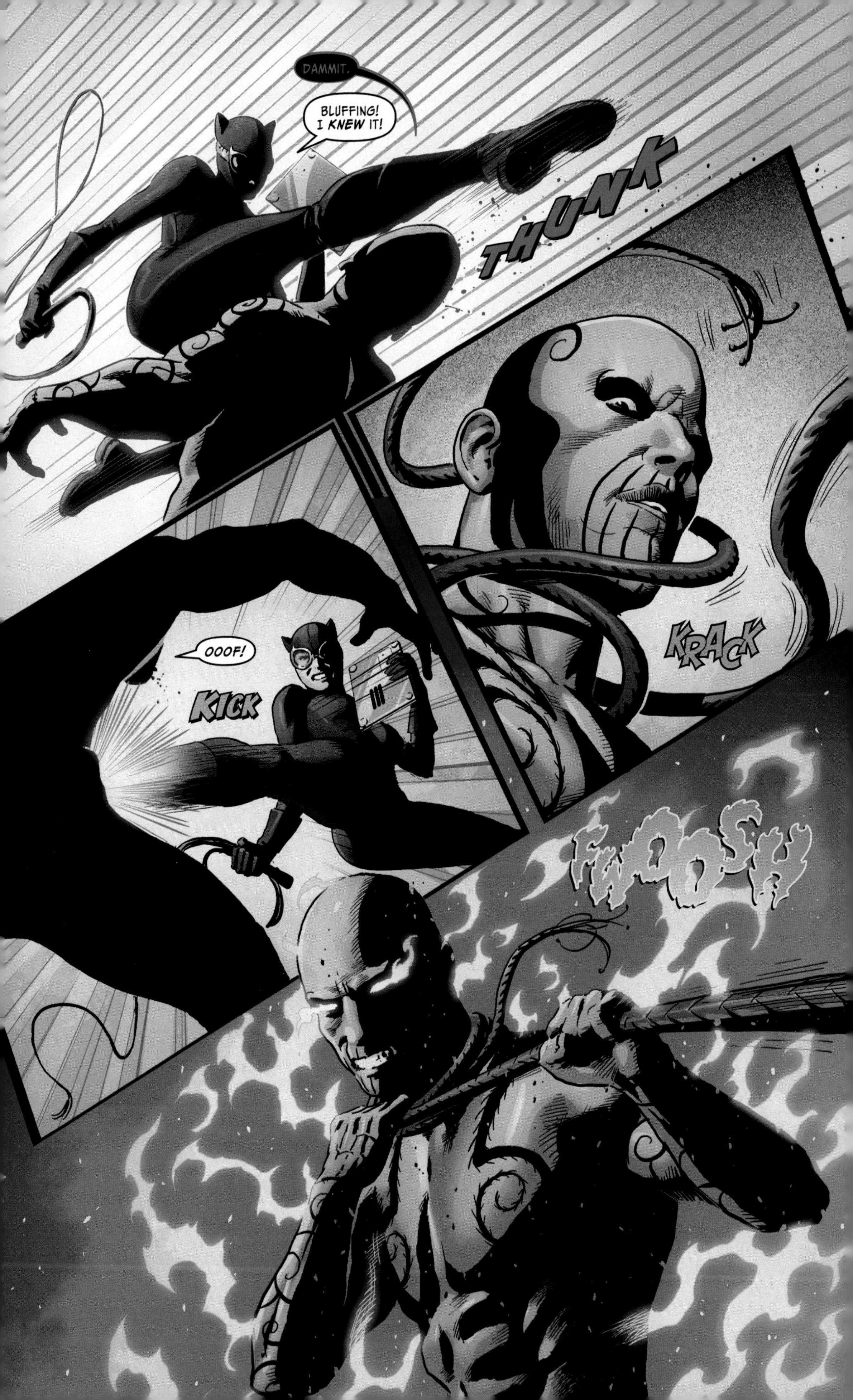
DAMMIT.
BLUFFING! I KNEW IT!
THUNK
OOOF!
KICK
KRACK
FWOOSH

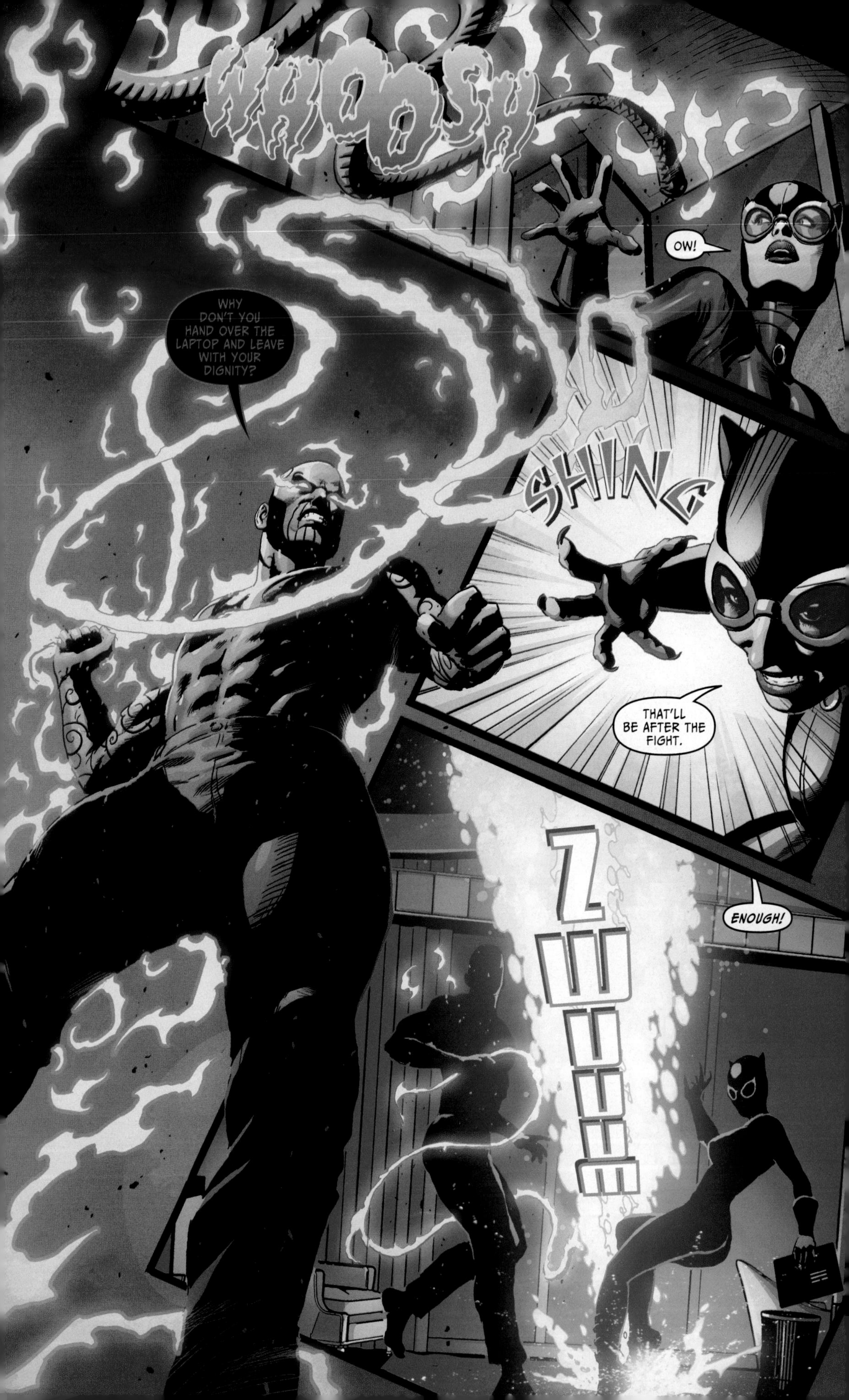
WHOOSH
OW!
WHY DON'T YOU HAND OVER THE LAPTOP AND LEAVE WITH YOUR DIGNITY?
SHING
THAT'LL BE AFTER THE FIGHT.
ZWEEEE
ENOUGH!

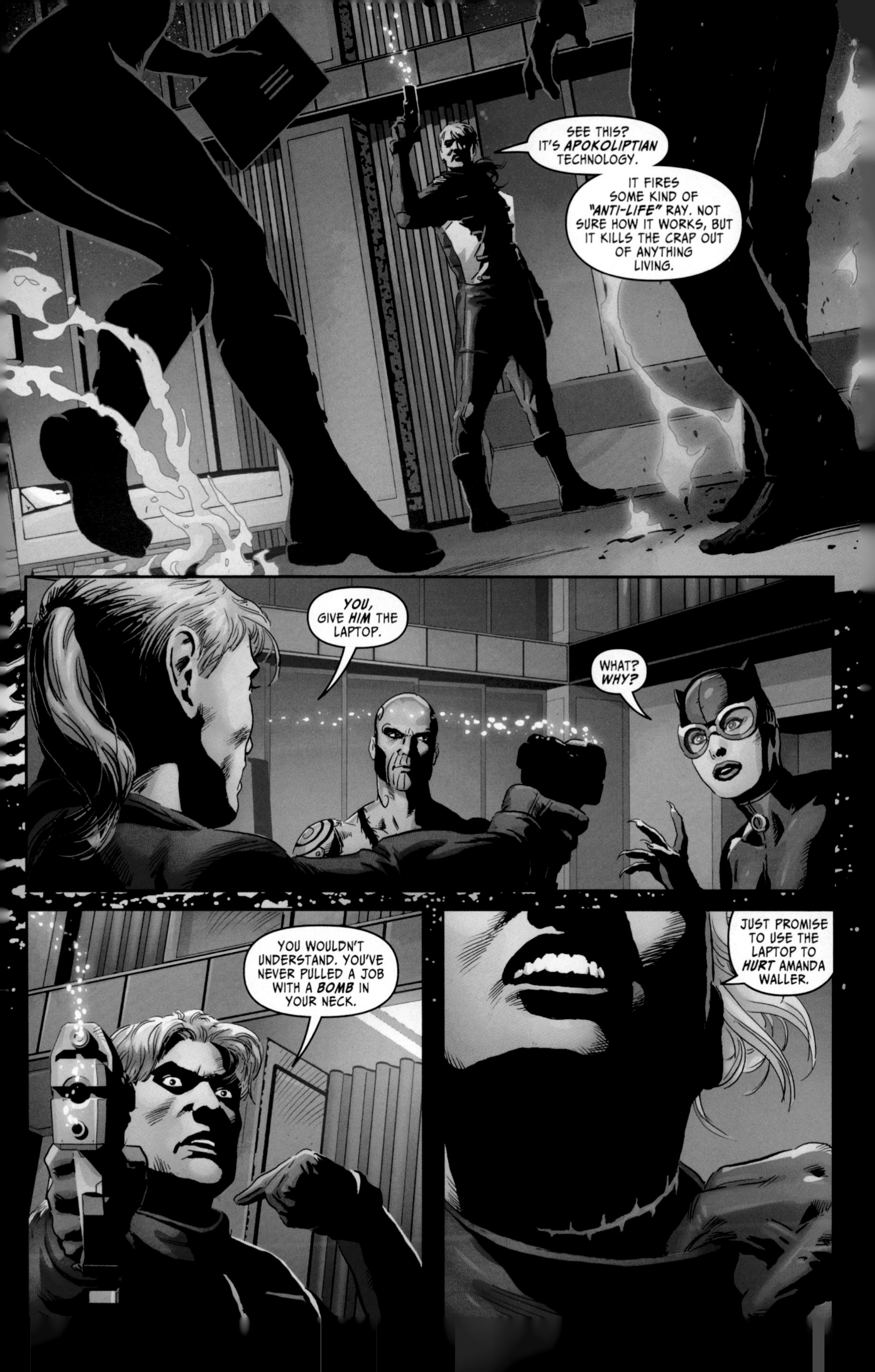
SEE THIS? IT'S APOKOLIPTIAN TECHNOLOGY.
IT FIRES SOME KIND OF "ANTI-LIFE" RAY. NOT SURE HOW IT WORKS, BUT IT KILLS THE CRAP OUT OF ANYTHING LIVING.
YOU, GIVE HIM THE LAPTOP.
WHAT? WHY?
YOU WOULDN'T UNDERSTAND. YOU'VE NEVER PULLED A JOB WITH A BOMB IN YOUR NECK.
JUST PROMISE TO USE THE LAPTOP TO HURT AMANDA WALLER.

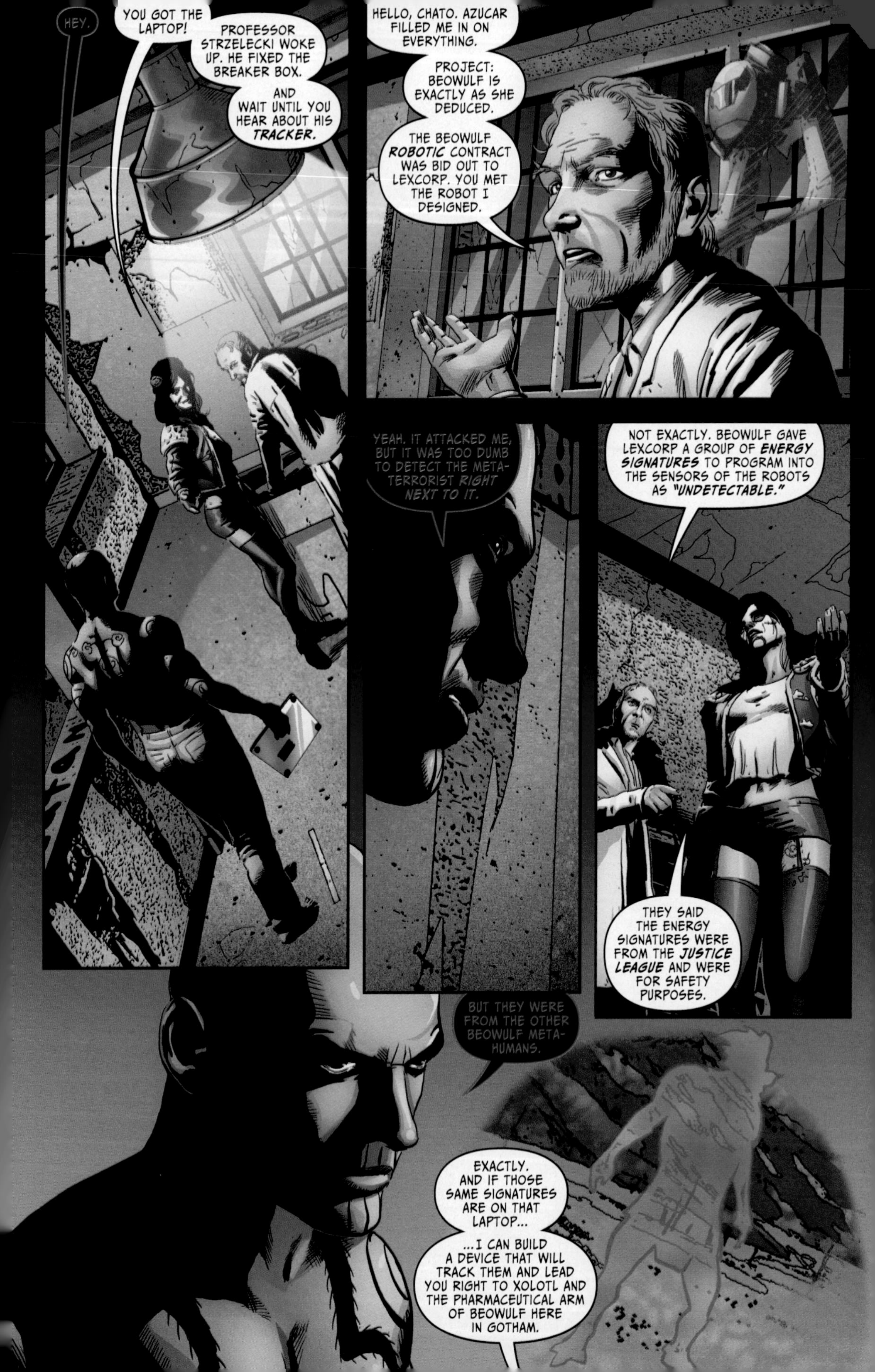
HEY.
YOU GOT THE LAPTOP!
PROFESSOR STRZELECKI WOKE UP. HE FIXED THE BREAKER BOX.
AND WAIT UNTIL YOU HEAR ABOUT HIS TRACKER.
HELLO, CHATO. AZUCAR FILLED ME IN ON EVERYTHING.
PROJECT: BEOWULF IS EXACTLY AS SHE DEDUCED.
THE BEOWULF ROBOTIC CONTRACT WAS BID OUT TO LEXCORP. YOU MET THE ROBOT I DESIGNED.
YEAH. IT ATTACKED ME, BUT IT WAS TOO DUMB TO DETECT THE META-TERRORIST RIGHT NEXT TO IT.
NOT EXACTLY. BEOWULF GAVE LEXCORP A GROUP OF ENERGY SIGNATURES TO PROGRAM INTO THE SENSORS OF THE ROBOTS AS "UNDETECTABLE."
THEY SAID THE ENERGY SIGNATURES WERE FROM THE JUSTICE LEAGUE AND WERE FOR SAFETY PURPOSES.
BUT THEY WERE FROM THE OTHER BEOWULF META-HUMANS.
EXACTLY. AND IF THOSE SAME SIGNATURES ARE ON THAT LAPTOP...
...I CAN BUILD A DEVICE THAT WILL TRACK THEM AND LEAD YOU RIGHT TO XOLOTL AND THE PHARMACEUTICAL ARM OF BEOWULF HERE IN GOTHAM.

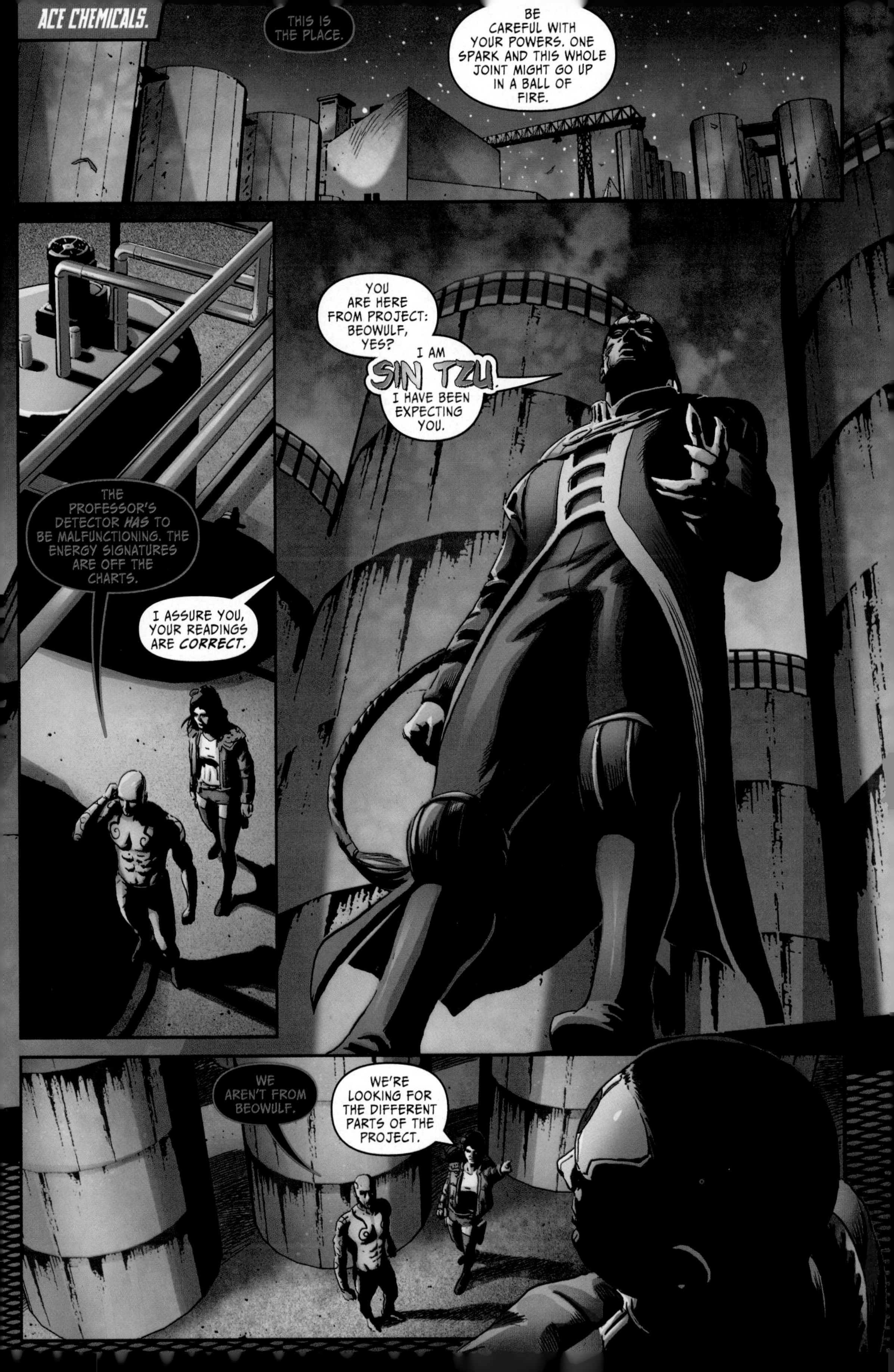
ACE CHEMICALS.
THIS IS THE PLACE.
BE CAREFUL WITH YOUR POWERS. ONE SPARK AND THIS WHOLE JOINT MIGHT GO UP IN A BALL OF FIRE.
YOU ARE HERE FROM PROJECT: BEOWULF, YES?
I AM SIN TZU. I HAVE BEEN EXPECTING YOU.
THE PROFESSOR'S DETECTOR HAS TO BE MALFUNCTIONING. THE ENERGY SIGNATURES ARE OFF THE CHARTS.
I ASSURE YOU, YOUR READINGS ARE CORRECT.
WE AREN'T FROM BEOWULF.
WE'RE LOOKING FOR THE DIFFERENT PARTS OF THE PROJECT.

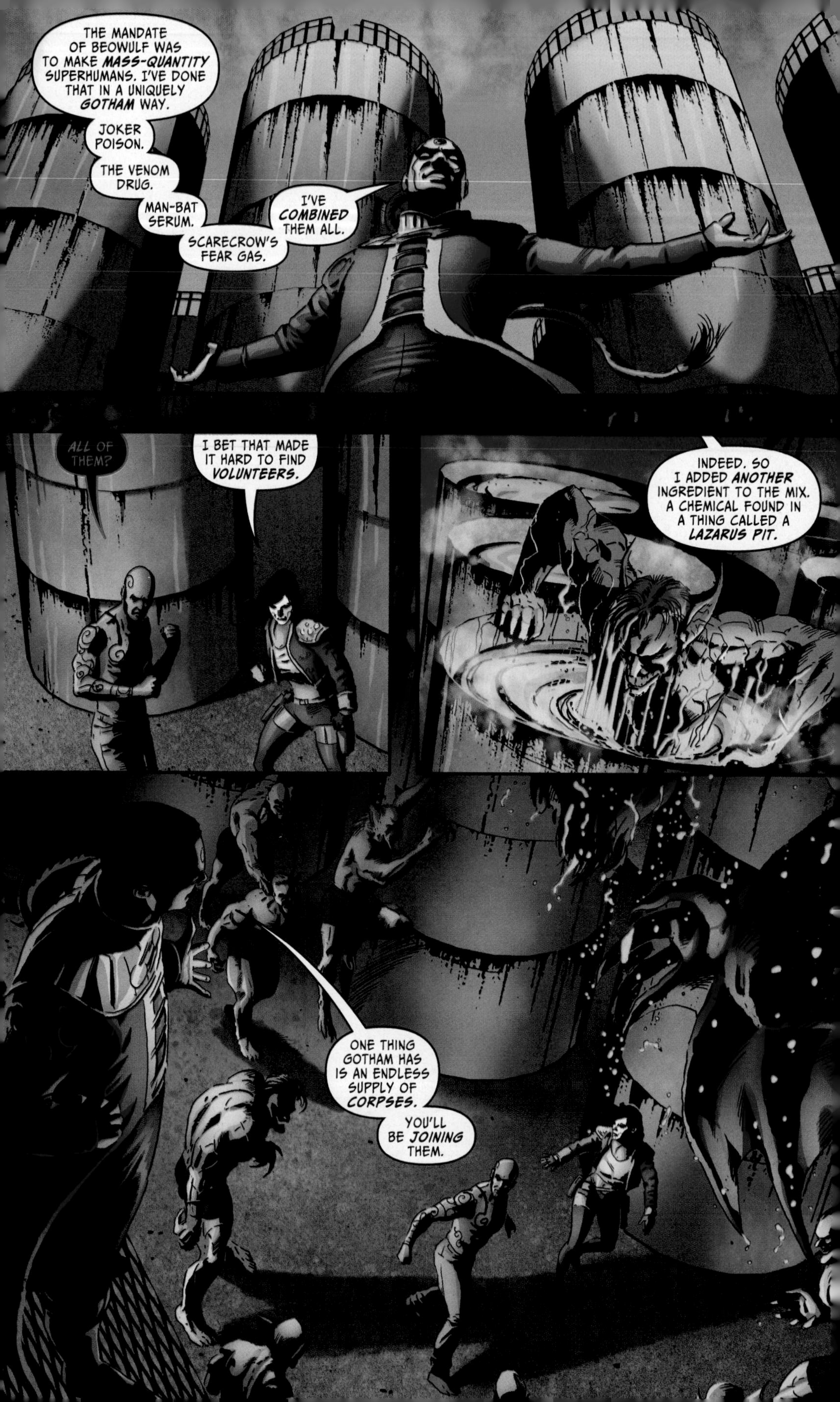
THE MANDATE OF BEOWULF WAS TO MAKE *MASS-QUANTITY* SUPERHUMANS. I'VE DONE THAT IN A UNIQUELY *GOTHAM* WAY.
JOKER POISON.
THE VENOM DRUG.
MAN-BAT SERUM.
SCARECROW'S FEAR GAS.
I'VE *COMBINED* THEM ALL.
ALL OF THEM?
I BET THAT MADE IT HARD TO FIND *VOLUNTEERS.*
INDEED. SO I ADDED *ANOTHER* INGREDIENT TO THE MIX. A CHEMICAL FOUND IN A THING CALLED A *LAZARUS PIT.*
ONE THING GOTHAM HAS IS AN ENDLESS SUPPLY OF *CORPSES.*
YOU'LL BE *JOINING* THEM.

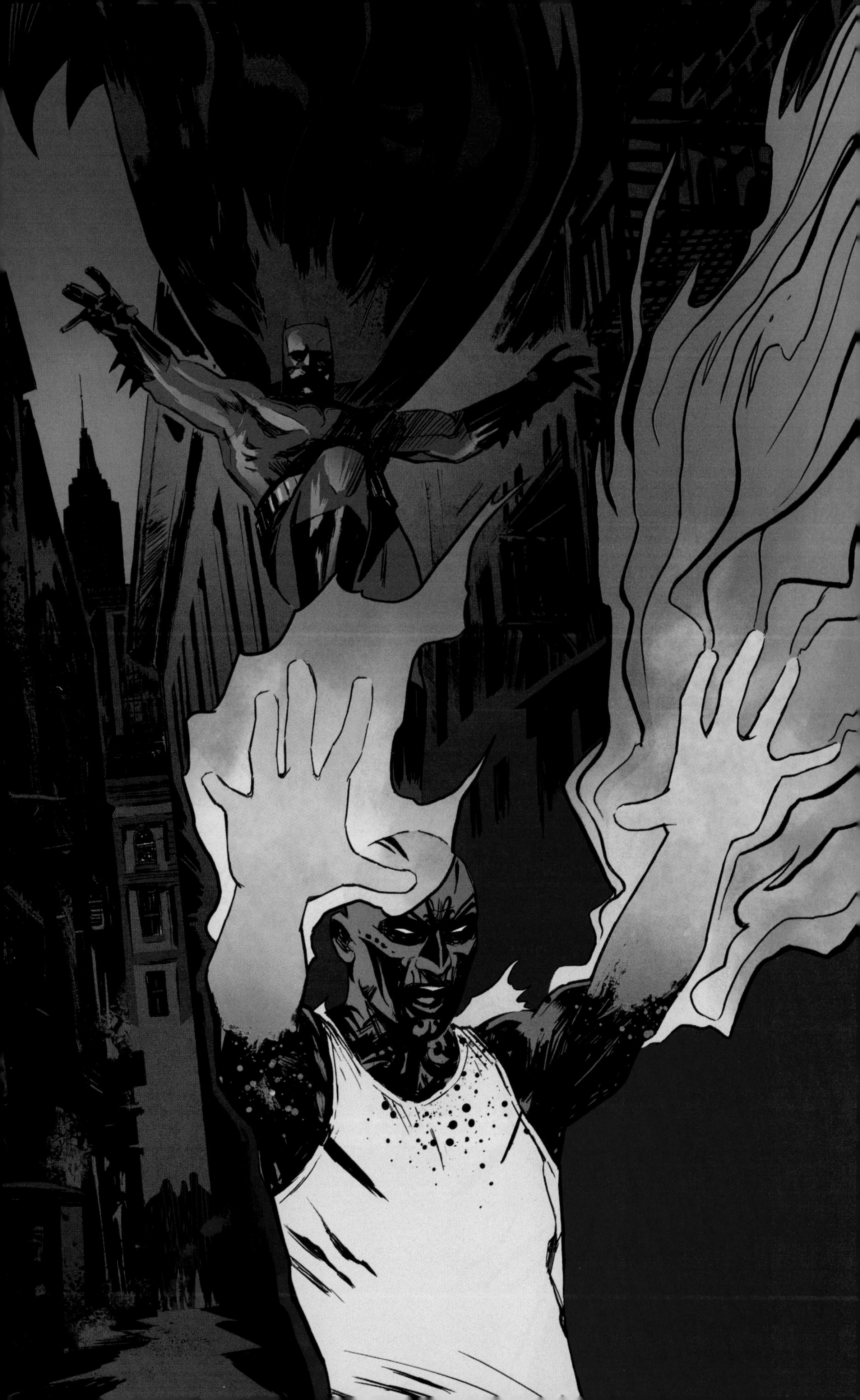

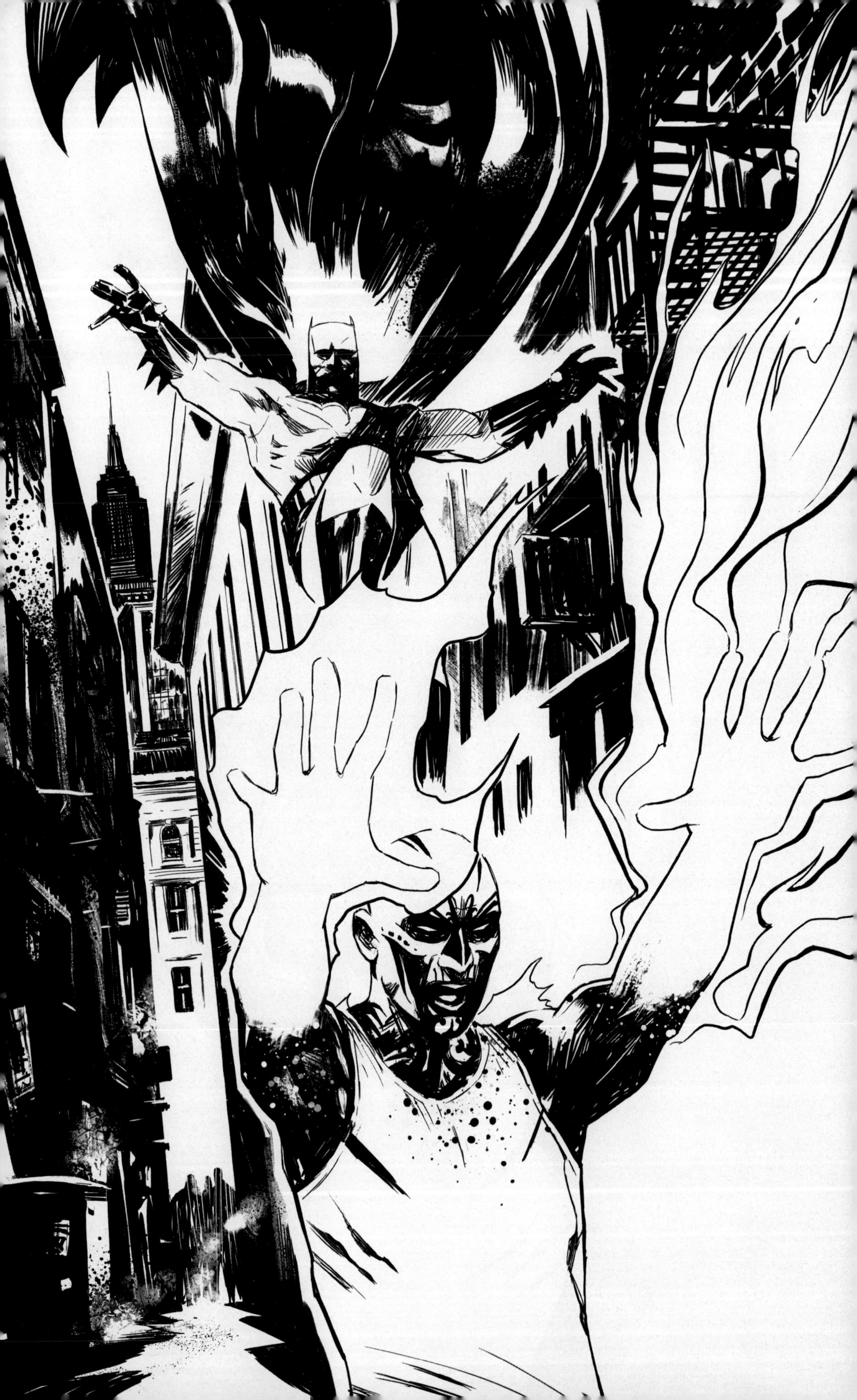

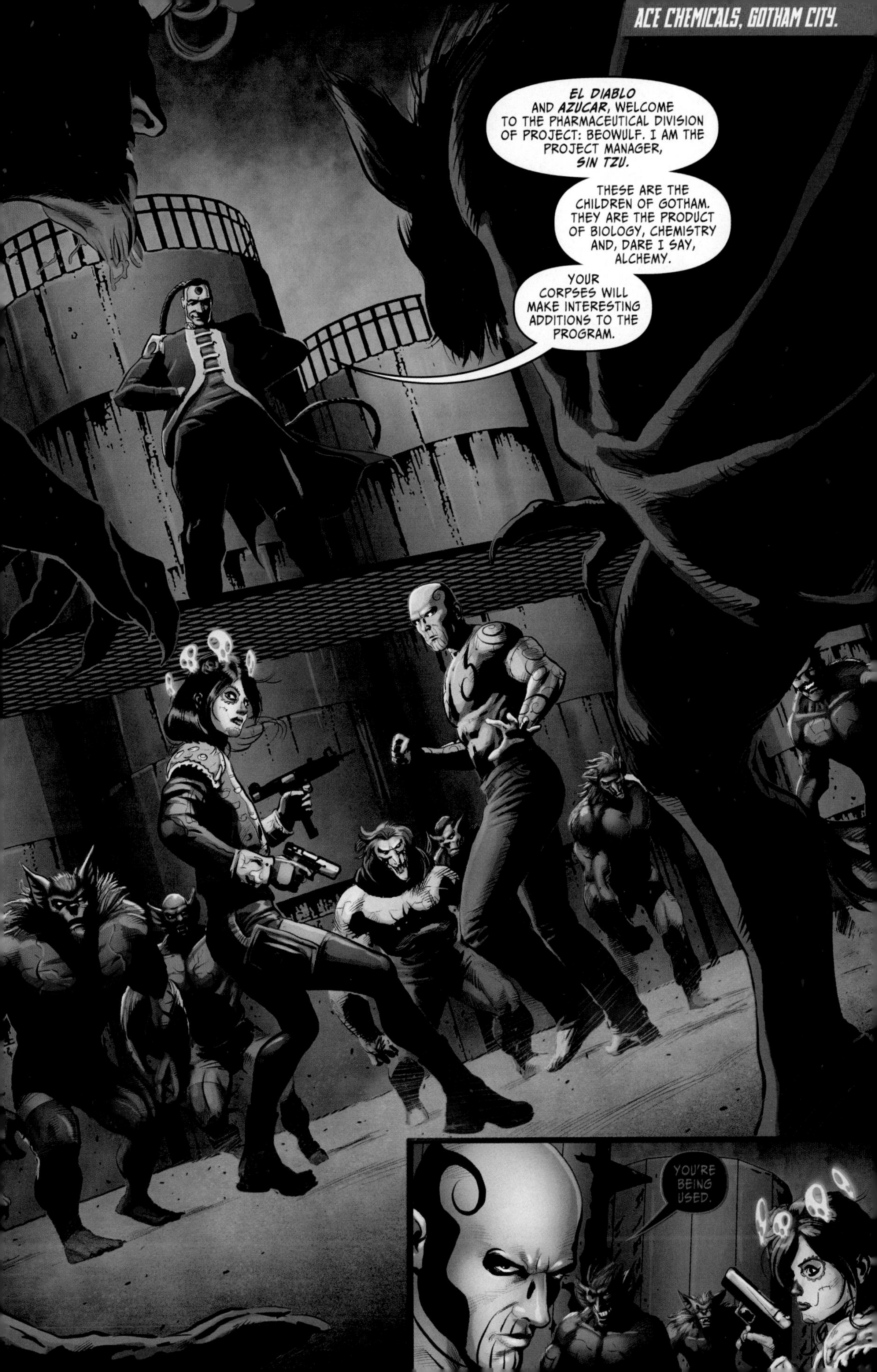
ACE CHEMICALS, GOTHAM CITY.
EL DIABLO AND AZUCAR, WELCOME TO THE PHARMACEUTICAL DIVISION OF PROJECT: BEOWULF. I AM THE PROJECT MANAGER, SIN TZU.
THESE ARE THE CHILDREN OF GOTHAM. THEY ARE THE PRODUCT OF BIOLOGY, CHEMISTRY AND, DARE I SAY, ALCHEMY.
YOUR CORPSES WILL MAKE INTERESTING ADDITIONS TO THE PROGRAM.
YOU'RE BEING USED.

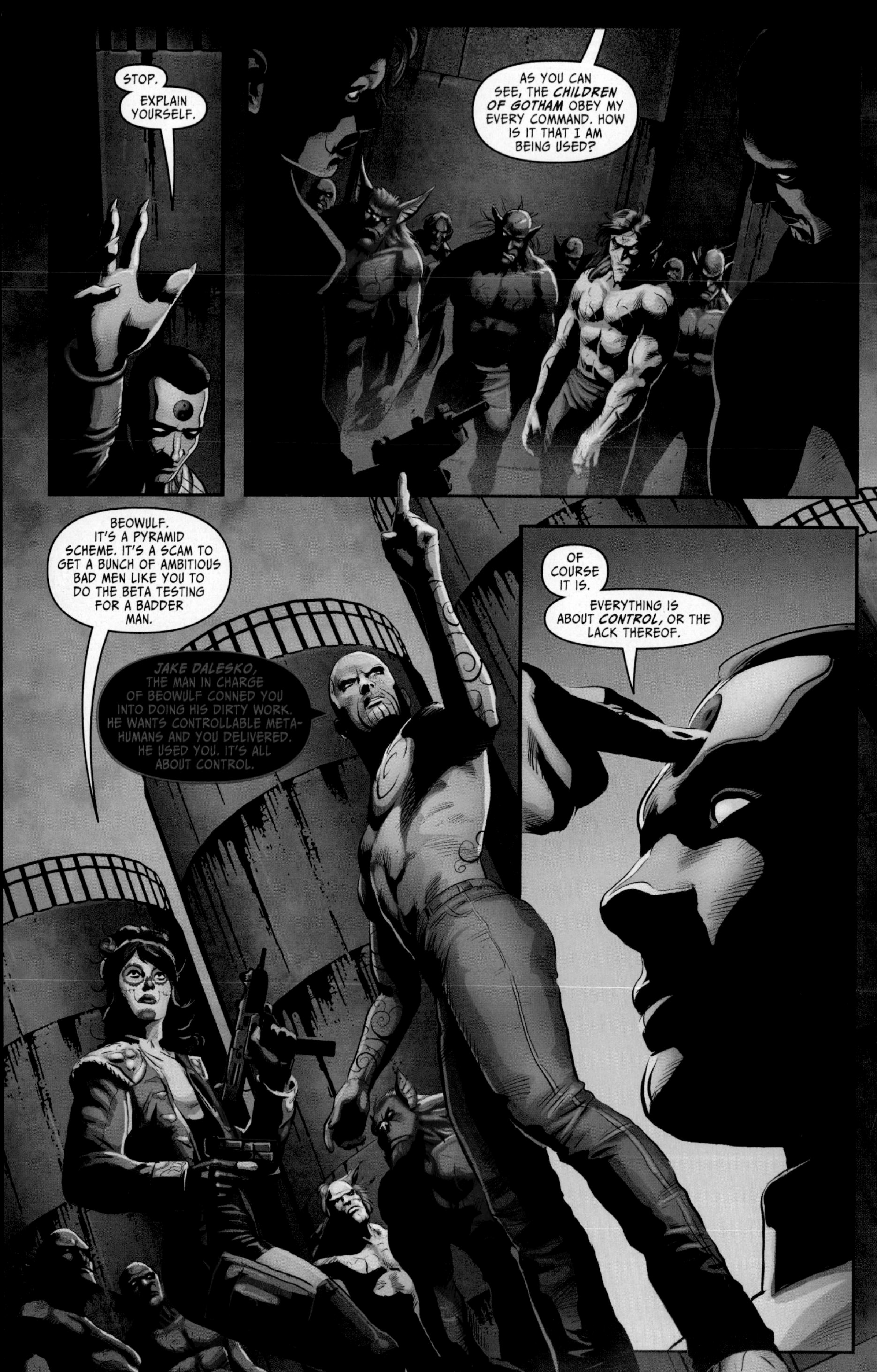

STOP.
EXPLAIN YOURSELF.
AS YOU CAN SEE, THE CHILDREN OF GOTHAM OBEY MY EVERY COMMAND. HOW IS IT THAT I AM BEING USED?
BEOWULF. IT'S A PYRAMID SCHEME. IT'S A SCAM TO GET A BUNCH OF AMBITIOUS BAD MEN LIKE YOU TO DO THE BETA TESTING FOR A BADDER MAN.
JAKE DALESKO, THE MAN IN CHARGE OF BEOWULF CONNED YOU INTO DOING HIS DIRTY WORK. HE WANTS CONTROLLABLE META-HUMANS AND YOU DELIVERED. HE USED YOU. IT'S ALL ABOUT CONTROL.
OF COURSE IT IS.
EVERYTHING IS ABOUT CONTROL, OR THE LACK THEREOF.

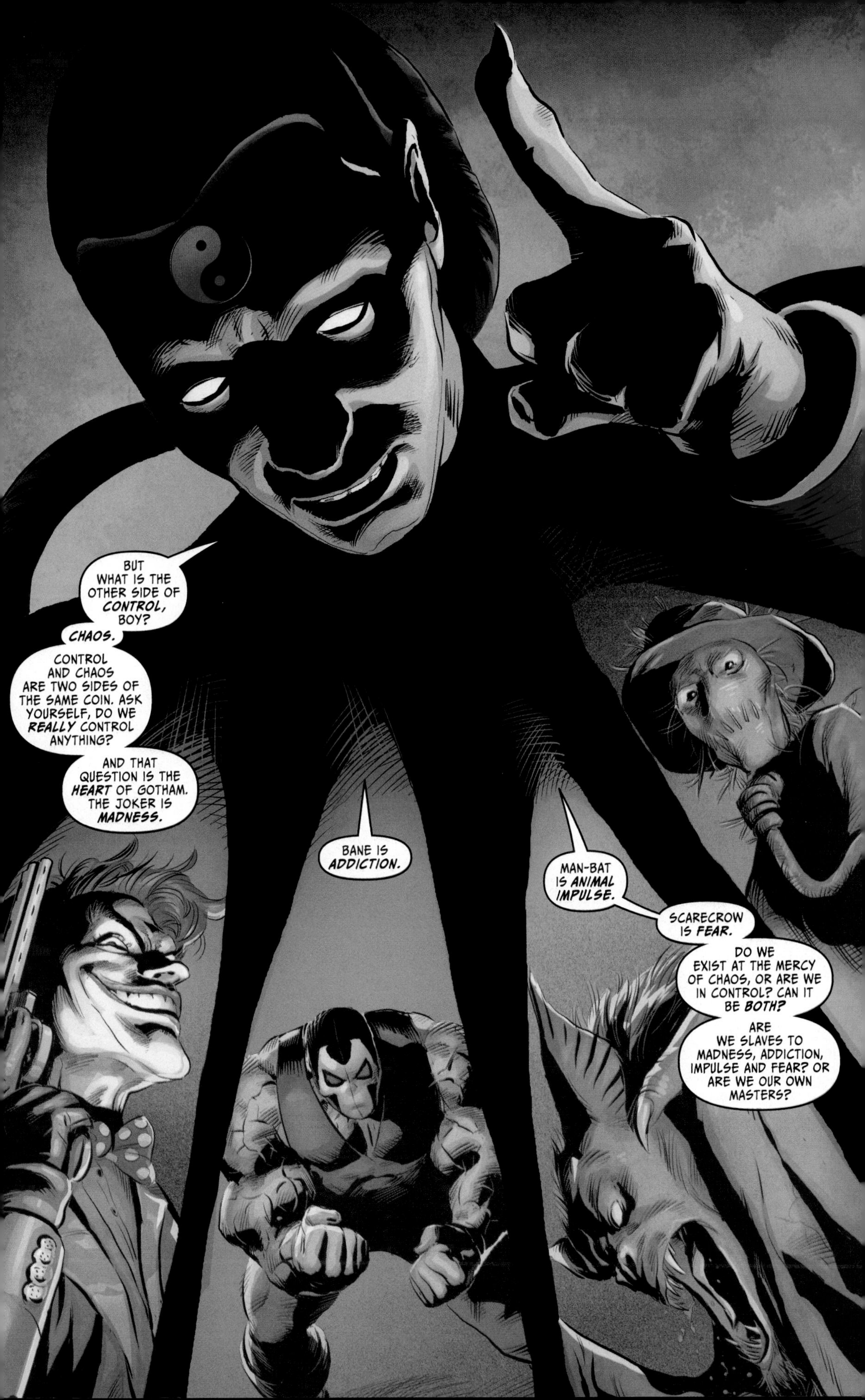
BUT WHAT IS THE OTHER SIDE OF *CONTROL,* BOY?
CHAOS.
CONTROL AND CHAOS ARE TWO SIDES OF THE SAME COIN. ASK YOURSELF, DO WE *REALLY* CONTROL ANYTHING?
AND THAT QUESTION IS THE *HEART* OF GOTHAM. THE JOKER IS *MADNESS.*
BANE IS *ADDICTION.*
MAN-BAT IS *ANIMAL IMPULSE.*
SCARECROW IS *FEAR.*
DO WE EXIST AT THE MERCY OF CHAOS, OR ARE WE IN CONTROL? CAN IT BE *BOTH?*
ARE WE SLAVES TO MADNESS, ADDICTION, IMPULSE AND FEAR? OR ARE WE OUR OWN MASTERS?

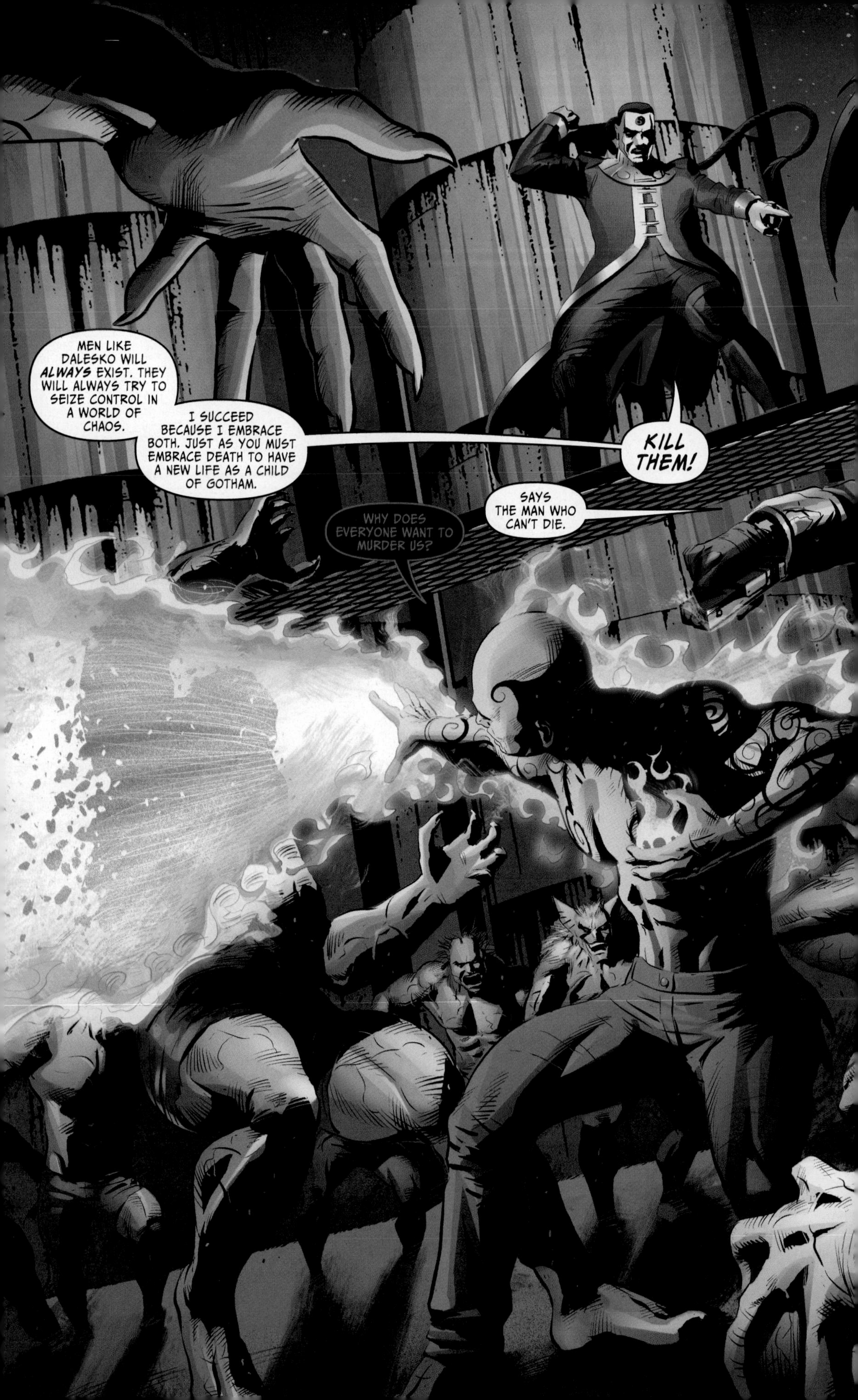
MEN LIKE DALESKO WILL ALWAYS EXIST. THEY WILL ALWAYS TRY TO SEIZE CONTROL IN A WORLD OF CHAOS.
I SUCCEED BECAUSE I EMBRACE BOTH. JUST AS YOU MUST EMBRACE DEATH TO HAVE A NEW LIFE AS A CHILD OF GOTHAM.
KILL THEM!
SAYS THE MAN WHO CAN'T DIE.
WHY DOES EVERYONE WANT TO MURDER US?

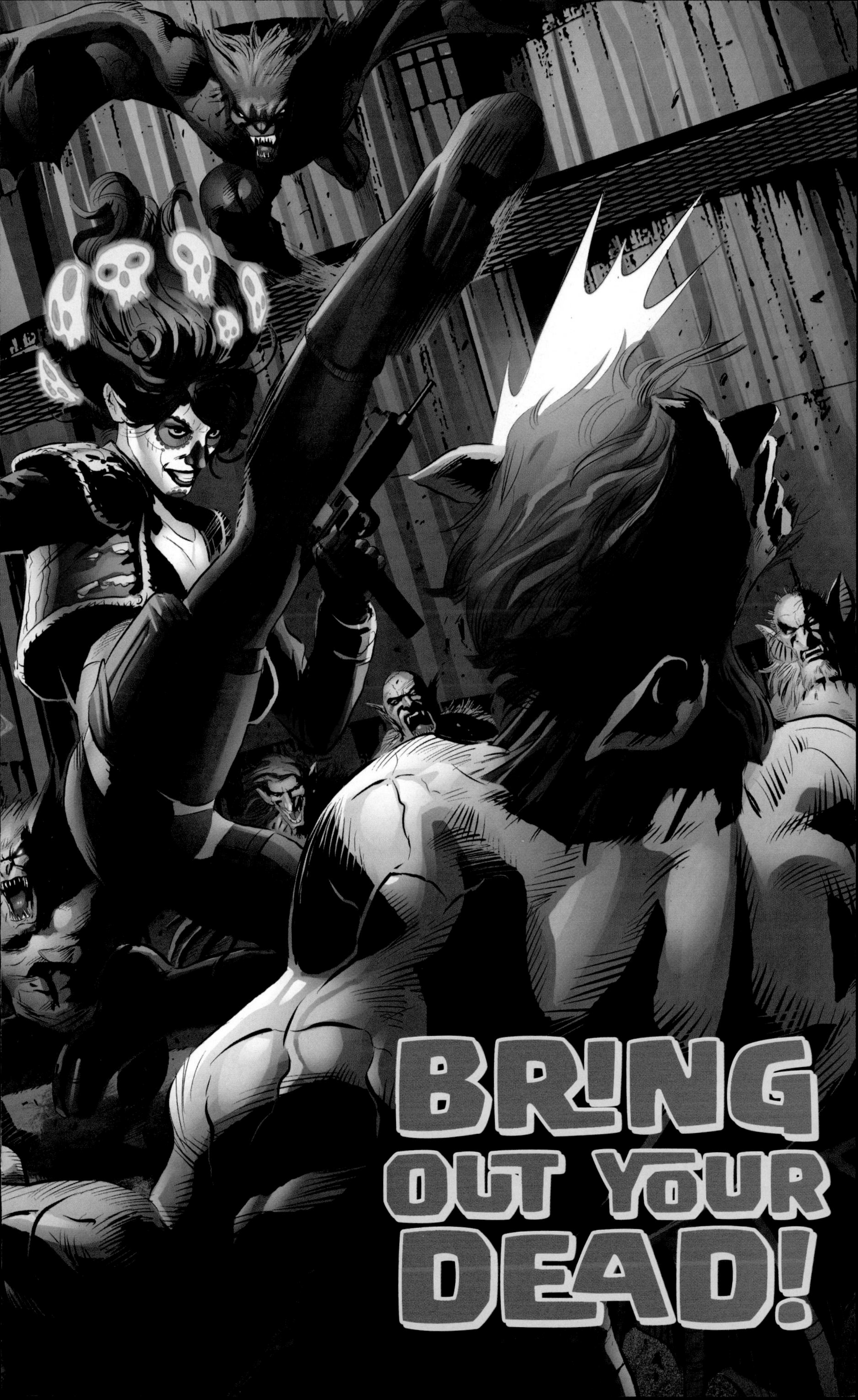
BR!NG
OUT YOUR
DEAD!

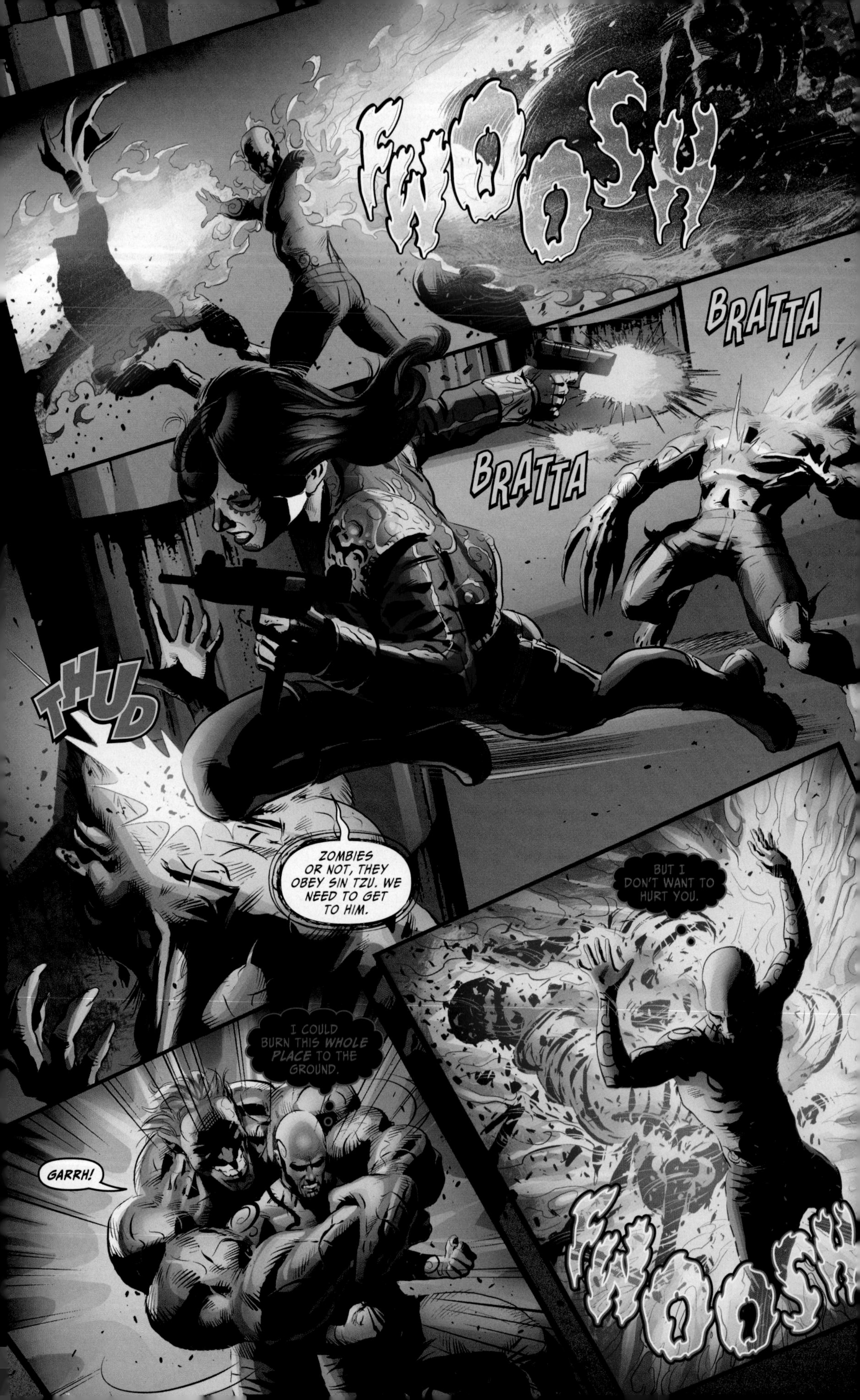
FWOOSH
BRATTA
BRATTA
THUD
ZOMBIES OR NOT, THEY OBEY SIN TZU. WE NEED TO GET TO HIM.
I COULD BURN THIS WHOLE PLACE TO THE GROUND.
GARRH!
BUT I DON'T WANT TO HURT YOU.
FWOOSH

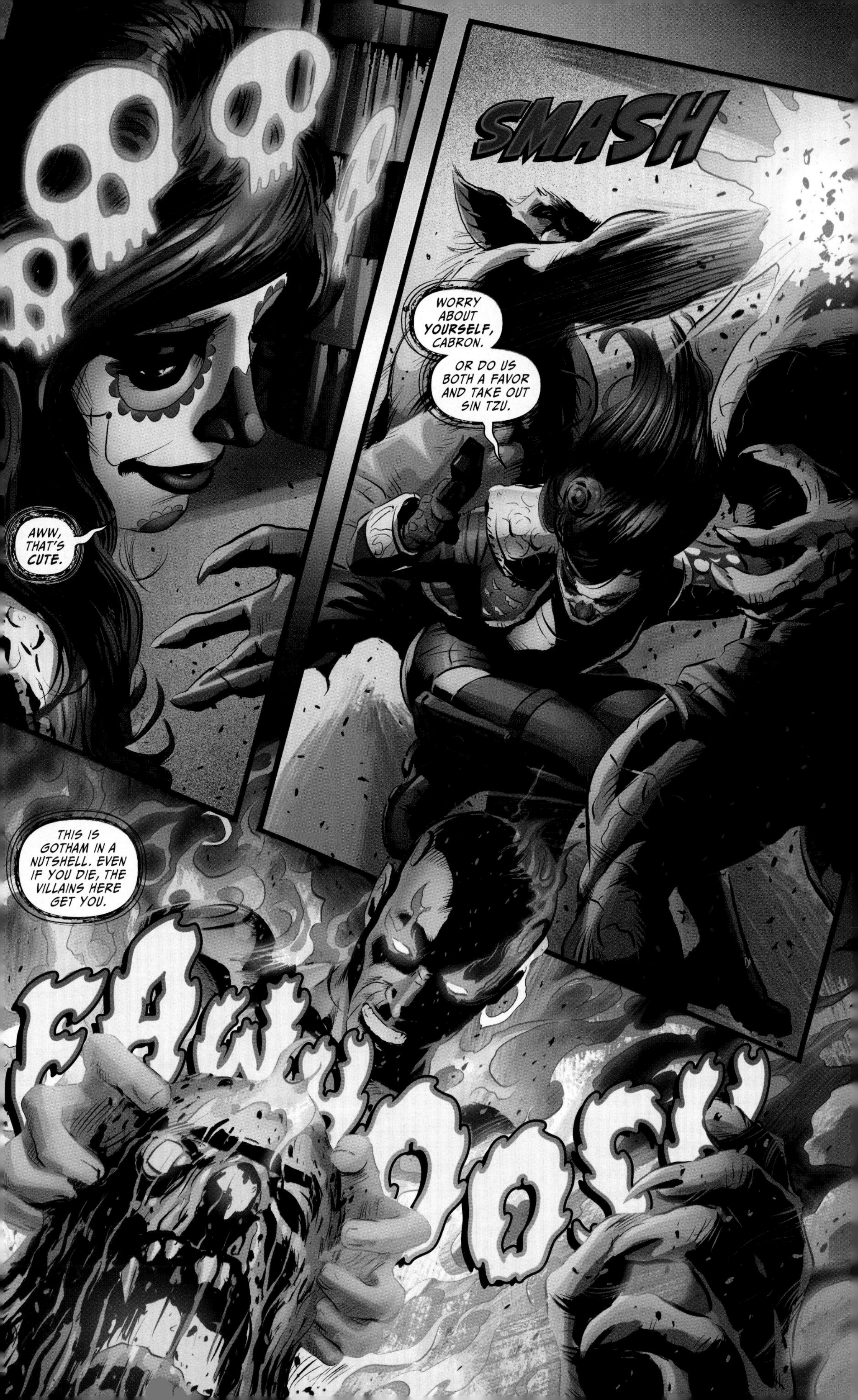
AWW, THAT'S CUTE.
SMASH
WORRY ABOUT YOURSELF, CABRON.
OR DO US BOTH A FAVOR AND TAKE OUT SIN TZU.
THIS IS GOTHAM IN A NUTSHELL. EVEN IF YOU DIE, THE VILLAINS HERE GET YOU.

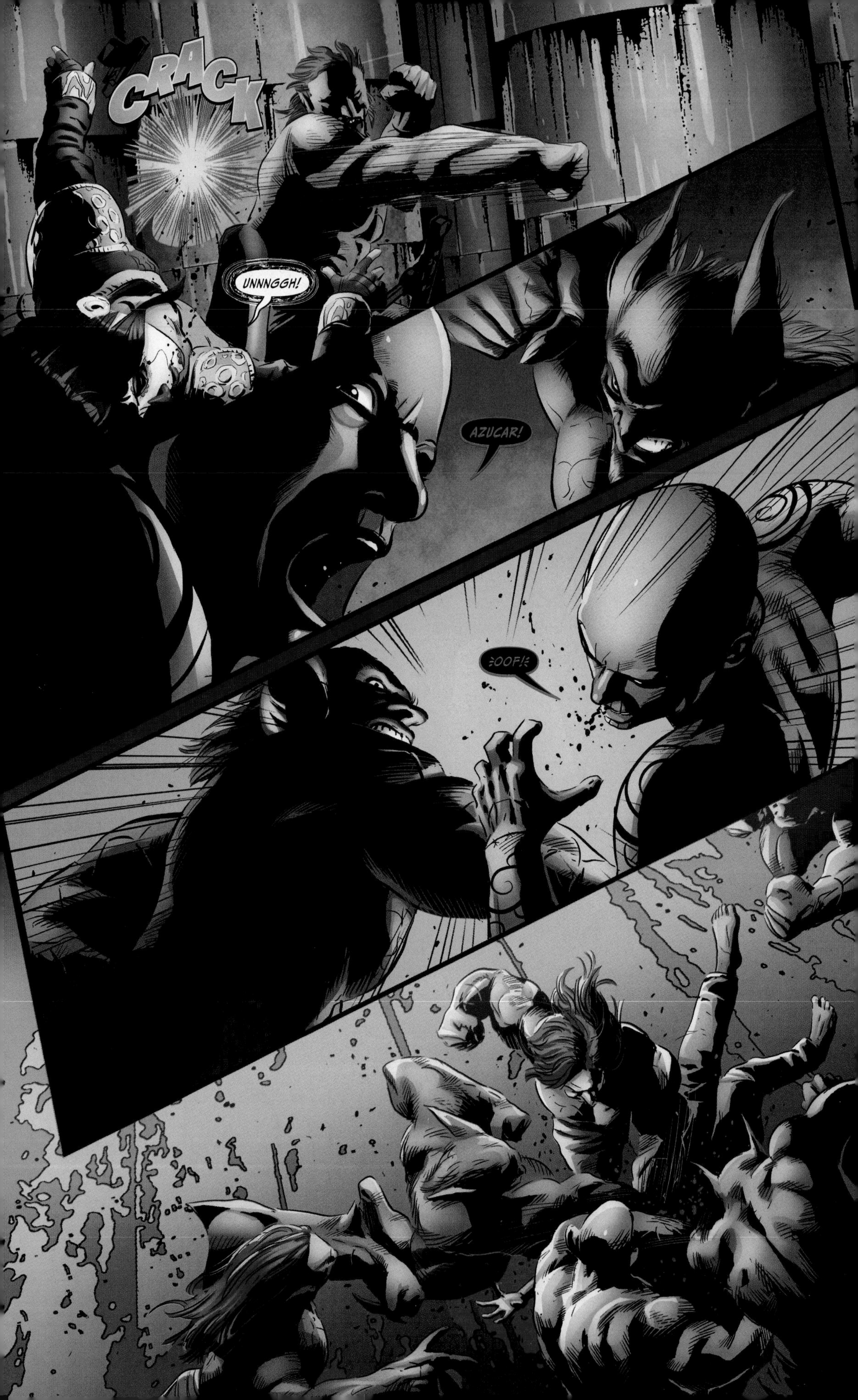
CRACK
UNNNGGH!
AZUCAR!
OOF!

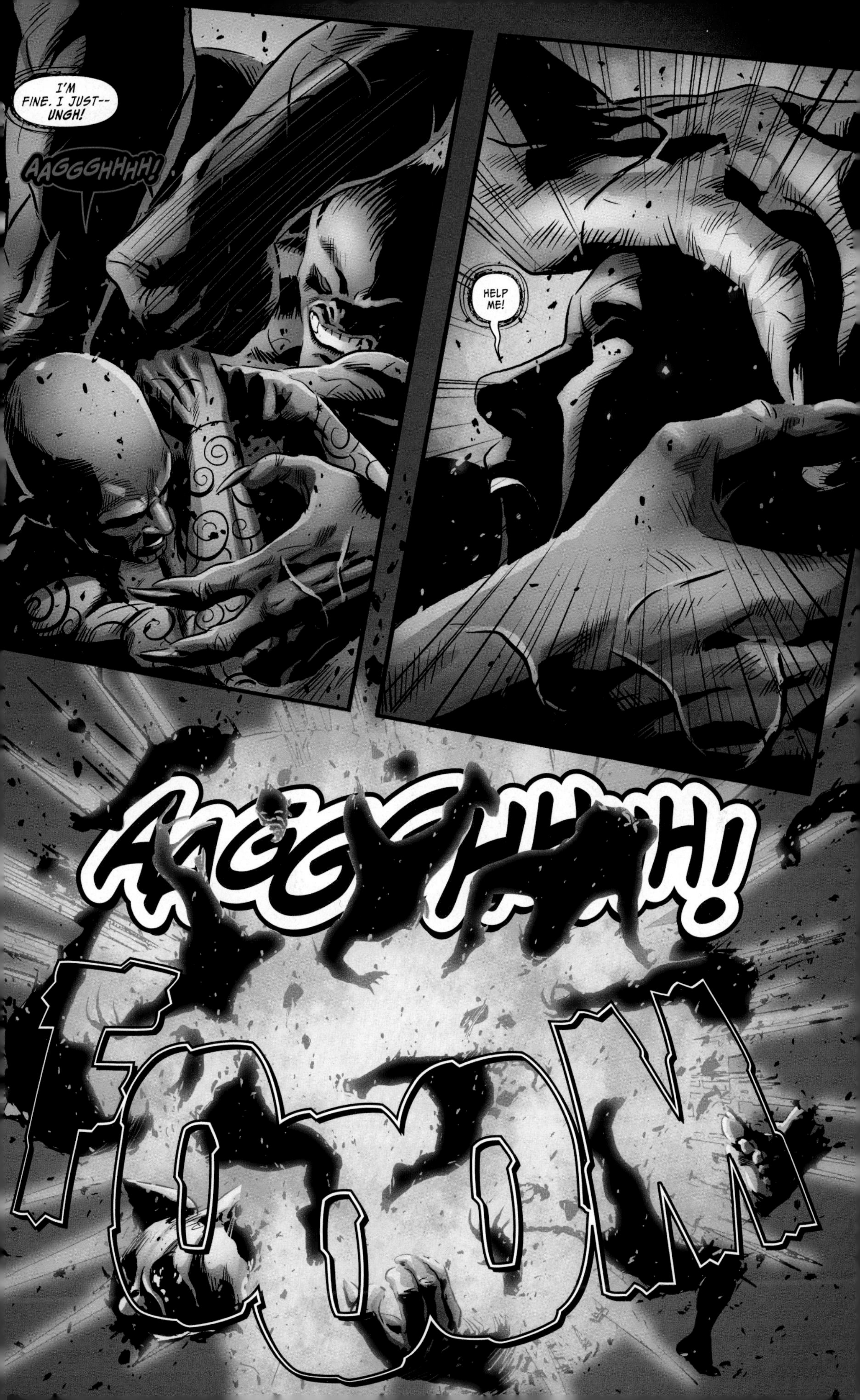
I'M FINE. I JUST-- UNGH!
AAGGGHHHH!
HELP ME!
AAGGGHHHH!
FOOOOM

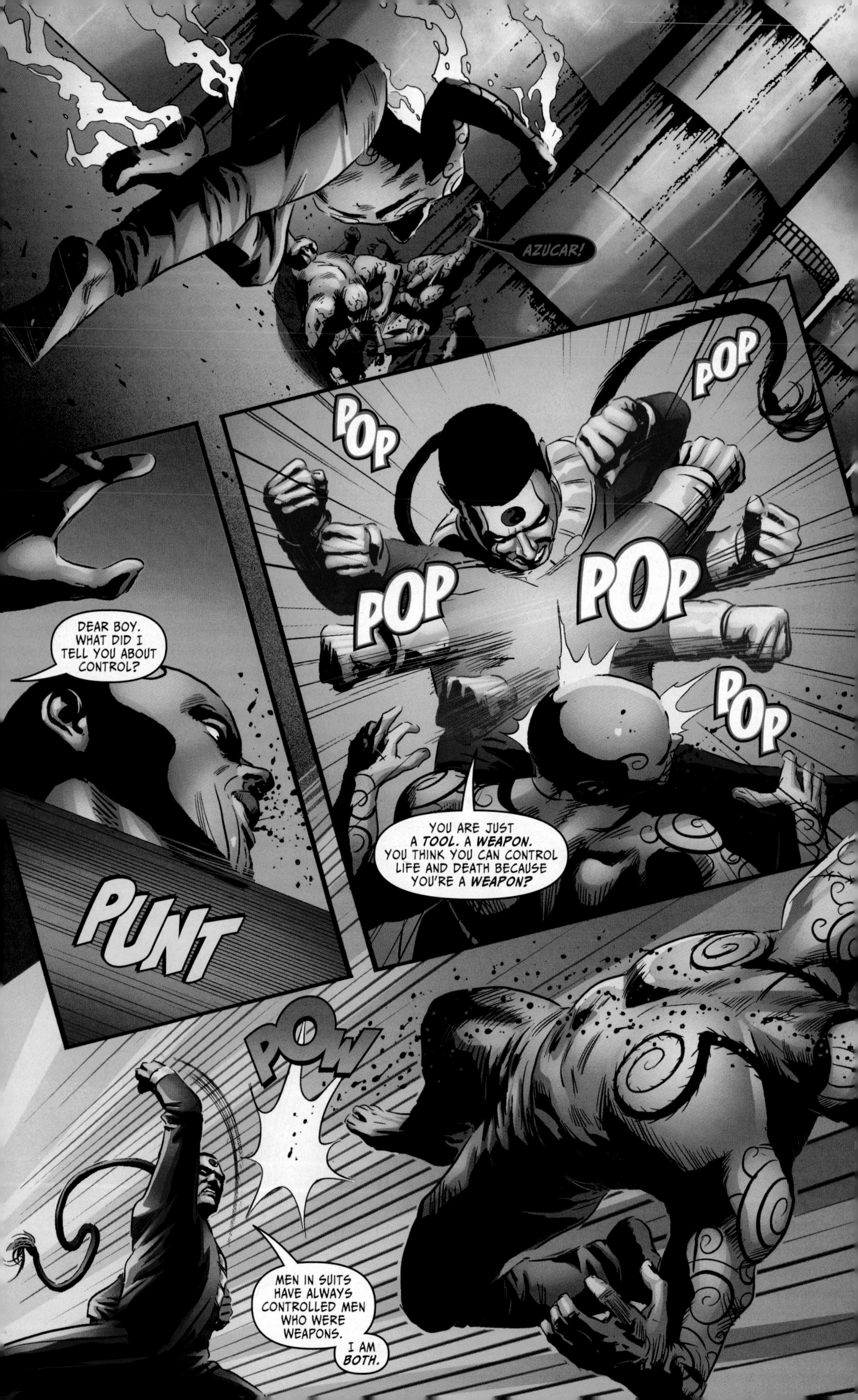
AZUCAR!
POP
POP
POP
POP
POP
DEAR BOY. WHAT DID I TELL YOU ABOUT CONTROL?
PUNT
YOU ARE JUST A TOOL. A WEAPON. YOU THINK YOU CAN CONTROL LIFE AND DEATH BECAUSE YOU'RE A WEAPON?
POW
MEN IN SUITS HAVE ALWAYS CONTROLLED MEN WHO WERE WEAPONS.
I AM BOTH.

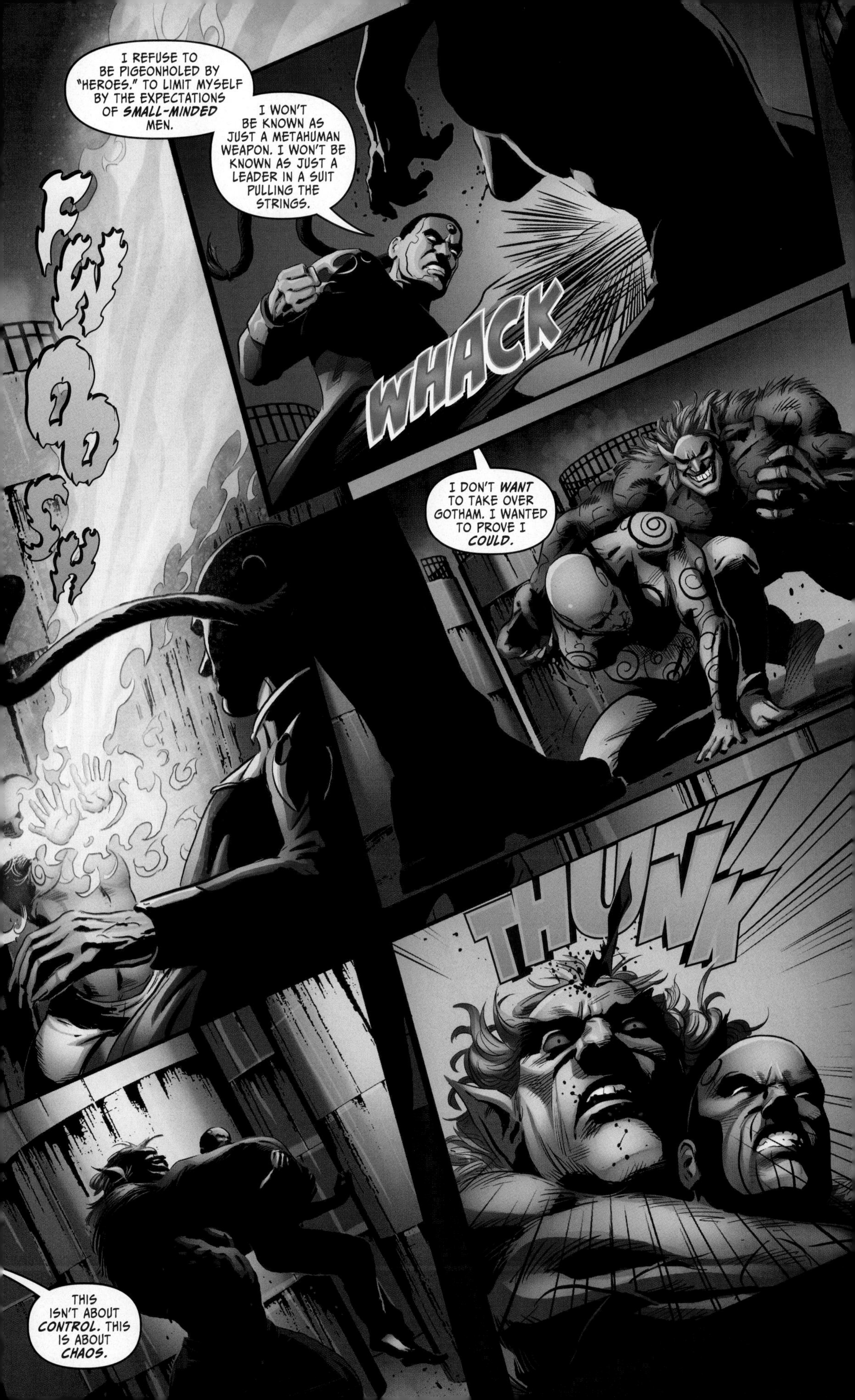

I REFUSE TO BE PIGEONHOLED BY "HEROES." TO LIMIT MYSELF BY THE EXPECTATIONS OF SMALL-MINDED MEN.
I WON'T BE KNOWN AS JUST A METAHUMAN WEAPON. I WON'T BE KNOWN AS JUST A LEADER IN A SUIT PULLING THE STRINGS.
WHACK
FWOOSH
I DON'T WANT TO TAKE OVER GOTHAM. I WANTED TO PROVE I COULD.
THUNK
THIS ISN'T ABOUT CONTROL. THIS IS ABOUT CHAOS.

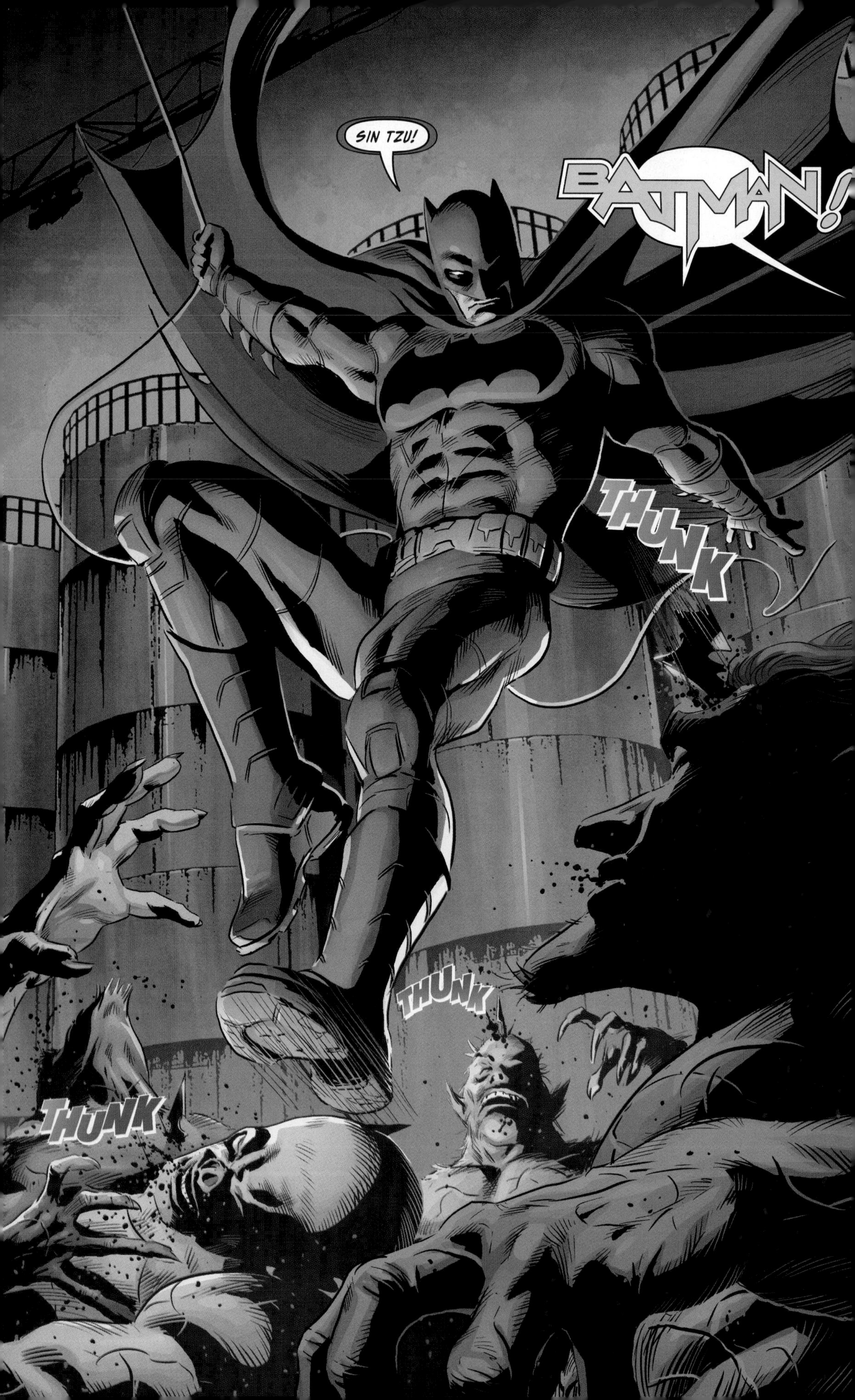
SIN TZU!
BATMAN!
THUNK
THUNK
THUNK

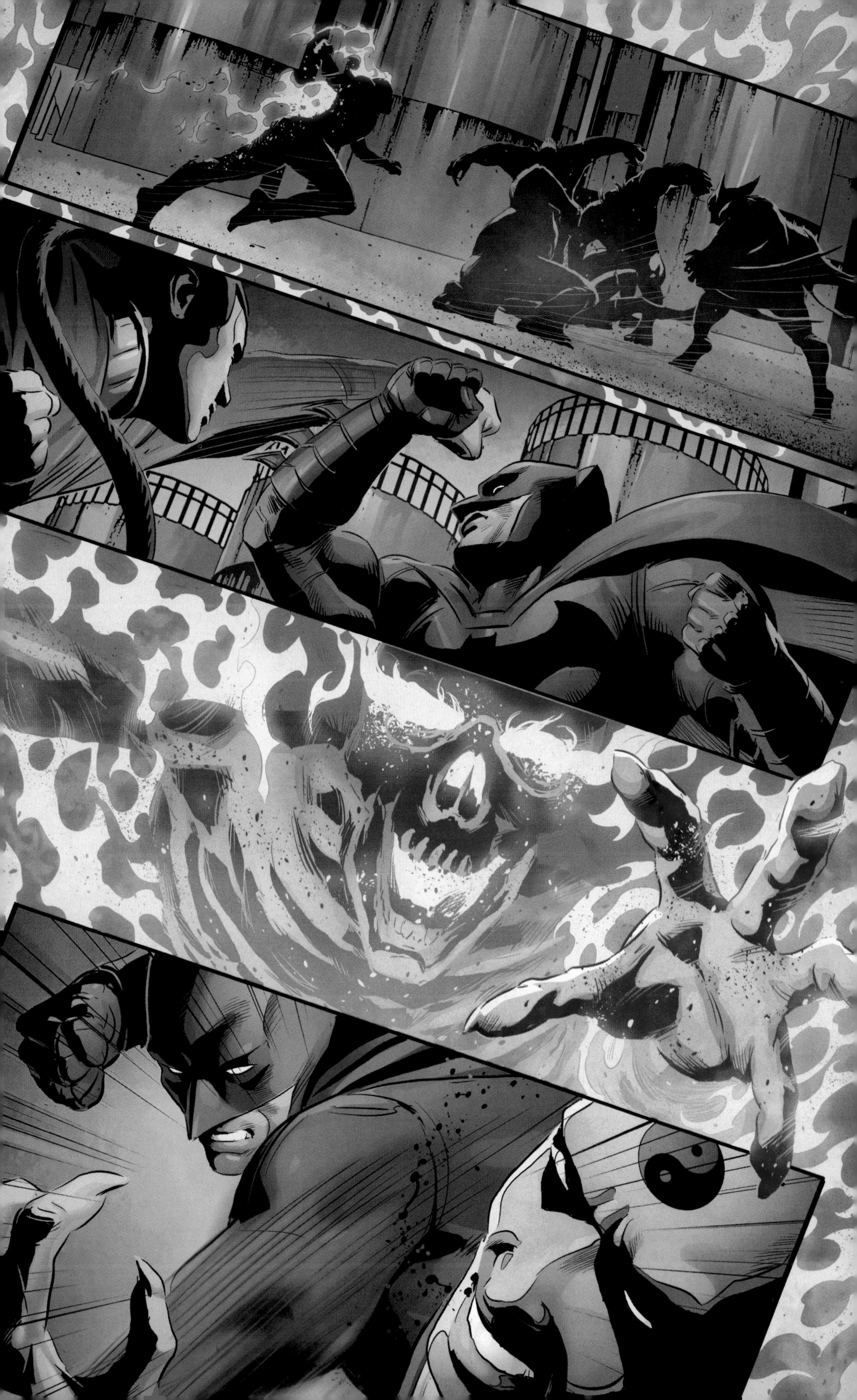

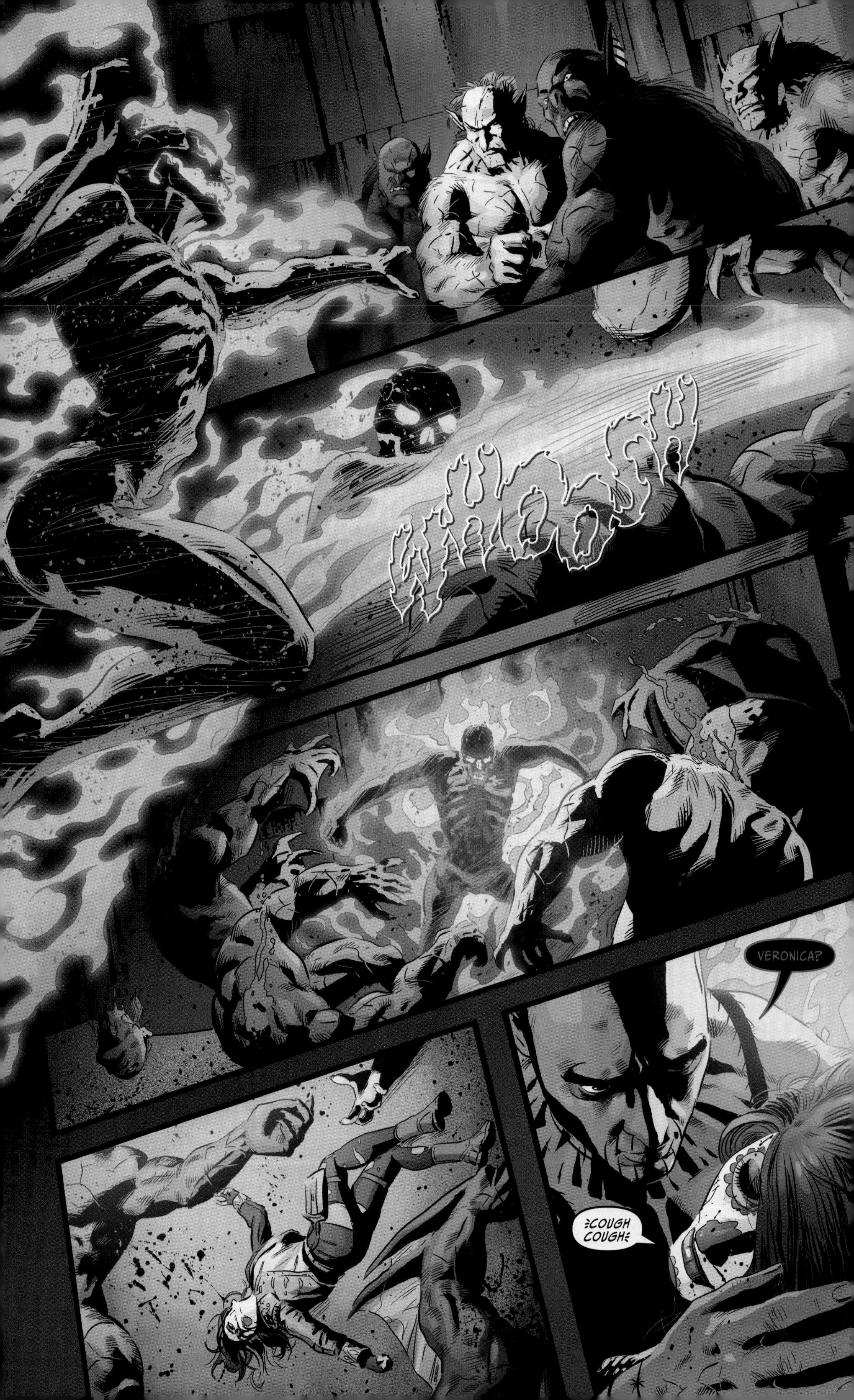
WHOOSH
VERONICA?
COUGH COUGH

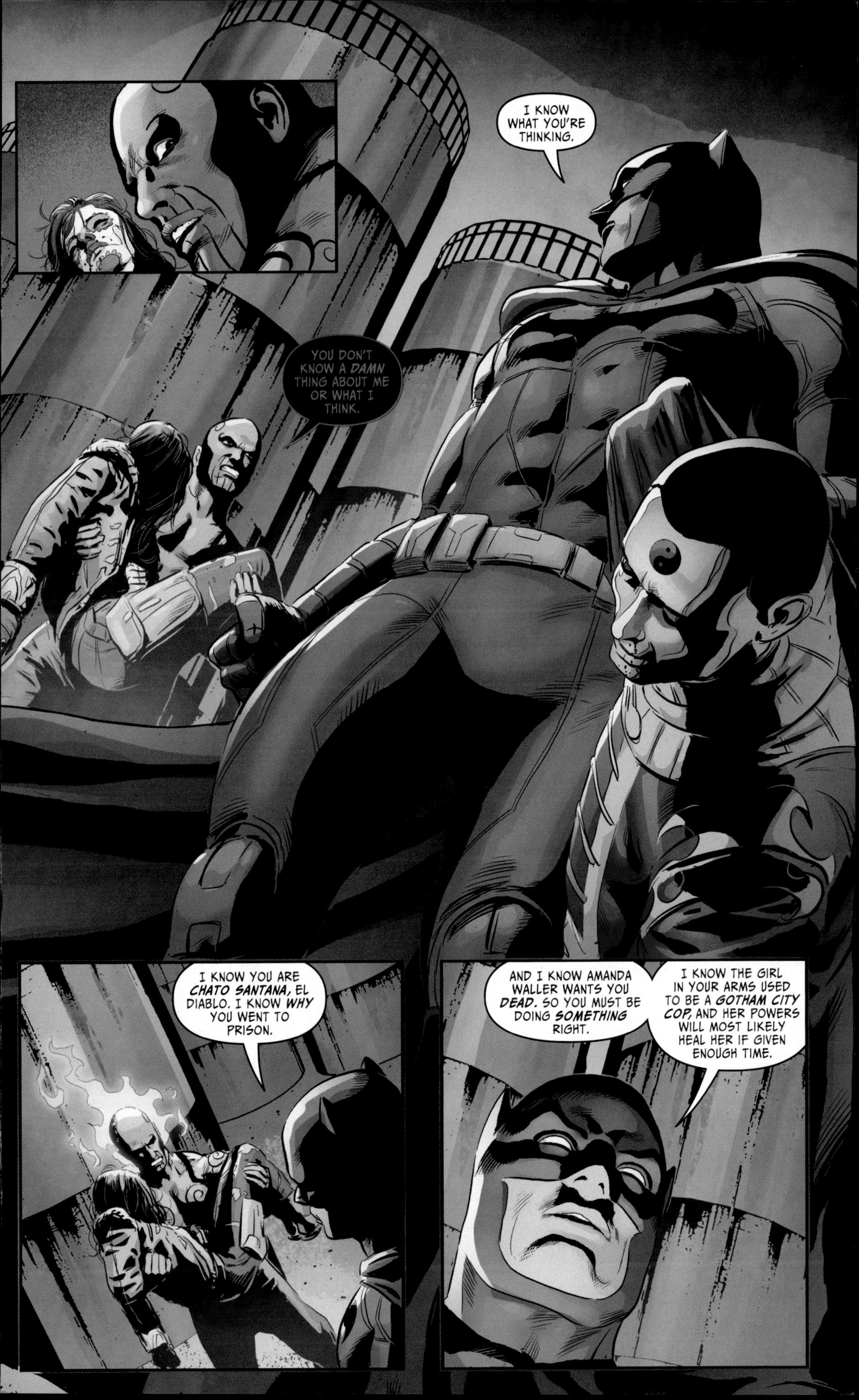
I KNOW WHAT YOU'RE THINKING.
YOU DON'T KNOW A *DAMN* THING ABOUT ME OR WHAT I THINK.
I KNOW YOU ARE *CHATO SANTANA,* EL DIABLO. I KNOW *WHY* YOU WENT TO PRISON.
AND I KNOW AMANDA WALLER WANTS YOU *DEAD.* SO YOU MUST BE DOING *SOMETHING* RIGHT.
I KNOW THE GIRL IN YOUR ARMS USED TO BE A *GOTHAM CITY COP,* AND HER POWERS WILL MOST LIKELY HEAL HER IF GIVEN ENOUGH TIME.

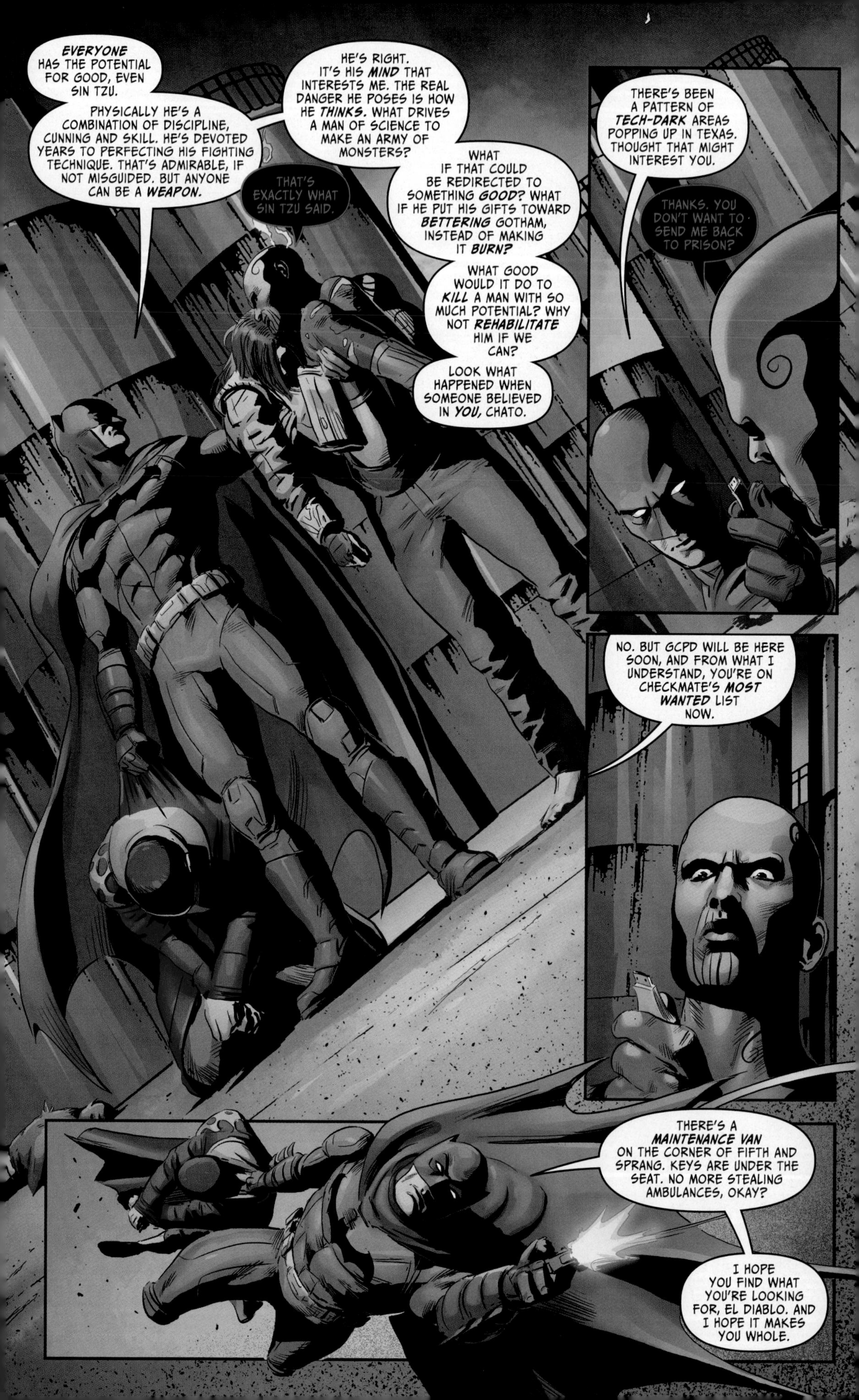
EVERYONE HAS THE POTENTIAL FOR GOOD, EVEN SIN TZU.
PHYSICALLY HE'S A COMBINATION OF DISCIPLINE, CUNNING AND SKILL. HE'S DEVOTED YEARS TO PERFECTING HIS FIGHTING TECHNIQUE. THAT'S ADMIRABLE, IF NOT MISGUIDED. BUT ANYONE CAN BE A WEAPON.
THAT'S EXACTLY WHAT SIN TZU SAID.
HE'S RIGHT. IT'S HIS MIND THAT INTERESTS ME. THE REAL DANGER HE POSES IS HOW HE THINKS. WHAT DRIVES A MAN OF SCIENCE TO MAKE AN ARMY OF MONSTERS?
WHAT IF THAT COULD BE REDIRECTED TO SOMETHING GOOD? WHAT IF HE PUT HIS GIFTS TOWARD BETTERING GOTHAM, INSTEAD OF MAKING IT BURN?
WHAT GOOD WOULD IT DO TO KILL A MAN WITH SO MUCH POTENTIAL? WHY NOT REHABILITATE HIM IF WE CAN?
LOOK WHAT HAPPENED WHEN SOMEONE BELIEVED IN YOU, CHATO.
THERE'S BEEN A PATTERN OF TECH-DARK AREAS POPPING UP IN TEXAS. THOUGHT THAT MIGHT INTEREST YOU.
THANKS. YOU DON'T WANT TO SEND ME BACK TO PRISON?
NO. BUT GCPD WILL BE HERE SOON, AND FROM WHAT I UNDERSTAND, YOU'RE ON CHECKMATE'S MOST WANTED LIST NOW.
THERE'S A MAINTENANCE VAN ON THE CORNER OF FIFTH AND SPRANG. KEYS ARE UNDER THE SEAT. NO MORE STEALING AMBULANCES, OKAY?
I HOPE YOU FIND WHAT YOU'RE LOOKING FOR, EL DIABLO. AND I HOPE IT MAKES YOU WHOLE.

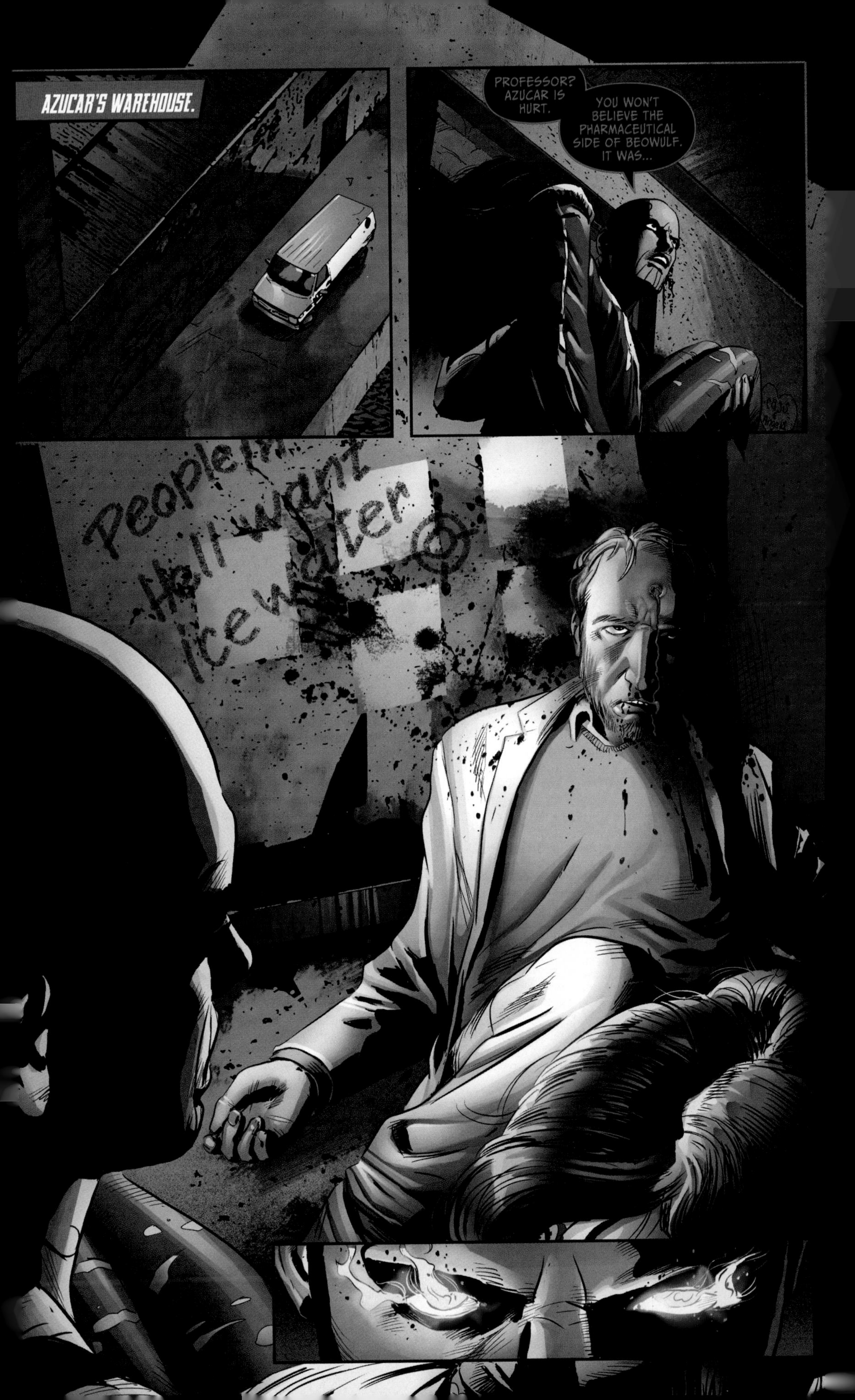
AZUCAR'S WAREHOUSE.
PROFESSOR? AZUCAR IS HURT.
YOU WON'T BELIEVE THE PHARMACEUTICAL SIDE OF BEOWULF. IT WAS...

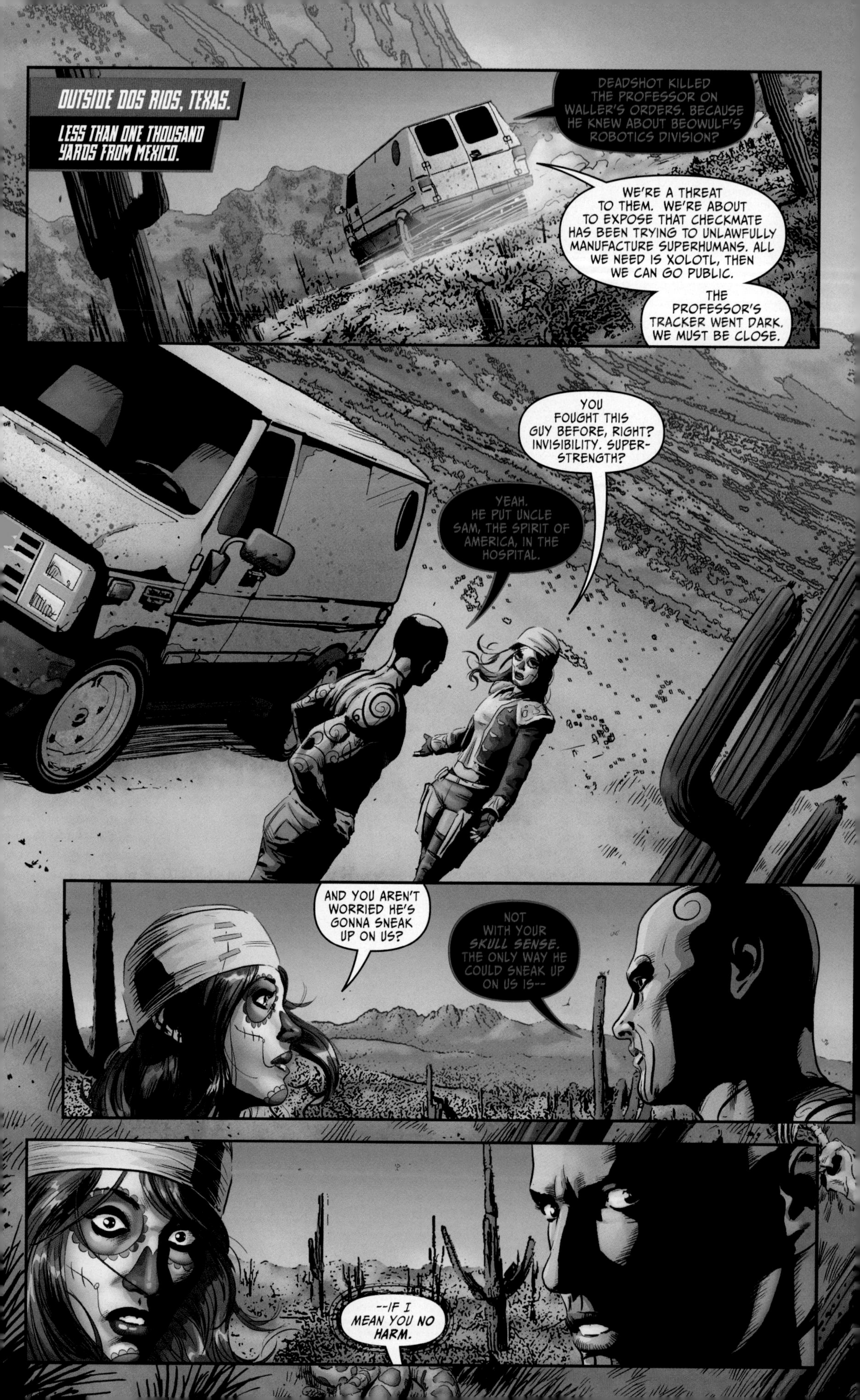
OUTSIDE DOS RIOS, TEXAS.
LESS THAN ONE THOUSAND YARDS FROM MEXICO.
DEADSHOT KILLED THE PROFESSOR ON WALLER'S ORDERS. BECAUSE HE KNEW ABOUT BEOWULF'S ROBOTICS DIVISION?
WE'RE A THREAT TO THEM. WE'RE ABOUT TO EXPOSE THAT CHECKMATE HAS BEEN TRYING TO UNLAWFULLY MANUFACTURE SUPERHUMANS. ALL WE NEED IS XOLOTL, THEN WE CAN GO PUBLIC.
THE PROFESSOR'S TRACKER WENT DARK. WE MUST BE CLOSE.
YOU FOUGHT THIS GUY BEFORE, RIGHT? INVISIBILITY. SUPER-STRENGTH?
YEAH. HE PUT UNCLE SAM, THE SPIRIT OF AMERICA, IN THE HOSPITAL.
AND YOU AREN'T WORRIED HE'S GONNA SNEAK UP ON US?
NOT WITH YOUR SKULL SENSE. THE ONLY WAY HE COULD SNEAK UP ON US IS--
--IF I MEAN YOU NO HARM.

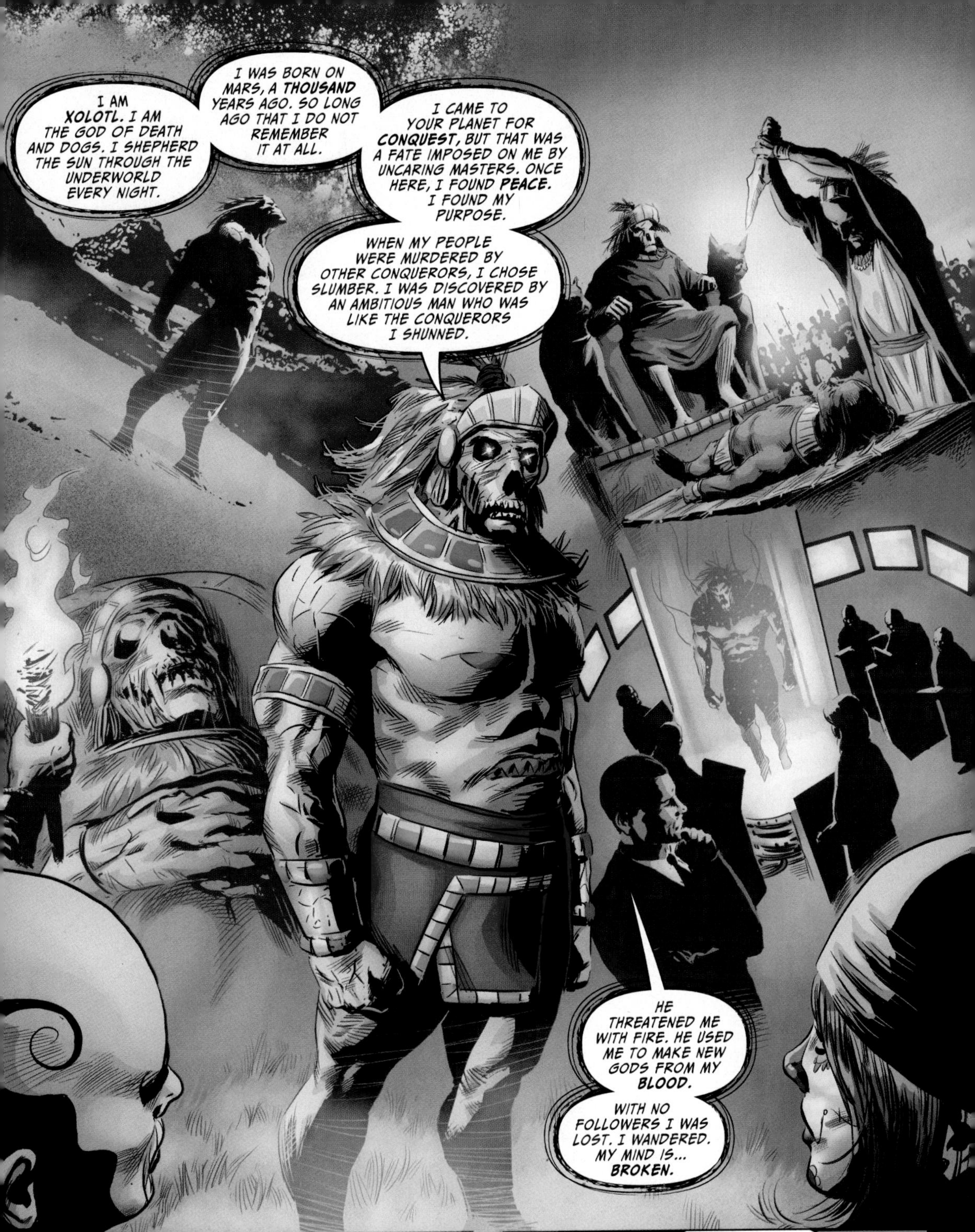
I AM XOLOTL. I AM THE GOD OF DEATH AND DOGS. I SHEPHERD THE SUN THROUGH THE UNDERWORLD EVERY NIGHT.
I WAS BORN ON MARS, A THOUSAND YEARS AGO. SO LONG AGO THAT I DO NOT REMEMBER IT AT ALL.
I CAME TO YOUR PLANET FOR CONQUEST, BUT THAT WAS A FATE IMPOSED ON ME BY UNCARING MASTERS. ONCE HERE, I FOUND PEACE. I FOUND MY PURPOSE.
WHEN MY PEOPLE WERE MURDERED BY OTHER CONQUERORS, I CHOSE SLUMBER. I WAS DISCOVERED BY AN AMBITIOUS MAN WHO WAS LIKE THE CONQUERORS I SHUNNED.
HE THREATENED ME WITH FIRE. HE USED ME TO MAKE NEW GODS FROM MY BLOOD.
WITH NO FOLLOWERS I WAS LOST. I WANDERED. MY MIND IS... BROKEN.
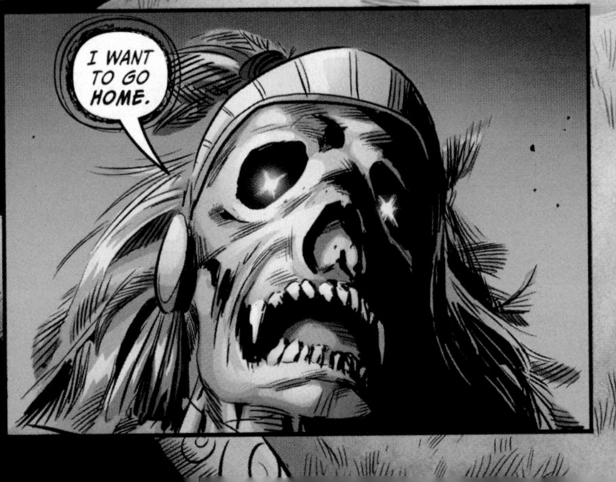
I WANT TO GO HOME.
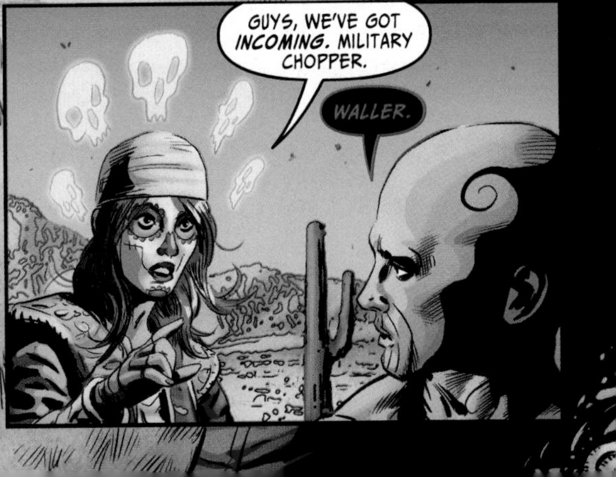
GUYS, WE'VE GOT INCOMING. MILITARY CHOPPER.
WALLER.

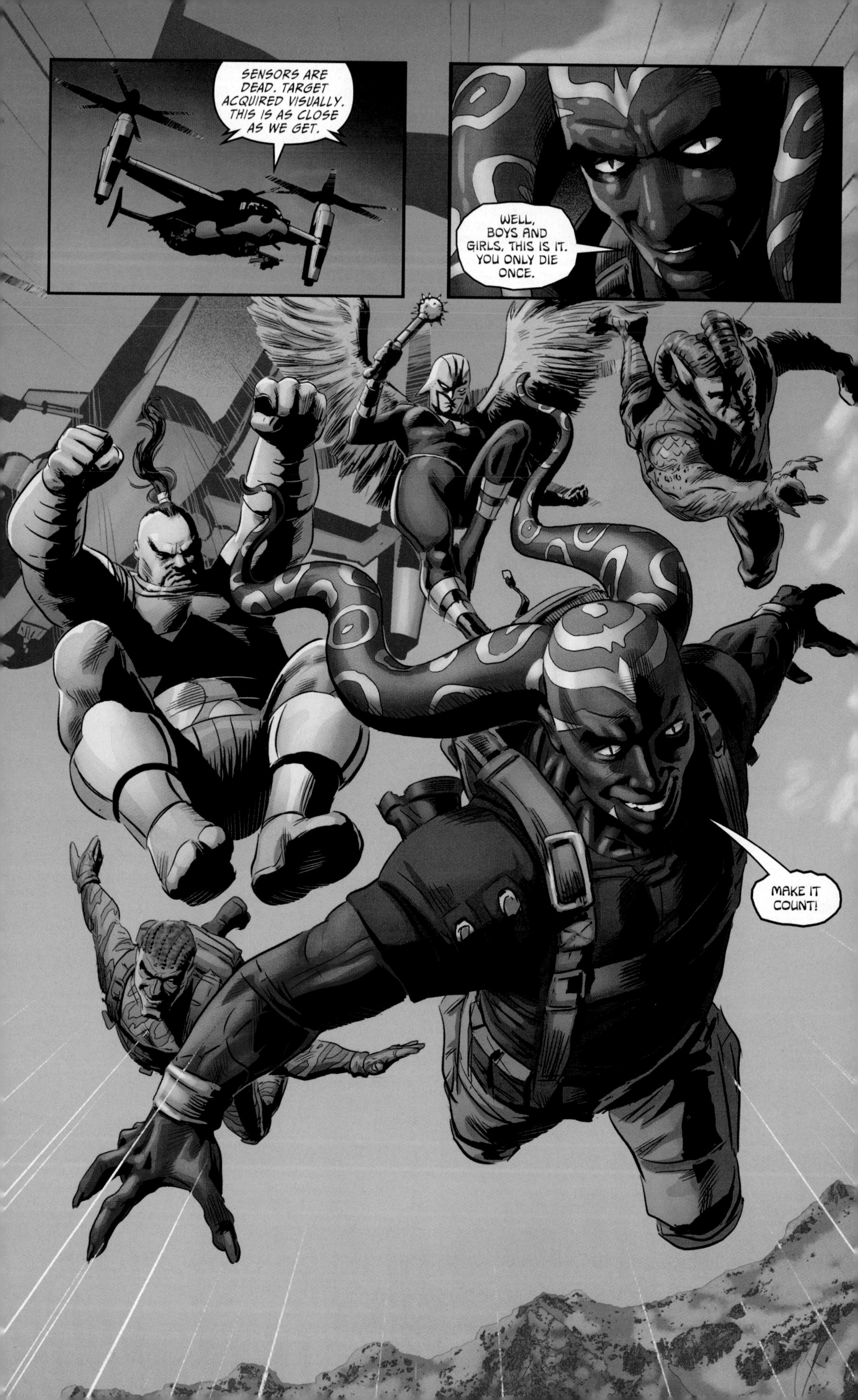
SENSORS ARE DEAD. TARGET ACQUIRED VISUALLY. THIS IS AS CLOSE AS WE GET.
WELL, BOYS AND GIRLS, THIS IS IT. YOU ONLY DIE ONCE.
MAKE IT COUNT!

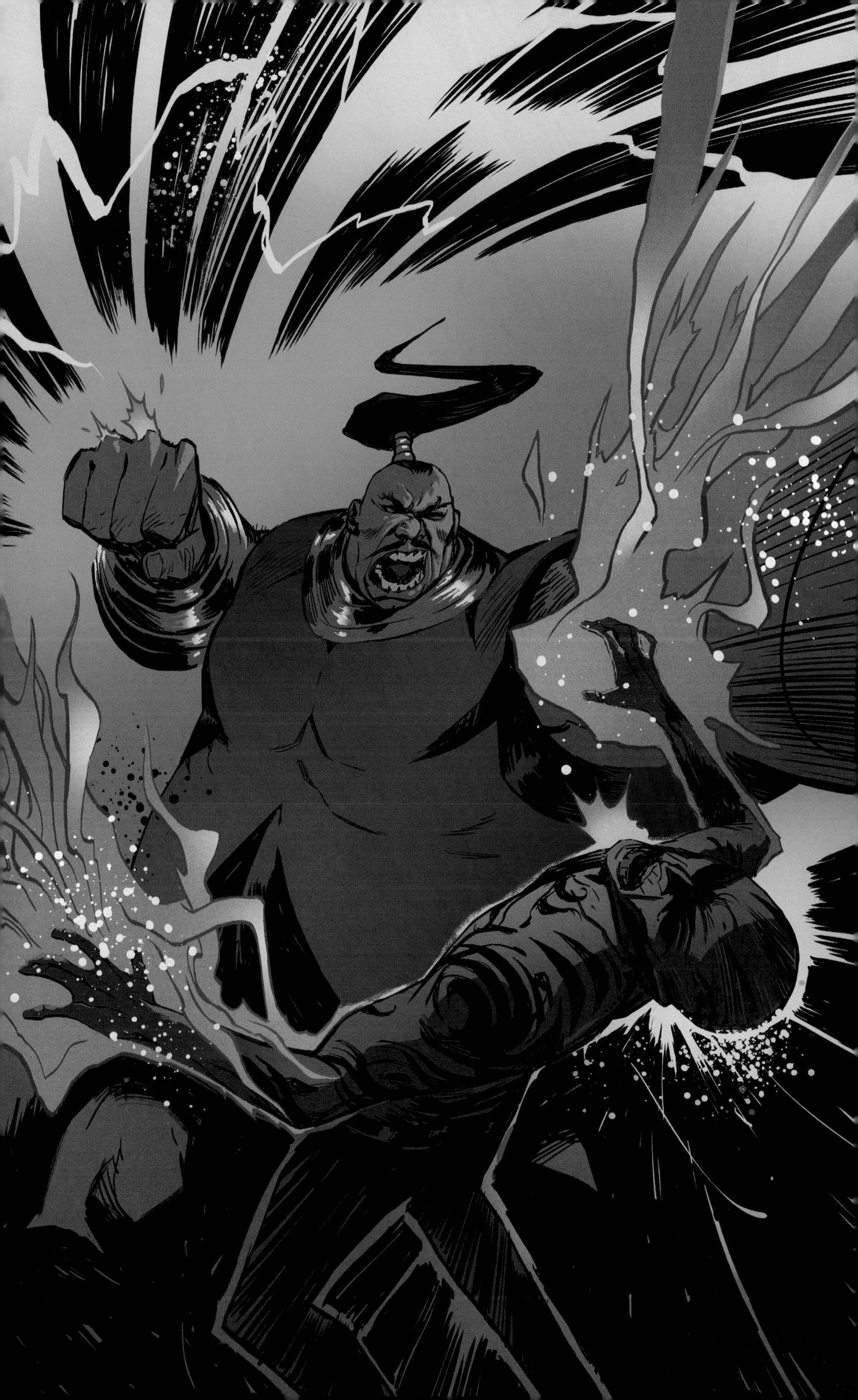

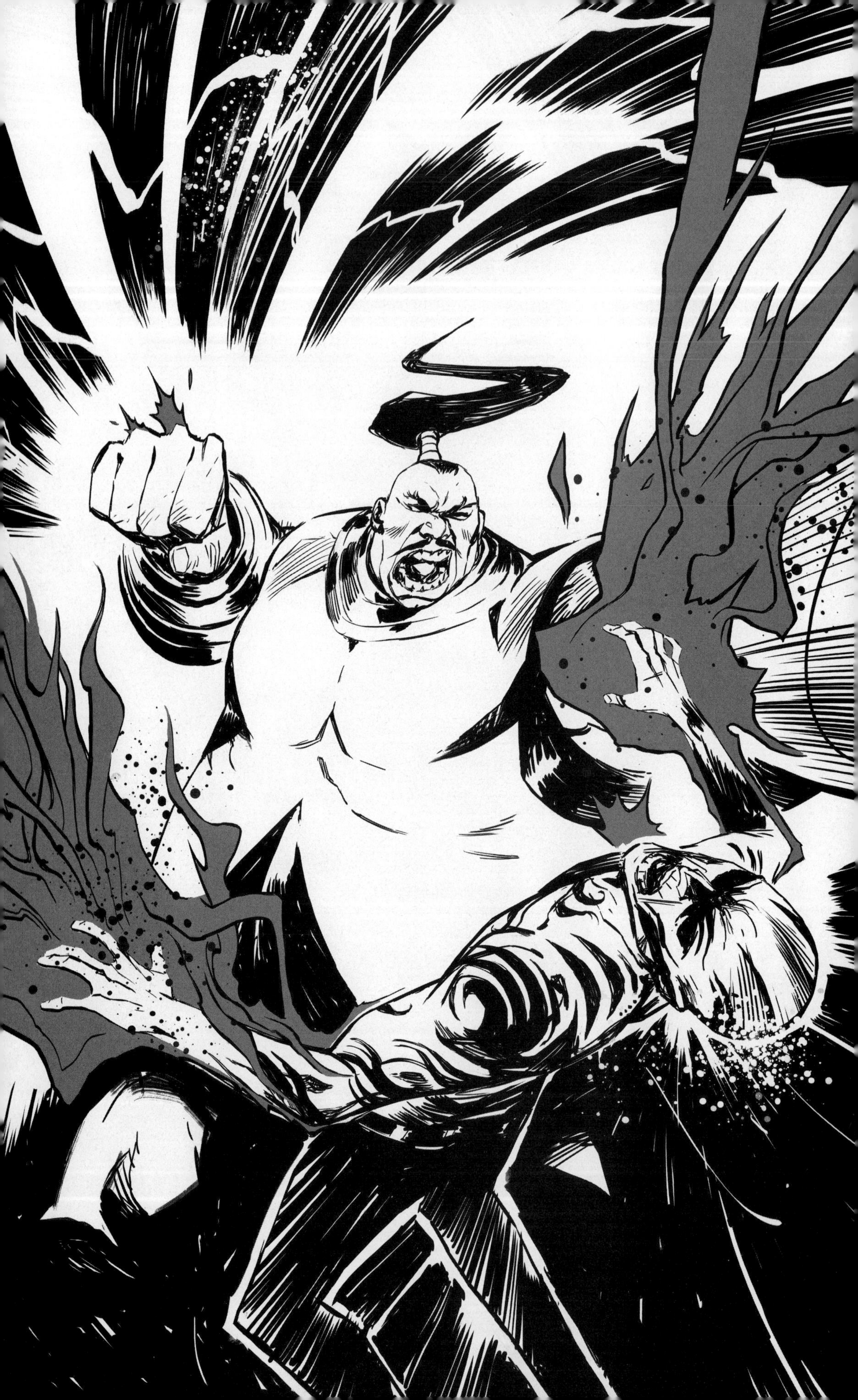

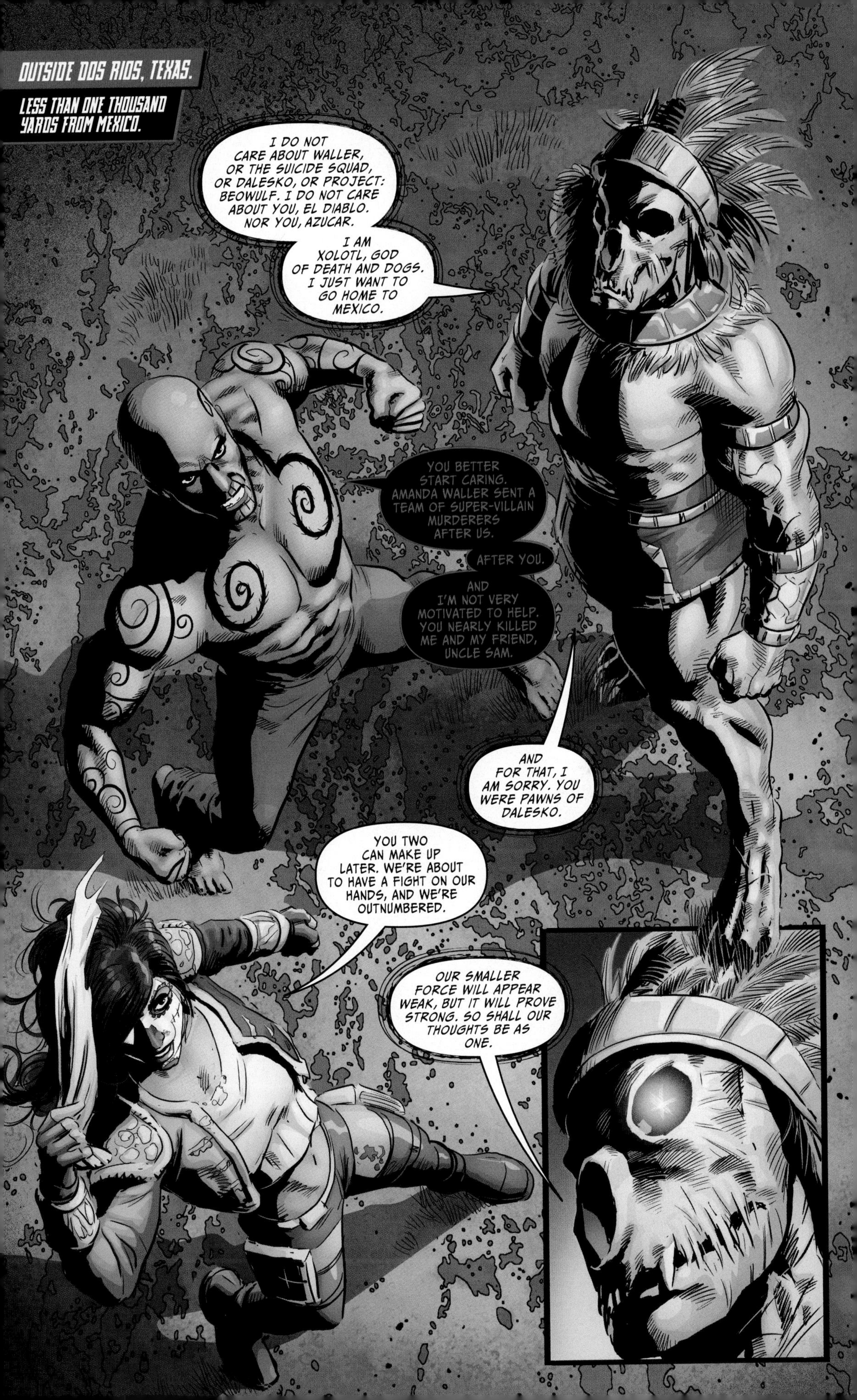
OUTSIDE DOS RIOS, TEXAS.
LESS THAN ONE THOUSAND YARDS FROM MEXICO.
I DO NOT CARE ABOUT WALLER, OR THE SUICIDE SQUAD, OR DALESKO, OR PROJECT: BEOWULF. I DO NOT CARE ABOUT YOU, EL DIABLO. NOR YOU, AZUCAR.
I AM XOLOTL, GOD OF DEATH AND DOGS. I JUST WANT TO GO HOME TO MEXICO.
YOU BETTER START CARING. AMANDA WALLER SENT A TEAM OF SUPER-VILLAIN MURDERERS AFTER US.
AFTER YOU.
AND I'M NOT VERY MOTIVATED TO HELP. YOU NEARLY KILLED ME AND MY FRIEND, UNCLE SAM.
AND FOR THAT, I AM SORRY. YOU WERE PAWNS OF DALESKO.
YOU TWO CAN MAKE UP LATER. WE'RE ABOUT TO HAVE A FIGHT ON OUR HANDS, AND WE'RE OUTNUMBERED.
OUR SMALLER FORCE WILL APPEAR WEAK, BUT IT WILL PROVE STRONG. SO SHALL OUR THOUGHTS BE AS ONE.

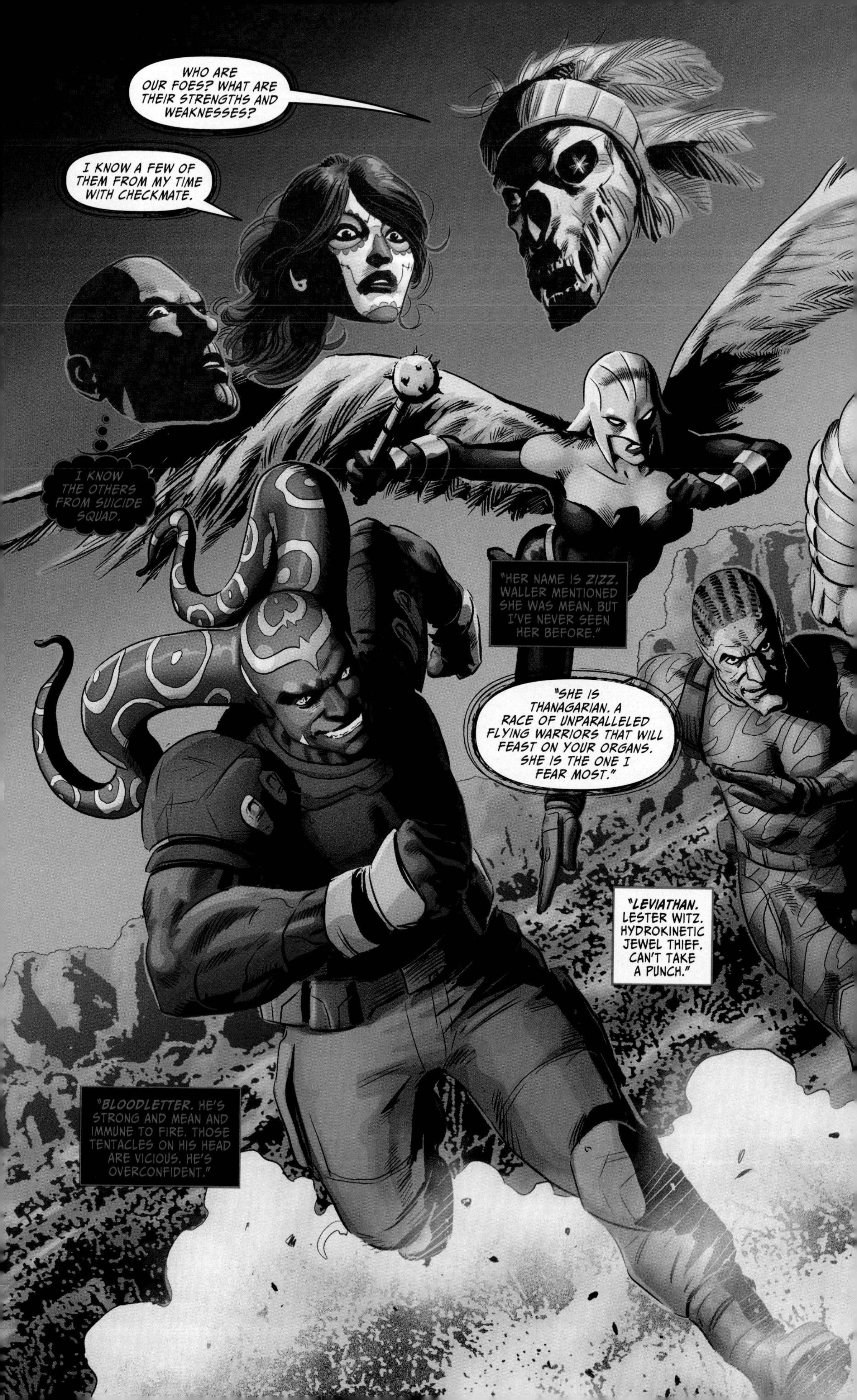
WHO ARE OUR FOES? WHAT ARE THEIR STRENGTHS AND WEAKNESSES?
I KNOW A FEW OF THEM FROM MY TIME WITH CHECKMATE.
I KNOW THE OTHERS FROM SUICIDE SQUAD.
"HER NAME IS ZIZZ. WALLER MENTIONED SHE WAS MEAN, BUT I'VE NEVER SEEN HER BEFORE."
"SHE IS THANAGARIAN. A RACE OF UNPARALLELED FLYING WARRIORS THAT WILL FEAST ON YOUR ORGANS. SHE IS THE ONE I FEAR MOST."
"LEVIATHAN. LESTER WITZ. HYDROKINETIC JEWEL THIEF. CAN'T TAKE A PUNCH."
"BLOODLETTER. HE'S STRONG AND MEAN AND IMMUNE TO FIRE. THOSE TENTACLES ON HIS HEAD ARE VICIOUS. HE'S OVERCONFIDENT."

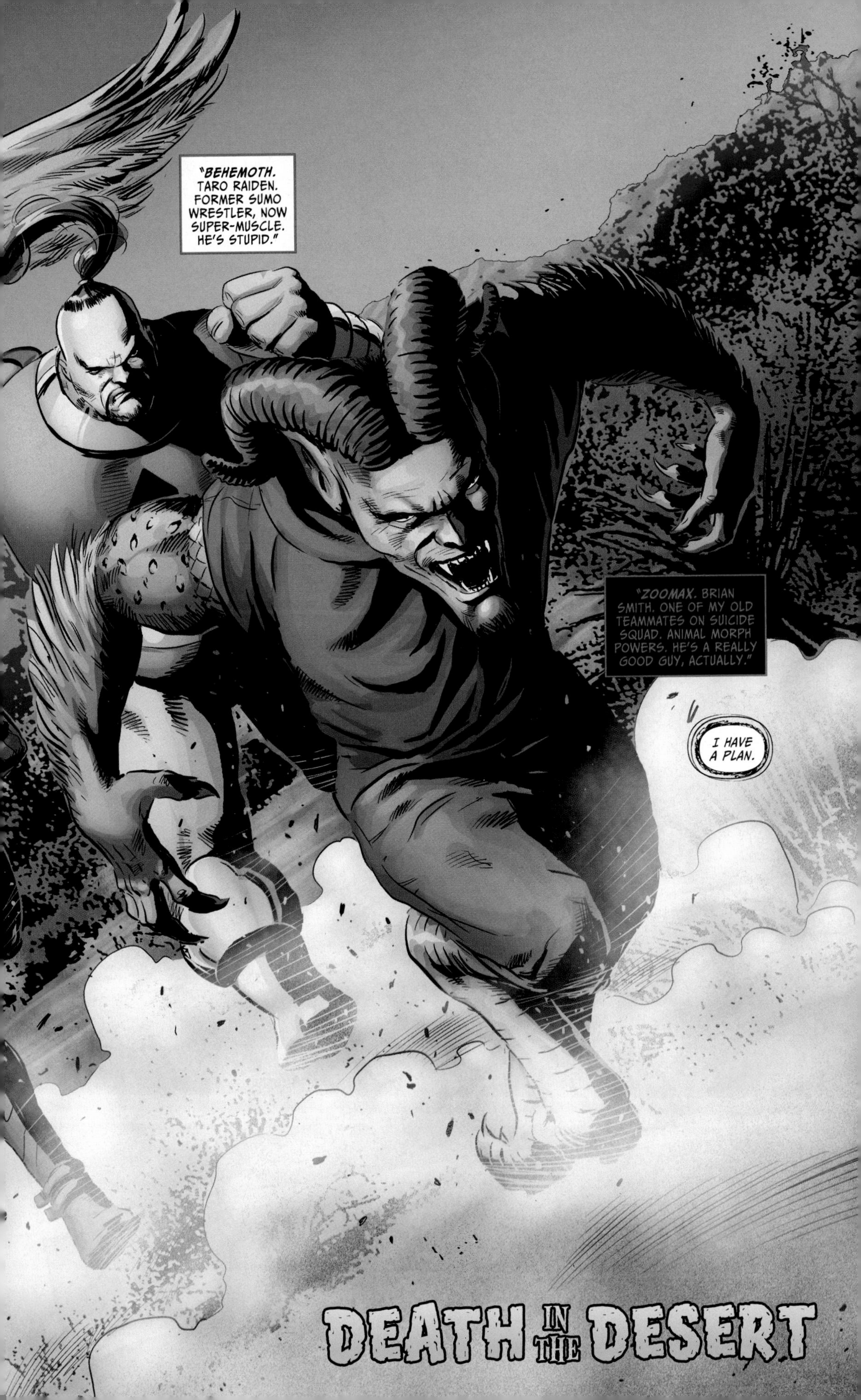
"BEHEMOTH. TARO RAIDEN. FORMER SUMO WRESTLER, NOW SUPER-MUSCLE. HE'S STUPID."
"ZOOMAX. BRIAN SMITH. ONE OF MY OLD TEAMMATES ON SUICIDE SQUAD. ANIMAL MORPH POWERS. HE'S A REALLY GOOD GUY, ACTUALLY."
I HAVE A PLAN.
DEATH IN THE DESERT

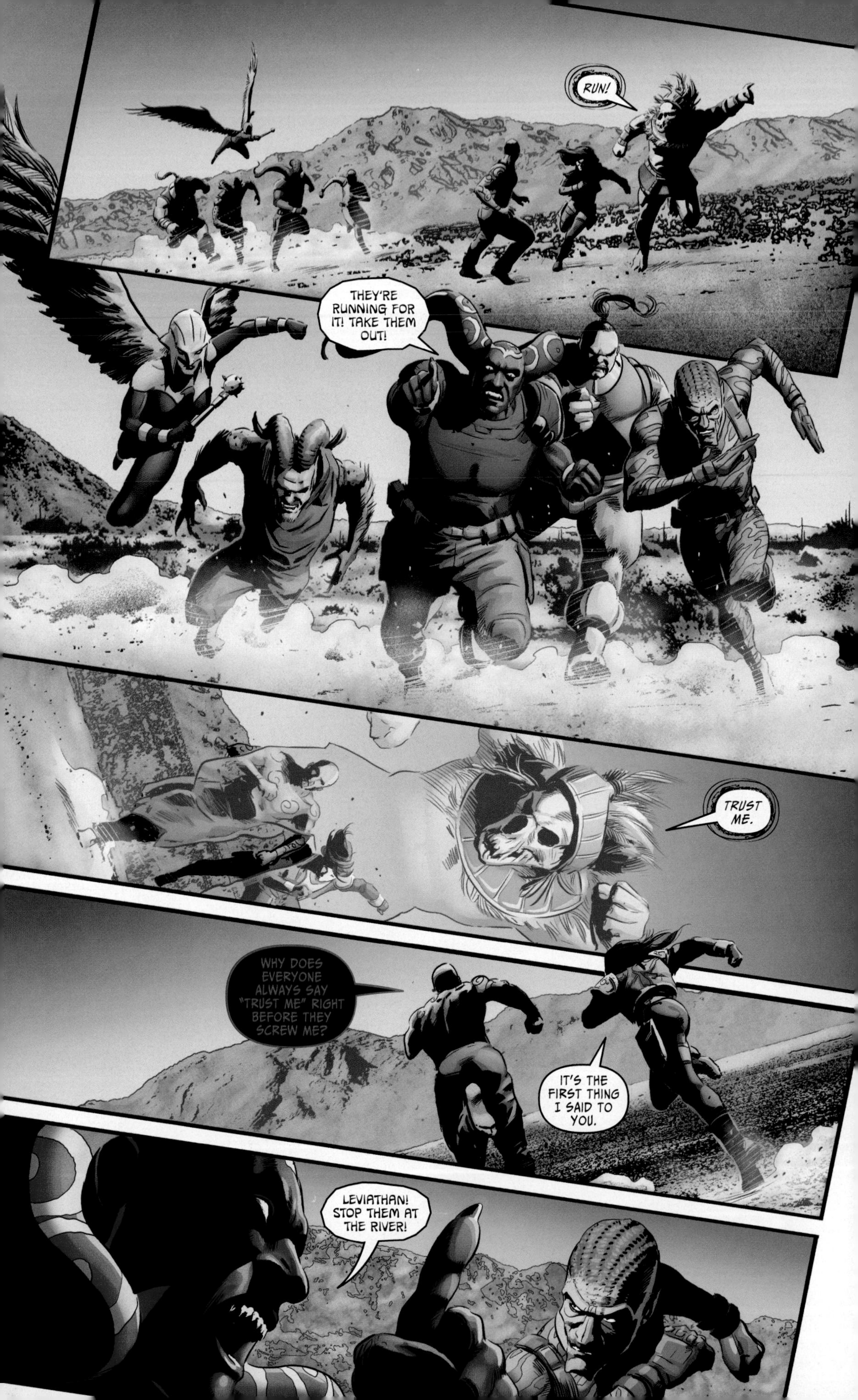
RUN!
THEY'RE RUNNING FOR IT! TAKE THEM OUT!
TRUST ME.
WHY DOES EVERYONE ALWAYS SAY "TRUST ME" RIGHT BEFORE THEY SCREW ME?
IT'S THE FIRST THING I SAID TO YOU.
LEVIATHAN! STOP THEM AT THE RIVER!

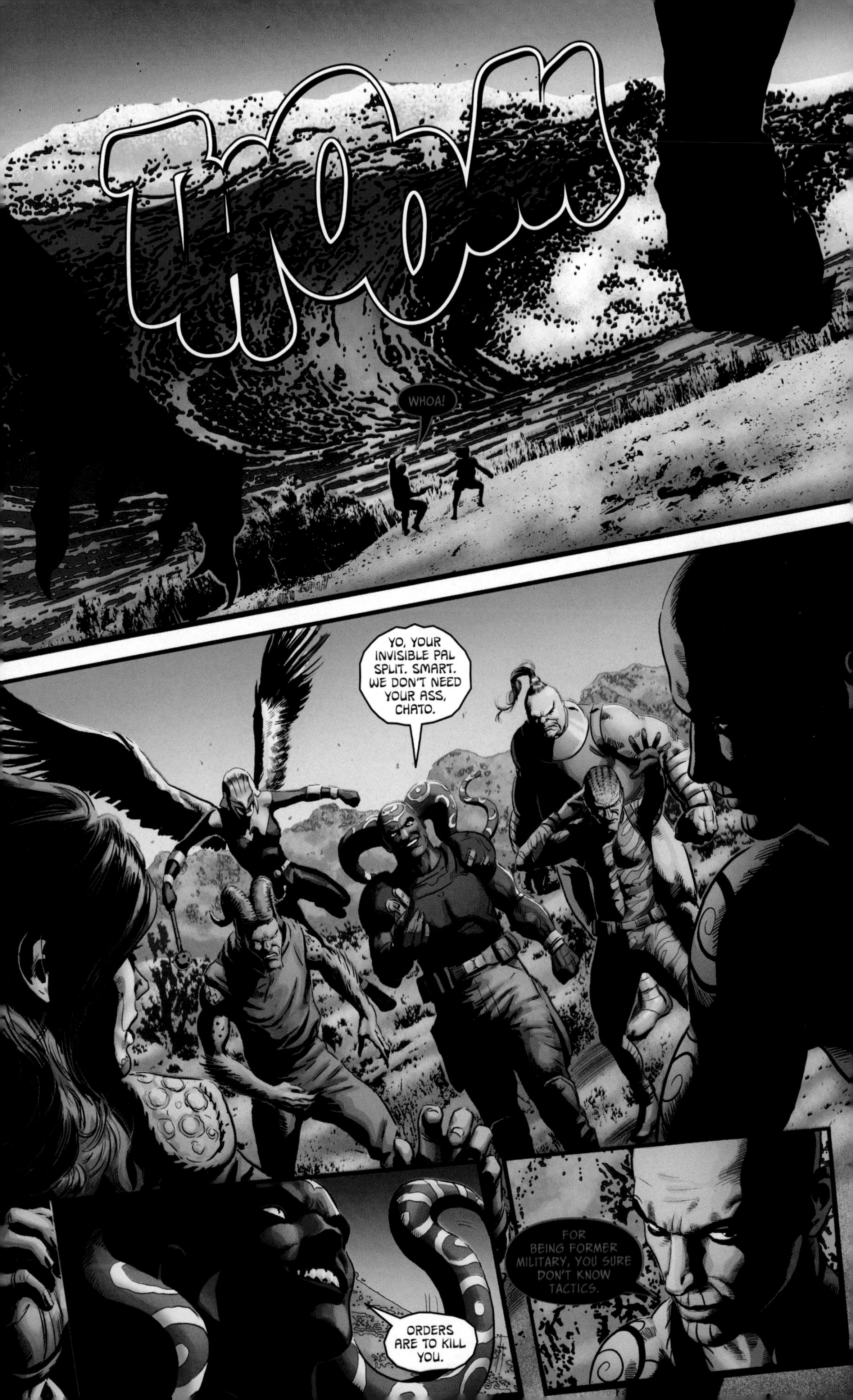
THOOM
WHOA!
YO, YOUR INVISIBLE PAL SPLIT. SMART. WE DON'T NEED YOUR ASS, CHATO.
ORDERS ARE TO KILL YOU.
FOR BEING FORMER MILITARY, YOU SURE DON'T KNOW TACTICS.

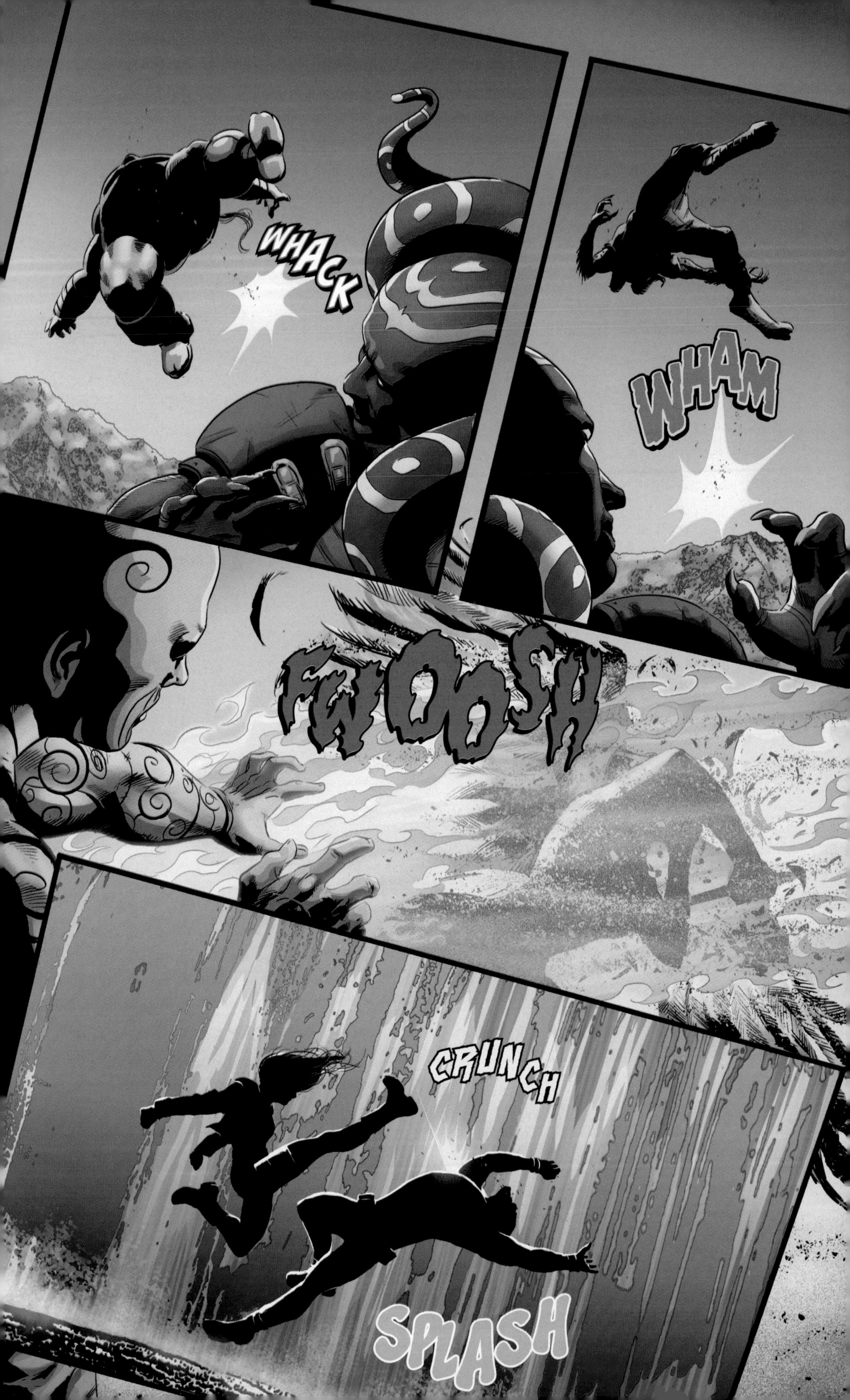
WHACK
WHAM
FWOOSH
CRUNCH
SPLASH

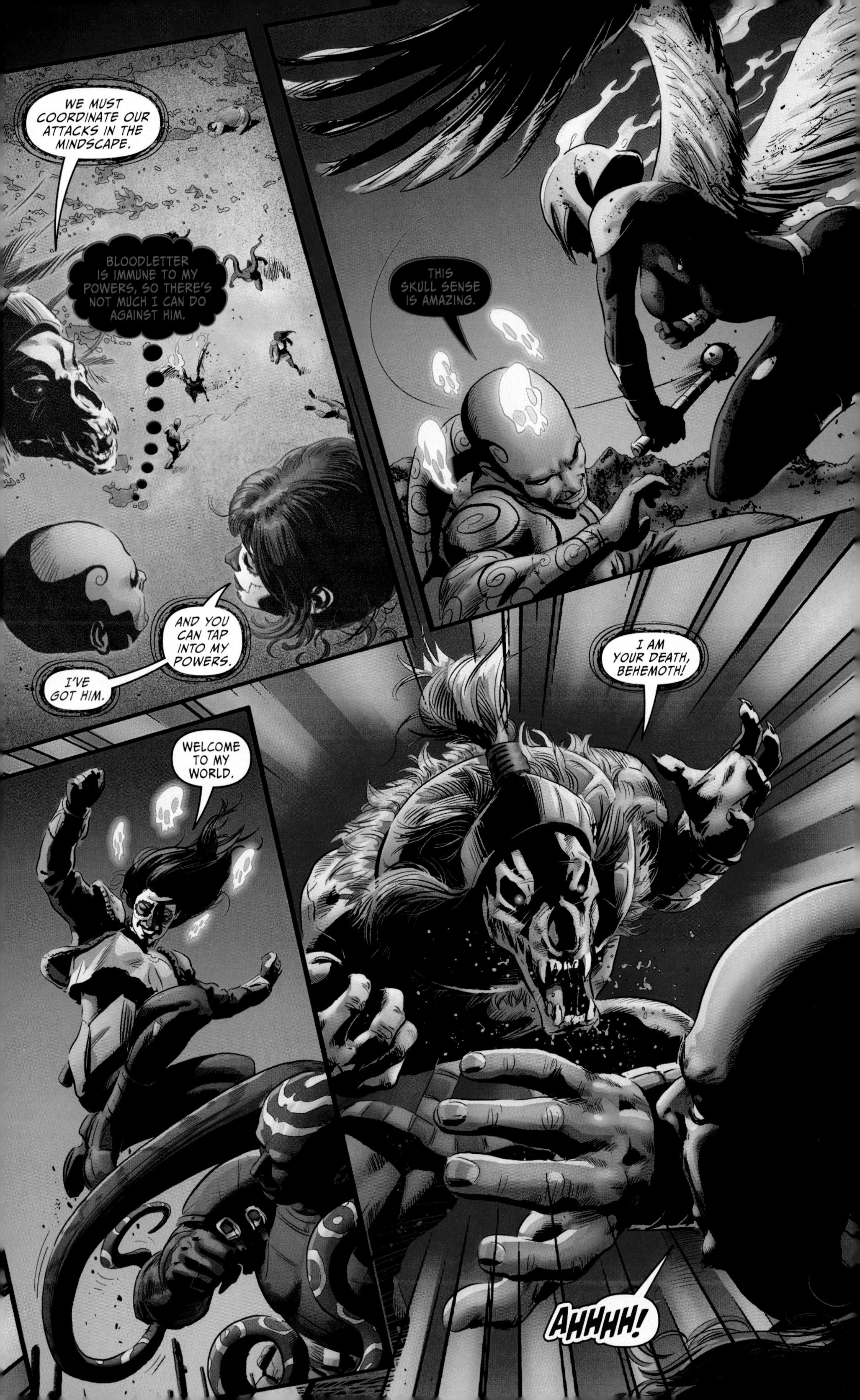
WE MUST COORDINATE OUR ATTACKS IN THE MINDSCAPE.
BLOODLETTER IS IMMUNE TO MY POWERS, SO THERE'S NOT MUCH I CAN DO AGAINST HIM.
AND YOU CAN TAP INTO MY POWERS.
I'VE GOT HIM.
THIS SKULL SENSE IS AMAZING.
WELCOME TO MY WORLD.
I AM YOUR DEATH, BEHEMOTH!
AHHHH!

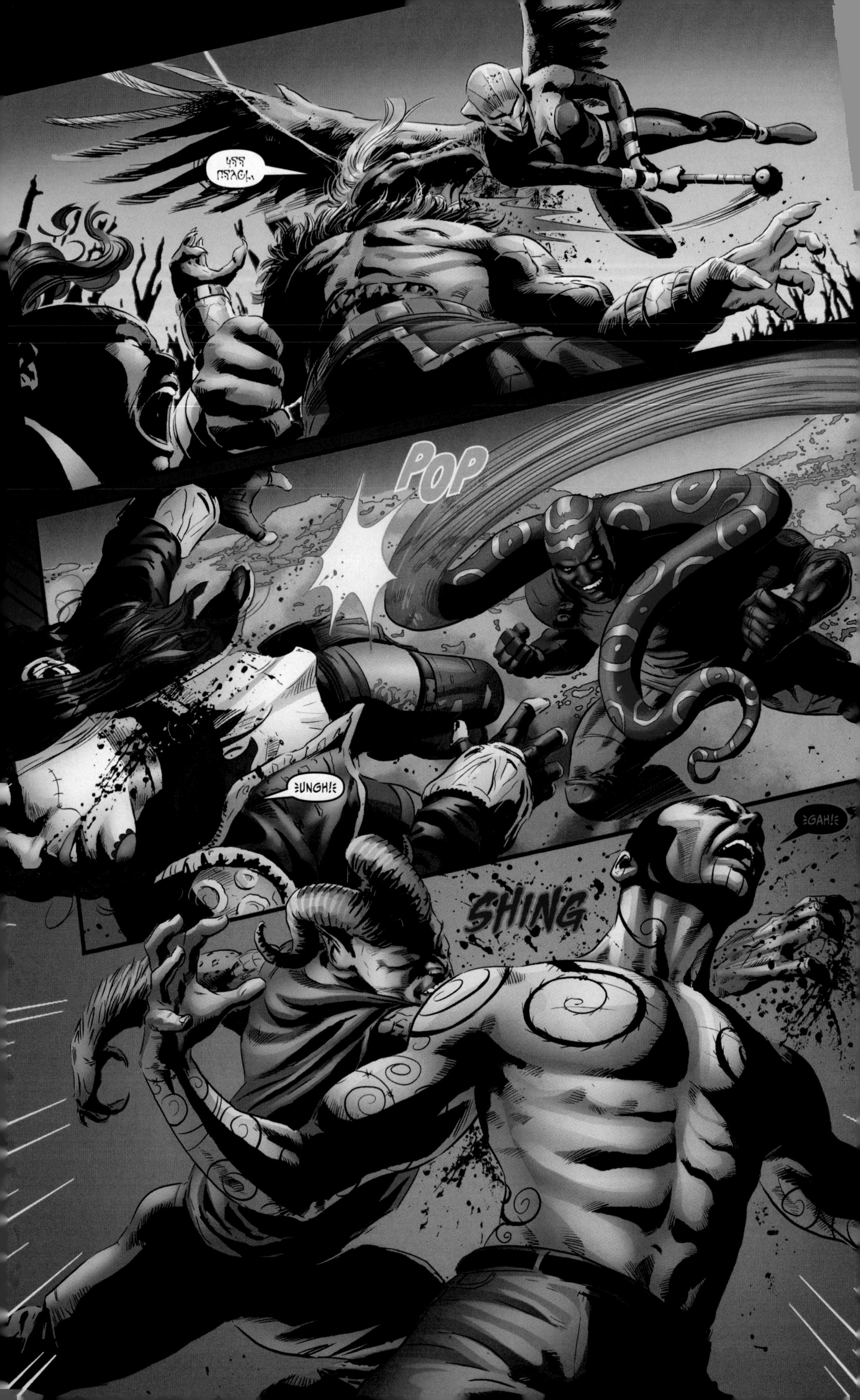
POP
UNGH!
GAH!
SHING

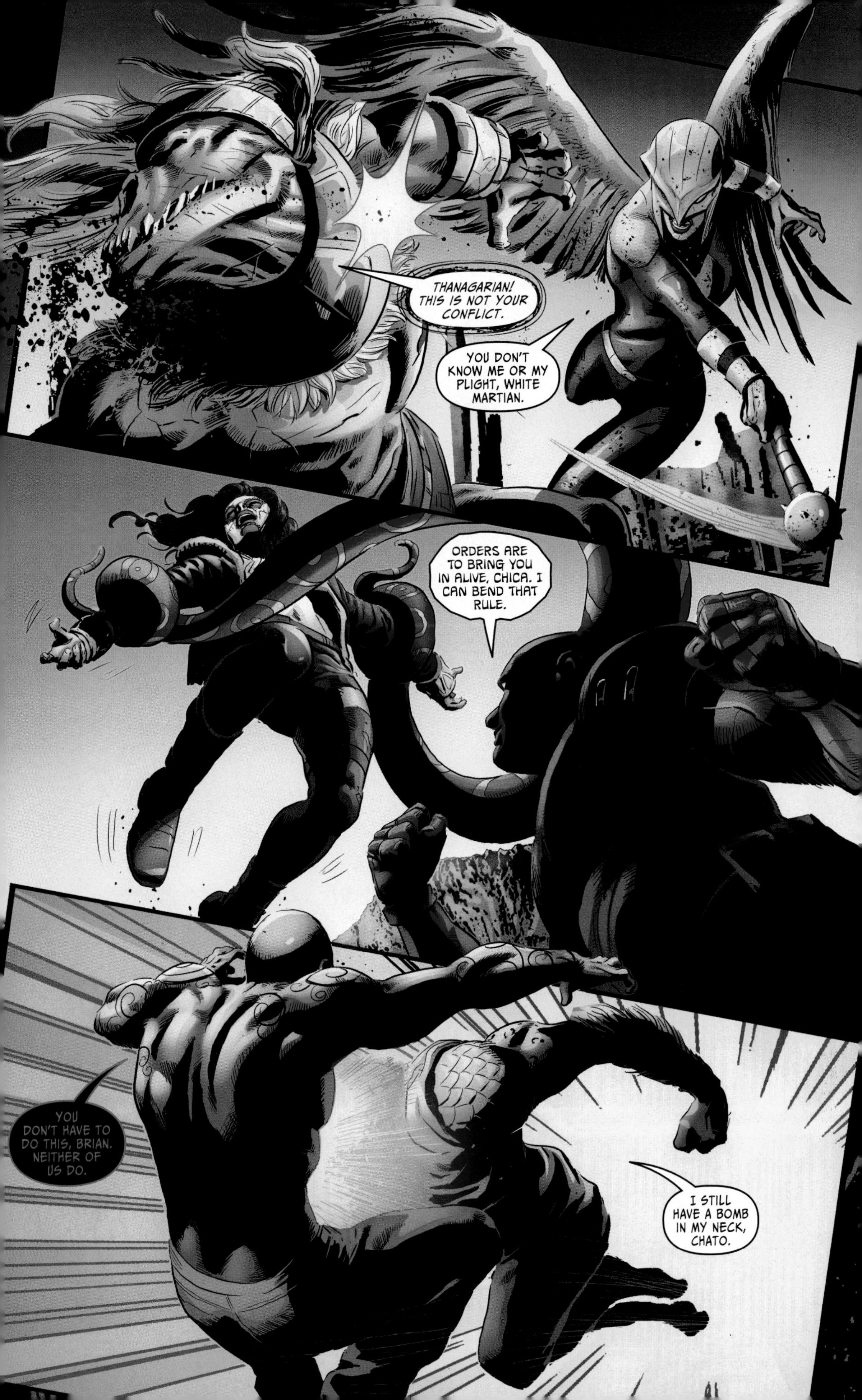
THANAGARIAN! THIS IS NOT YOUR CONFLICT.
YOU DON'T KNOW ME OR MY PLIGHT, WHITE MARTIAN.
ORDERS ARE TO BRING YOU IN ALIVE, CHICA. I CAN BEND THAT RULE.
YOU DON'T HAVE TO DO THIS, BRIAN. NEITHER OF US DO.
I STILL HAVE A BOMB IN MY NECK, CHATO.

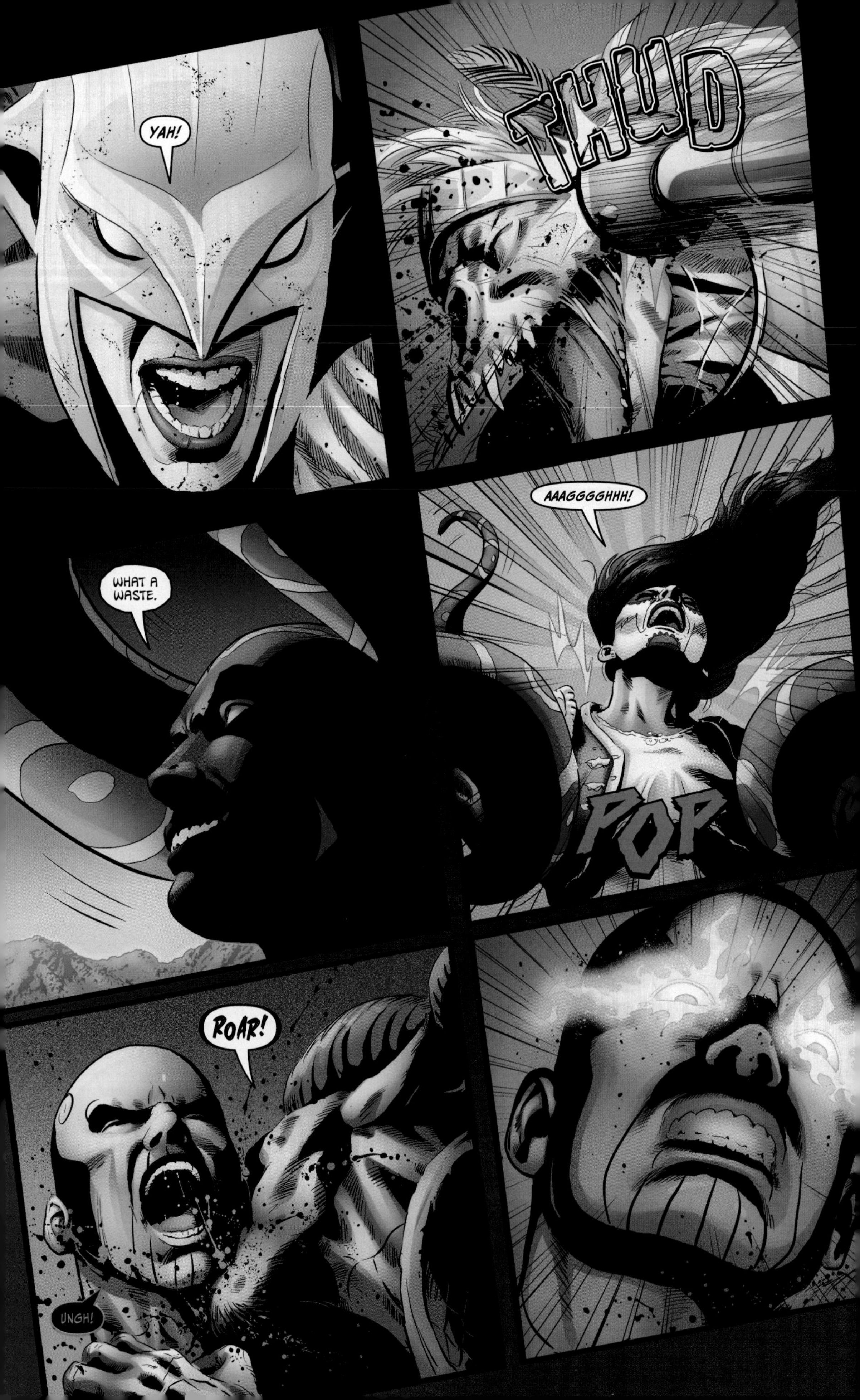
YAH!
THUD
WHAT A WASTE.
AAAGGGGHHH!
POP
ROAR!
UNGH!

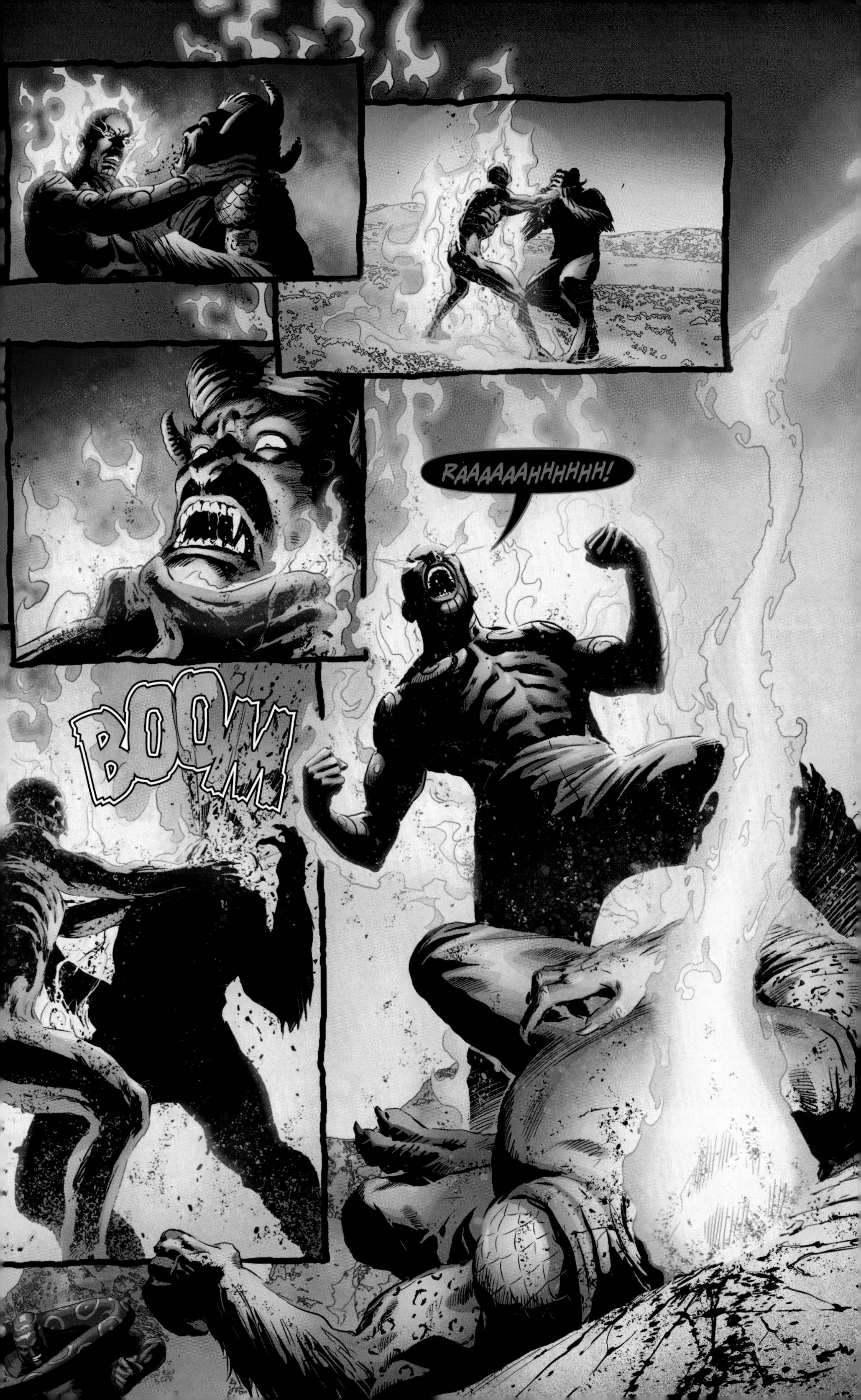
RAAAAAAHHHHHH!
BOOM

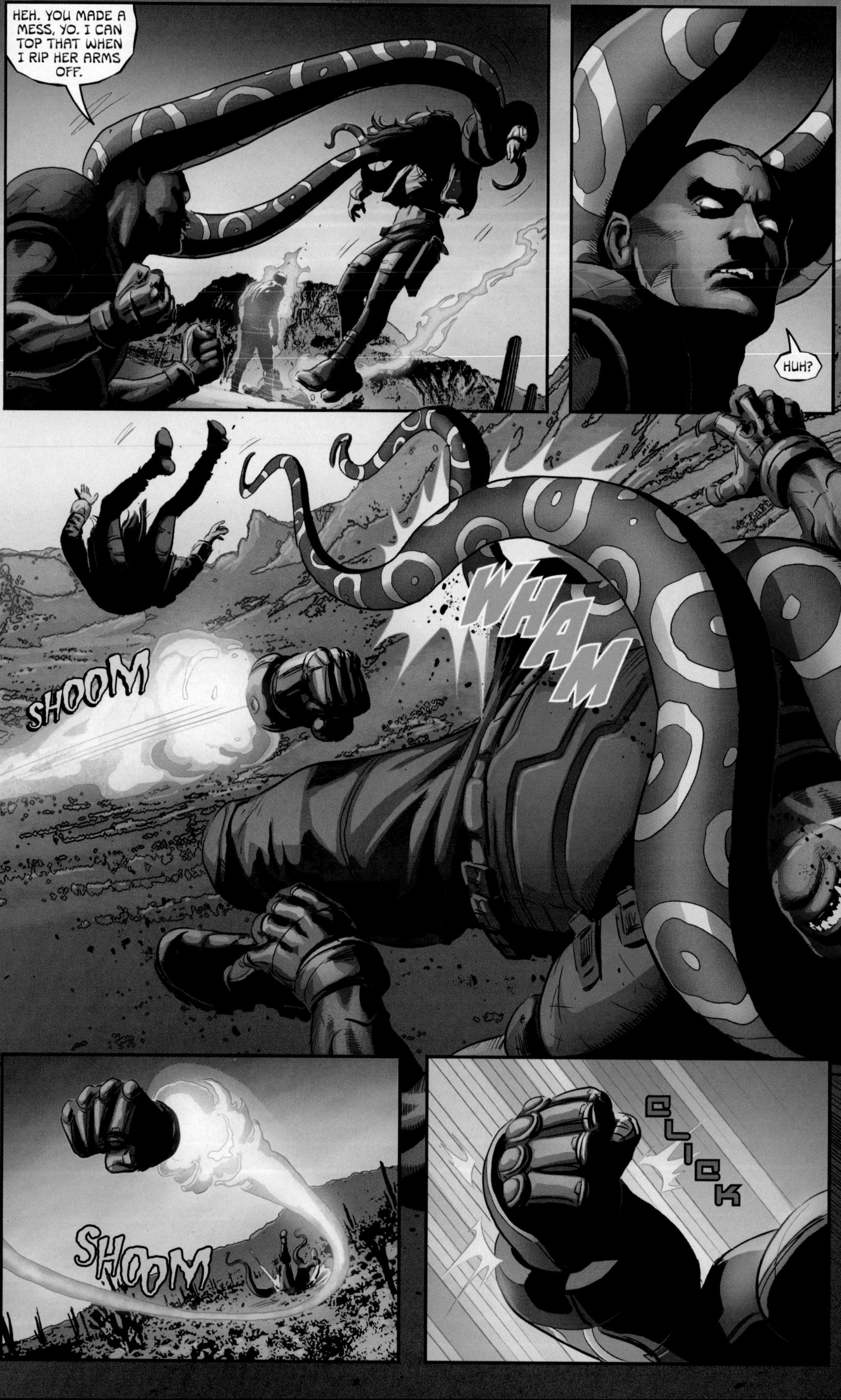
HEH. YOU MADE A MESS, YO. I CAN TOP THAT WHEN I RIP HER ARMS OFF.
HUH?
WHAM
SHOOM
SHOOM
CLICK

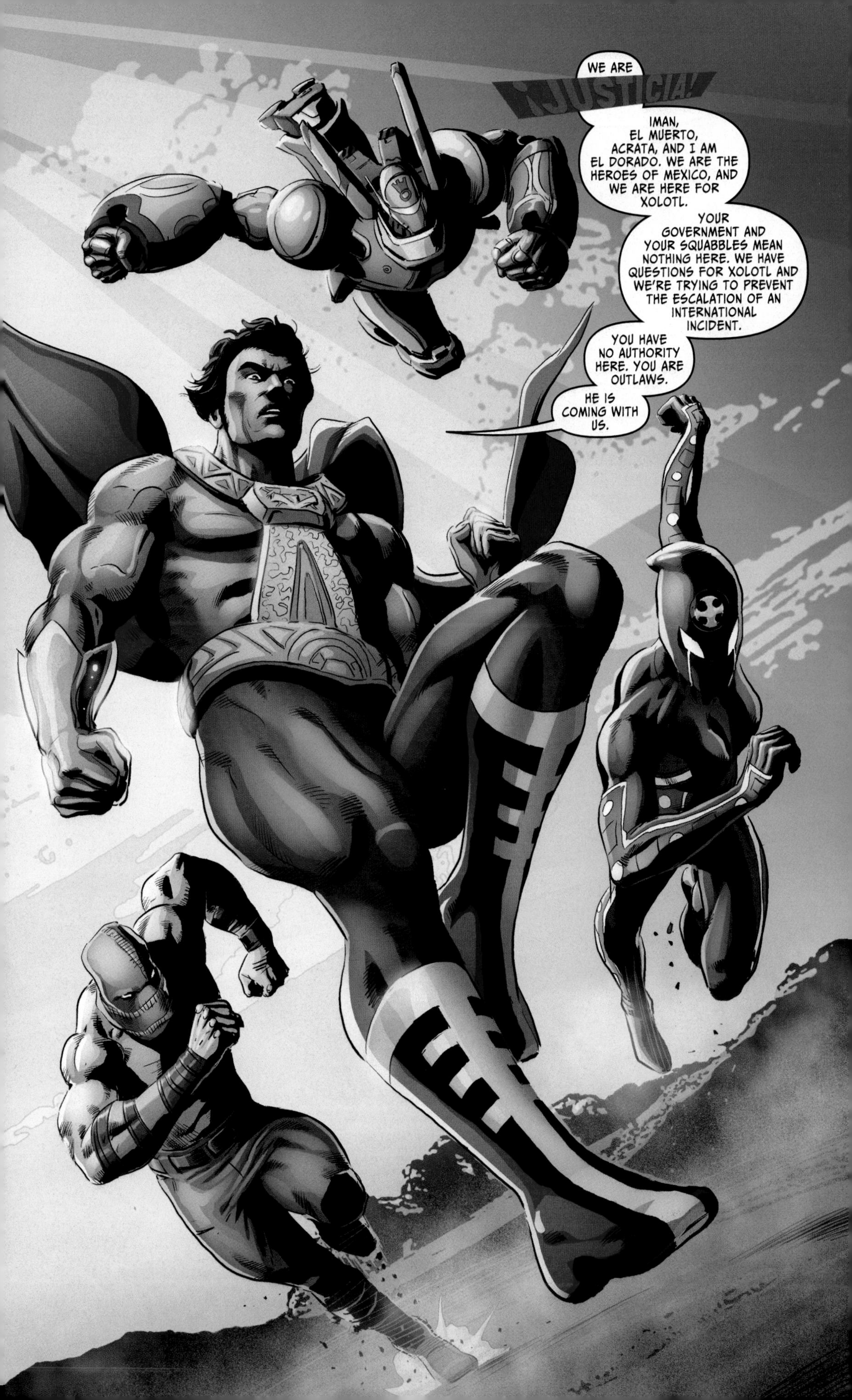
WE ARE
¡JUSTICIA!
IMAN, EL MUERTO, ACRATA, AND I AM EL DORADO. WE ARE THE HEROES OF MEXICO, AND WE ARE HERE FOR XOLOTL.
YOUR GOVERNMENT AND YOUR SQUABBLES MEAN NOTHING HERE. WE HAVE QUESTIONS FOR XOLOTL AND WE'RE TRYING TO PREVENT THE ESCALATION OF AN INTERNATIONAL INCIDENT.
YOU HAVE NO AUTHORITY HERE. YOU ARE OUTLAWS.
HE IS COMING WITH US.

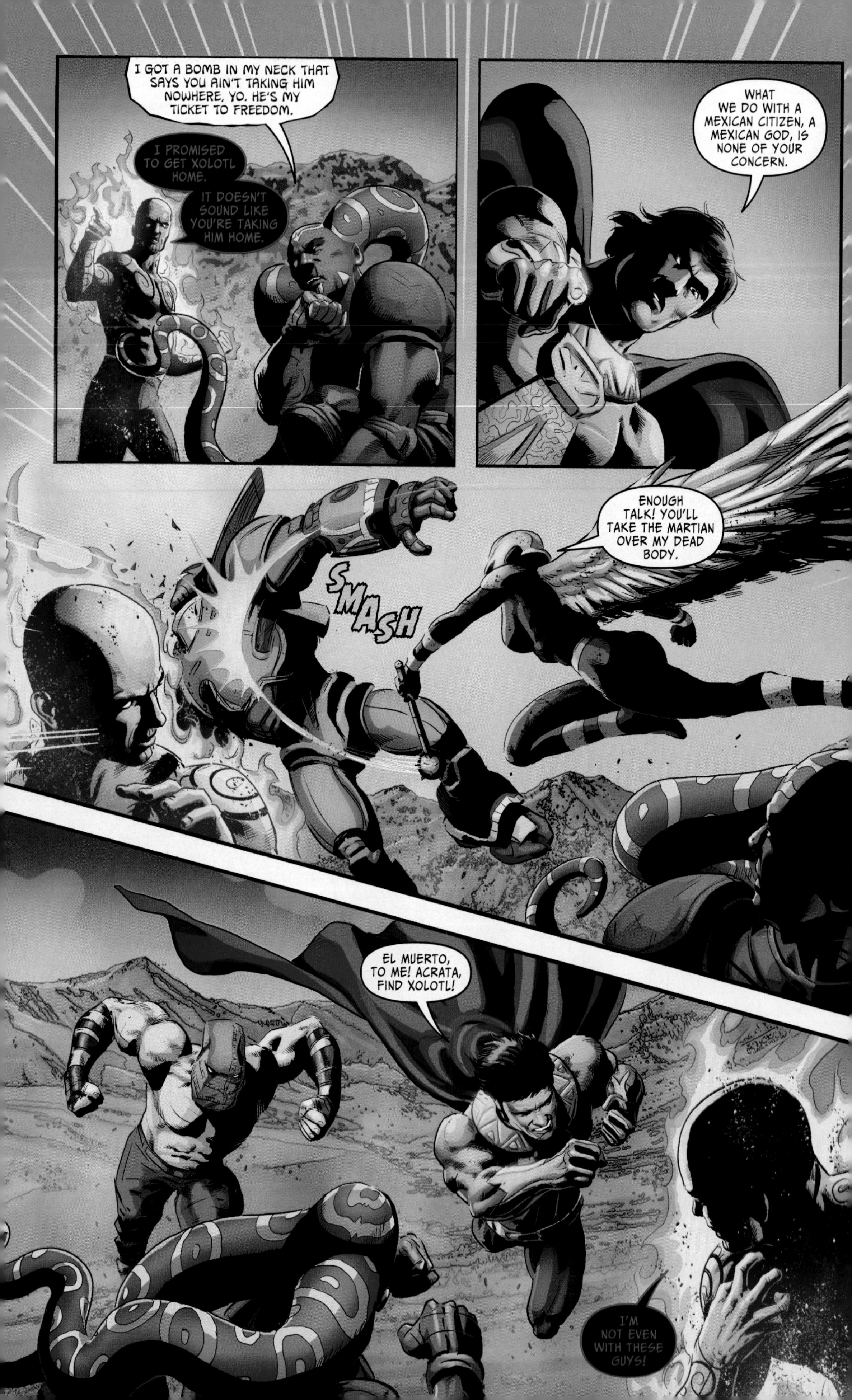
I GOT A BOMB IN MY NECK THAT SAYS YOU AIN'T TAKING HIM NOWHERE, YO. HE'S MY TICKET TO FREEDOM.
I PROMISED TO GET XOLOTL HOME.
IT DOESN'T SOUND LIKE YOU'RE TAKING HIM HOME.
WHAT WE DO WITH A MEXICAN CITIZEN, A MEXICAN GOD, IS NONE OF YOUR CONCERN.
ENOUGH TALK! YOU'LL TAKE THE MARTIAN OVER MY DEAD BODY.
SMASH
EL MUERTO, TO ME! ACRATA, FIND XOLOTL!
I'M NOT EVEN WITH THESE GUYS!

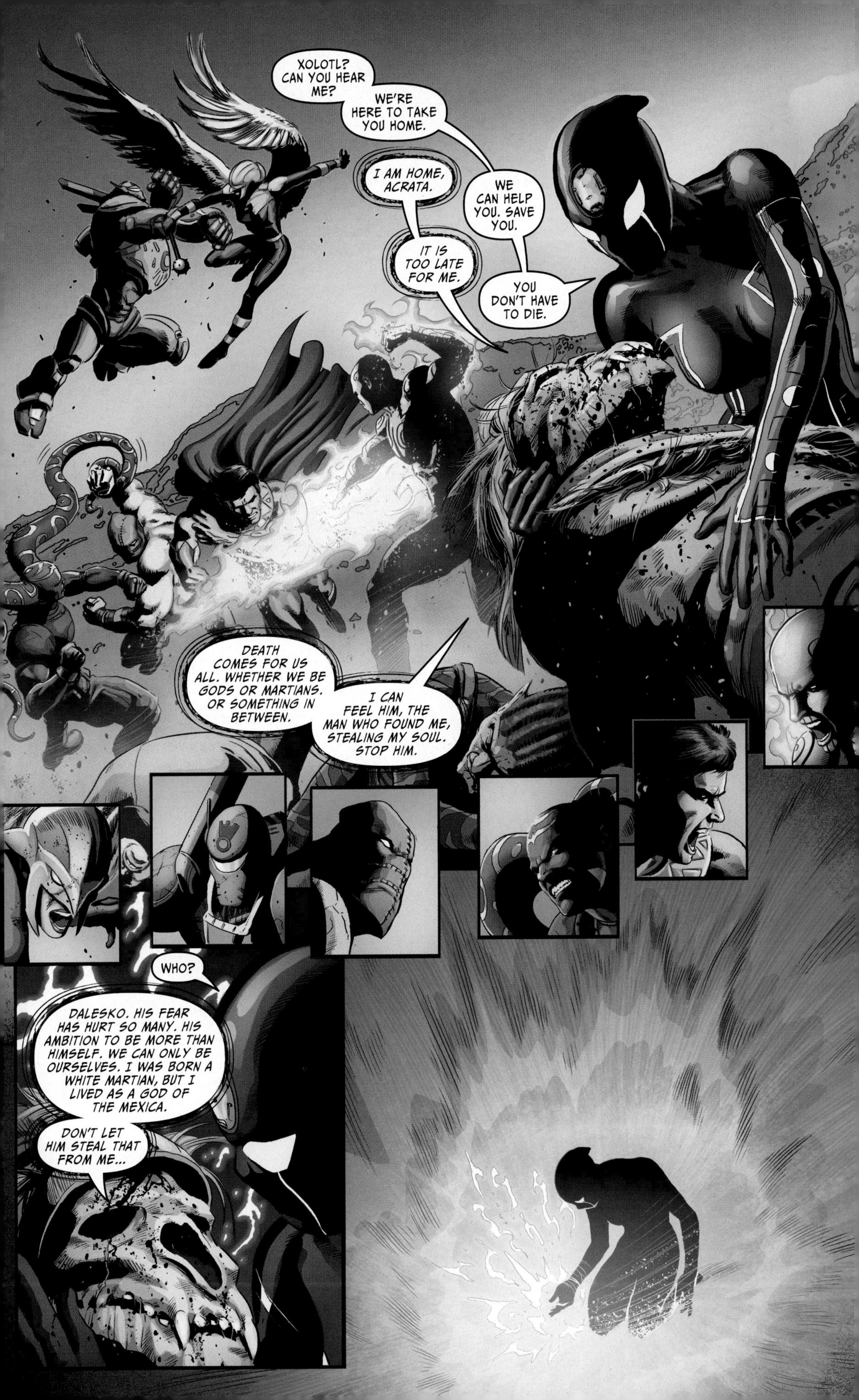
XOLOTL? CAN YOU HEAR ME?
WE'RE HERE TO TAKE YOU HOME.
I AM HOME, ACRATA.
IT IS TOO LATE FOR ME.
WE CAN HELP YOU. SAVE YOU.
YOU DON'T HAVE TO DIE.
DEATH COMES FOR US ALL. WHETHER WE BE GODS OR MARTIANS. OR SOMETHING IN BETWEEN.
I CAN FEEL HIM, THE MAN WHO FOUND ME, STEALING MY SOUL. STOP HIM.
WHO?
DALESKO. HIS FEAR HAS HURT SO MANY. HIS AMBITION TO BE MORE THAN HIMSELF. WE CAN ONLY BE OURSELVES. I WAS BORN A WHITE MARTIAN, BUT I LIVED AS A GOD OF THE MEXICA.
DON'T LET HIM STEAL THAT FROM ME...

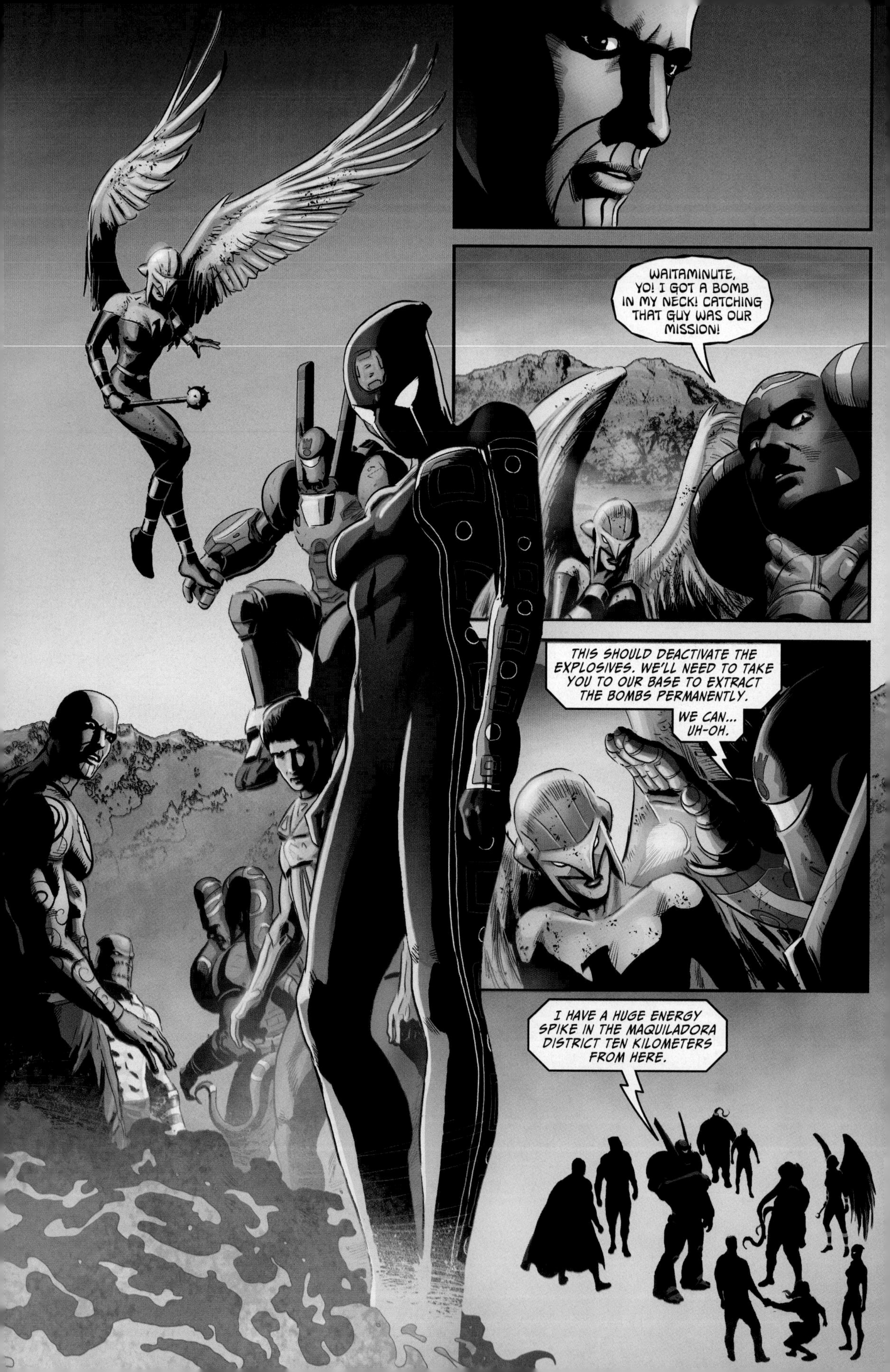
WAITAMINUTE, YO! I GOT A BOMB IN MY NECK! CATCHING THAT GUY WAS OUR MISSION!
THIS SHOULD DEACTIVATE THE EXPLOSIVES. WE'LL NEED TO TAKE YOU TO OUR BASE TO EXTRACT THE BOMBS PERMANENTLY.
WE CAN... UH-OH.
I HAVE A HUGE ENERGY SPIKE IN THE MAQUILADORA DISTRICT TEN KILOMETERS FROM HERE.

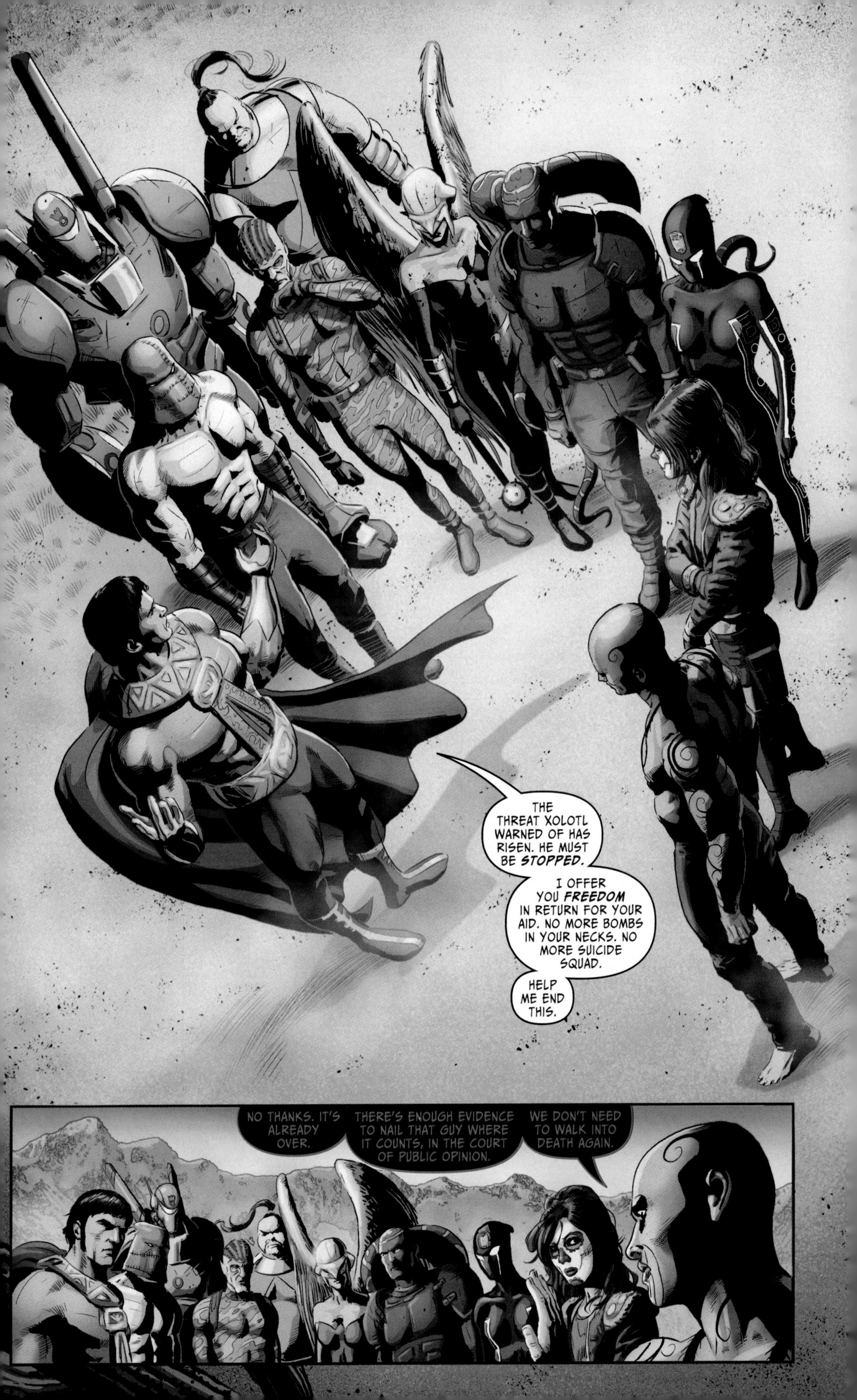
THE THREAT XOLOTL WARNED OF HAS RISEN. HE MUST BE STOPPED.
I OFFER YOU FREEDOM IN RETURN FOR YOUR AID. NO MORE BOMBS IN YOUR NECKS. NO MORE SUICIDE SQUAD.
HELP ME END THIS.
NO THANKS. IT'S ALREADY OVER.
THERE'S ENOUGH EVIDENCE TO NAIL THAT GUY WHERE IT COUNTS, IN THE COURT OF PUBLIC OPINION.
WE DON'T NEED TO WALK INTO DEATH AGAIN.

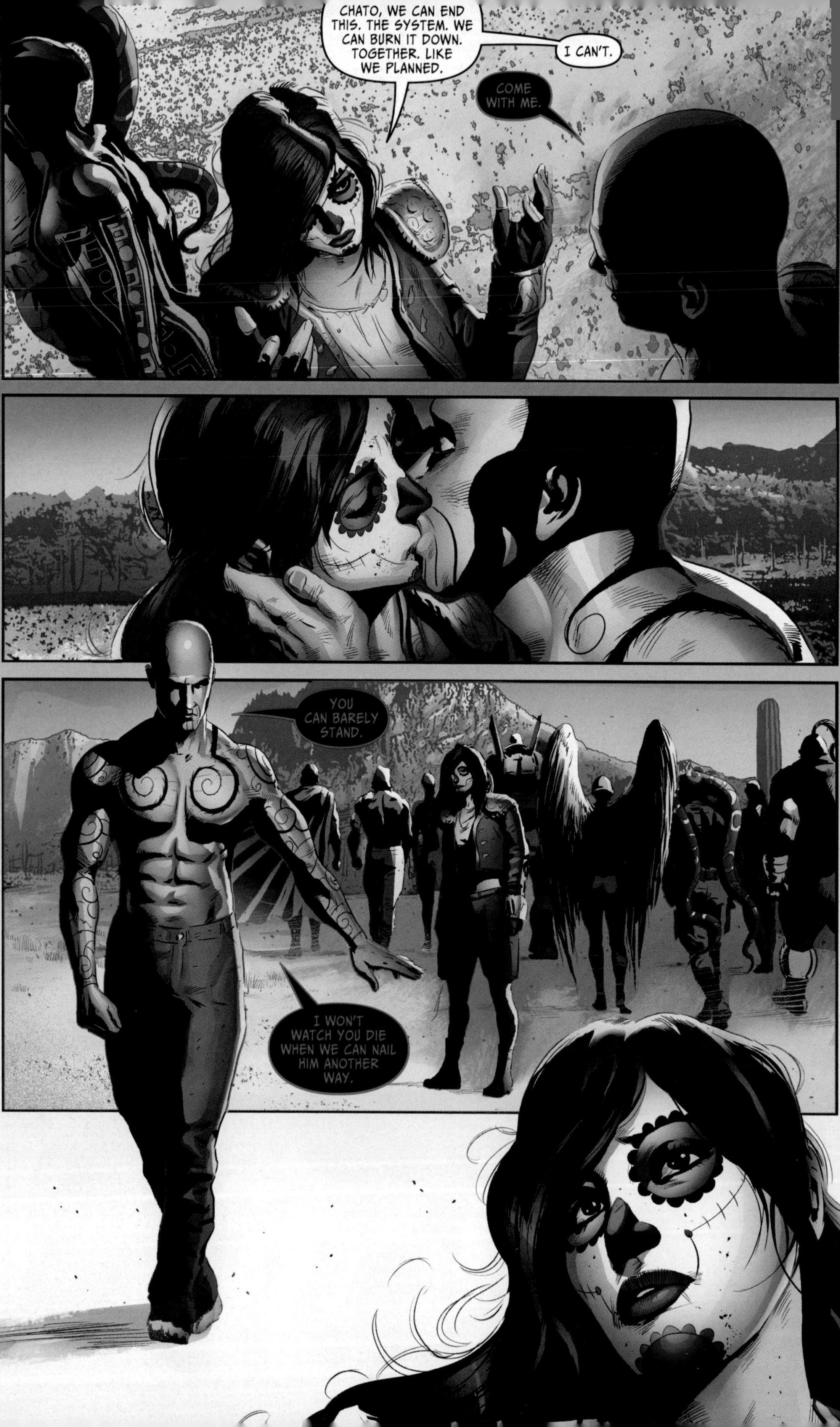
CHATO, WE CAN END THIS. THE SYSTEM. WE CAN BURN IT DOWN. TOGETHER. LIKE WE PLANNED.
I CAN'T.
COME WITH ME.
YOU CAN BARELY STAND.
I WON'T WATCH YOU DIE WHEN WE CAN NAIL HIM ANOTHER WAY.

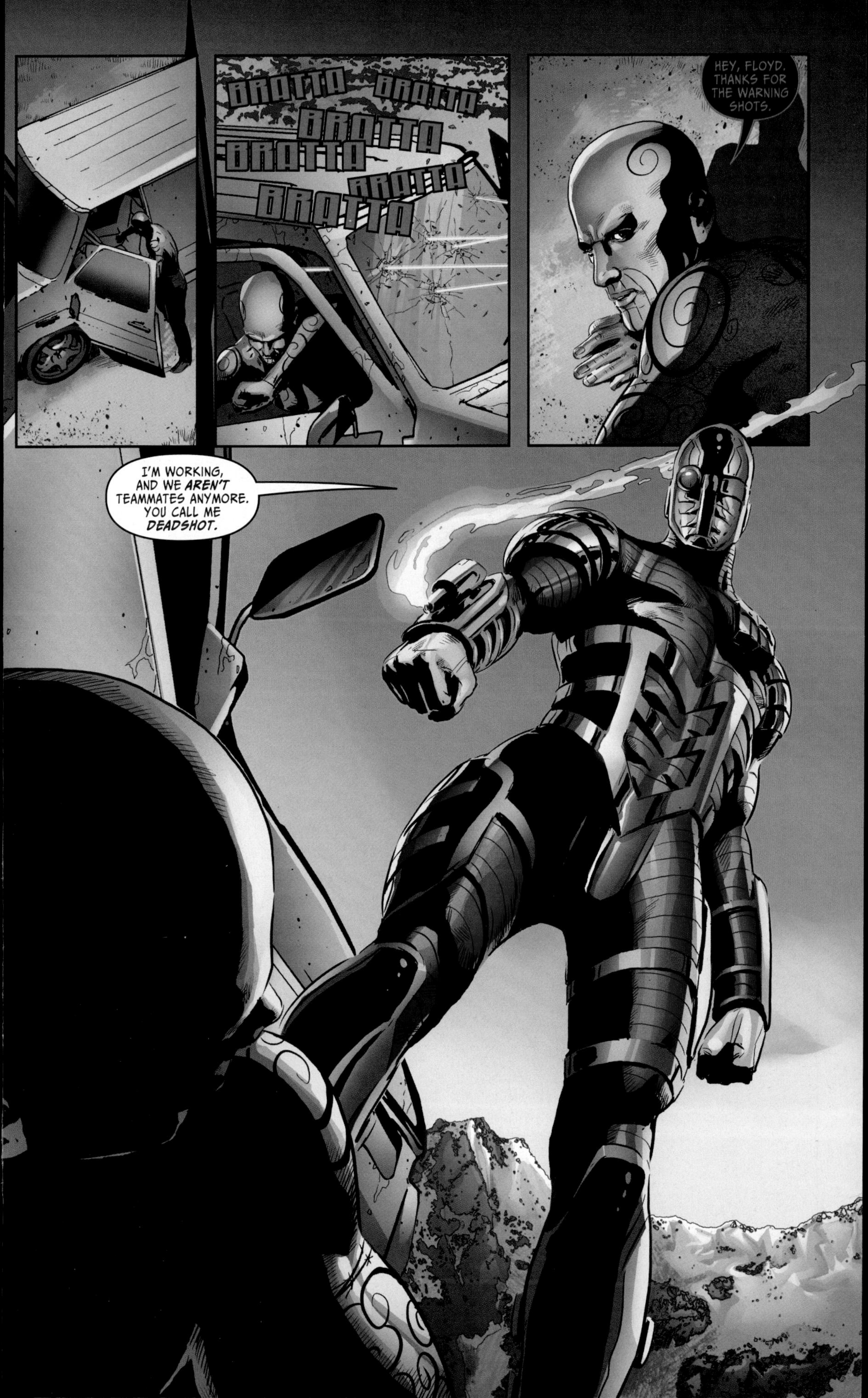
BRATTA BRATTA BRATTA BRATTA BRATTA BRATTA
HEY, FLOYD. THANKS FOR THE WARNING SHOTS.
I'M WORKING, AND WE AREN'T TEAMMATES ANYMORE. YOU CALL ME DEADSHOT.

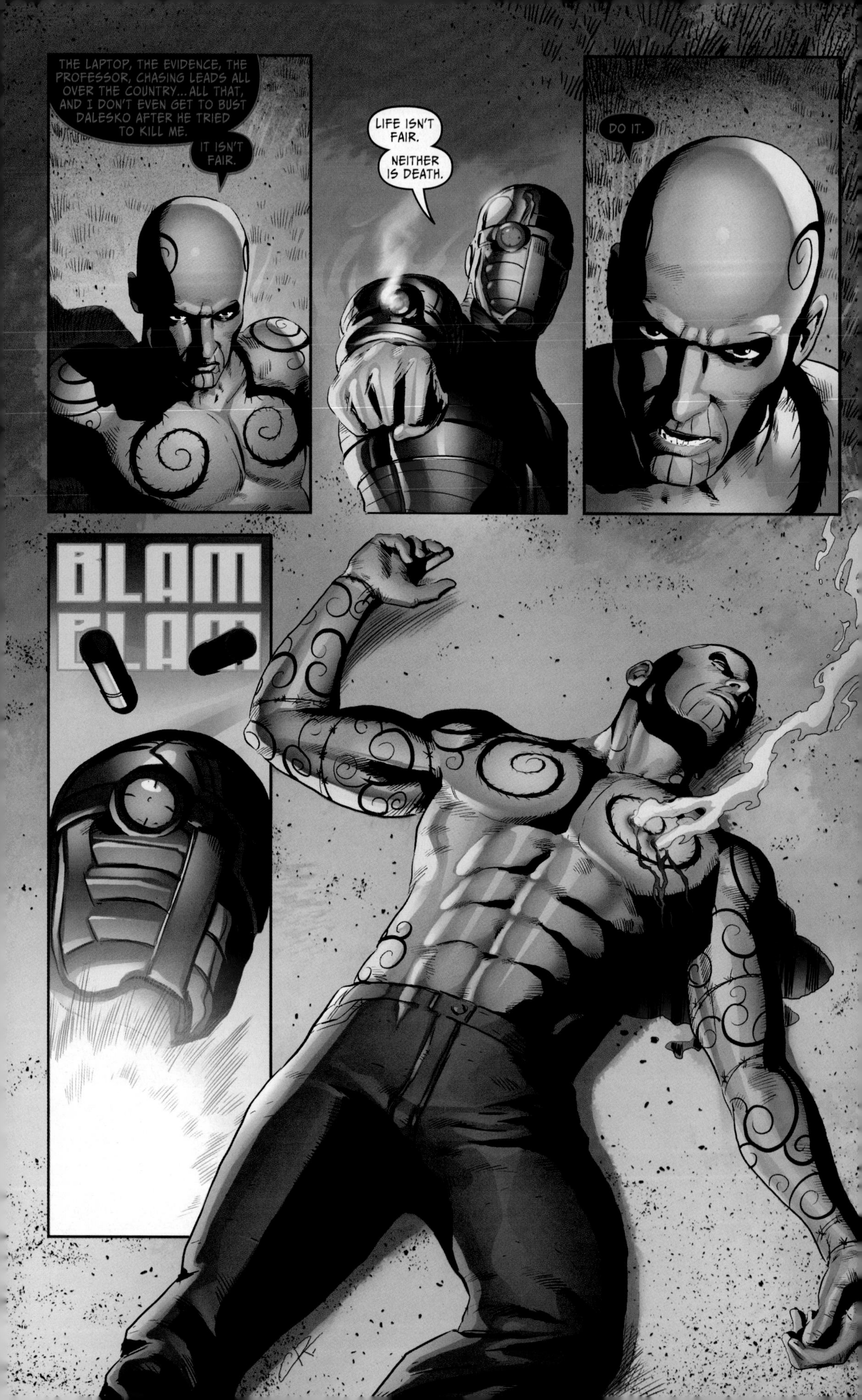

THE LAPTOP, THE EVIDENCE, THE PROFESSOR, CHASING LEADS ALL OVER THE COUNTRY... ALL THAT, AND I DON'T EVEN GET TO BUST DALESKO AFTER HE TRIED TO KILL ME.
IT ISN'T FAIR.
LIFE ISN'T FAIR.
NEITHER IS DEATH.
DO IT.
BLAM
BLAM

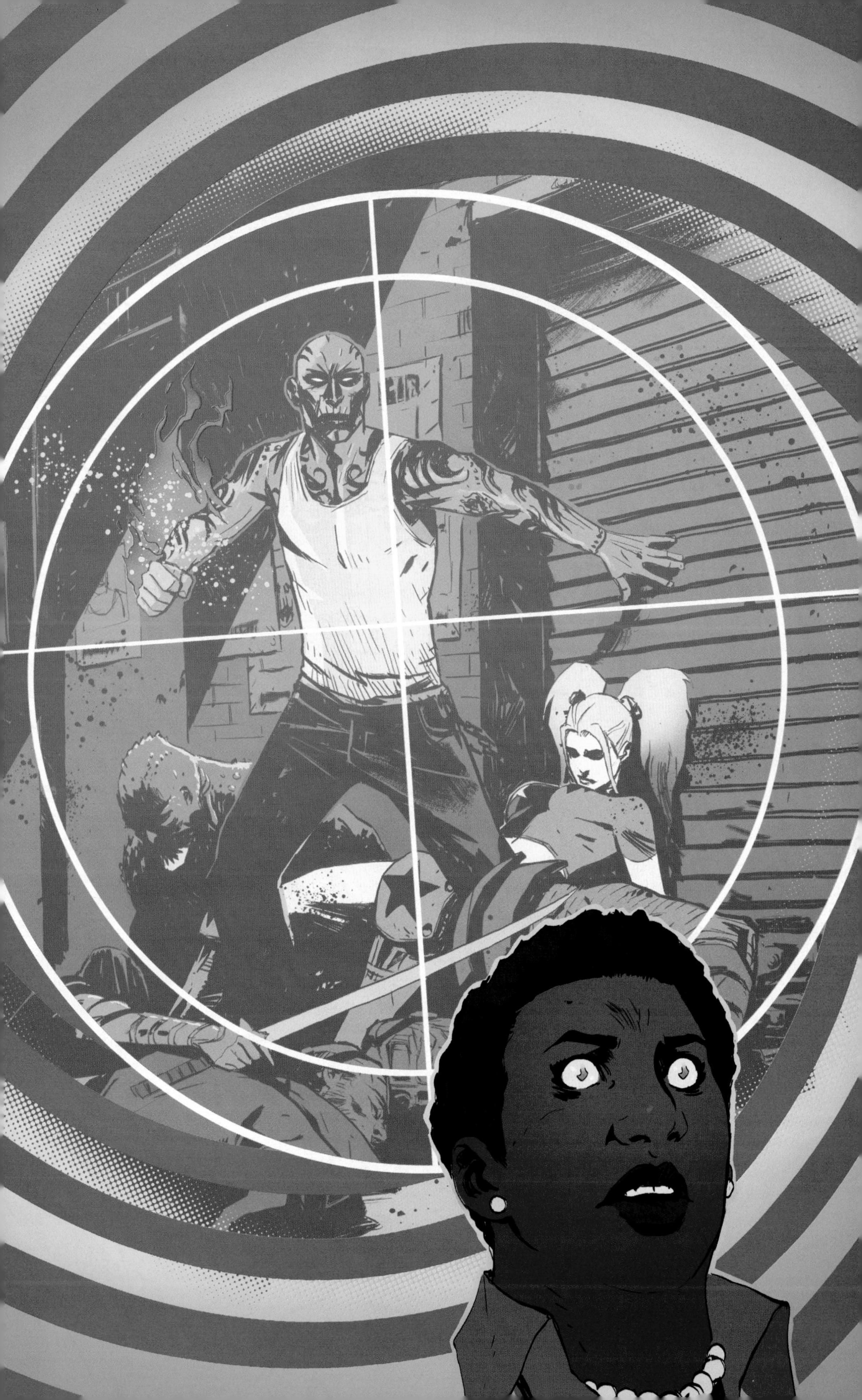

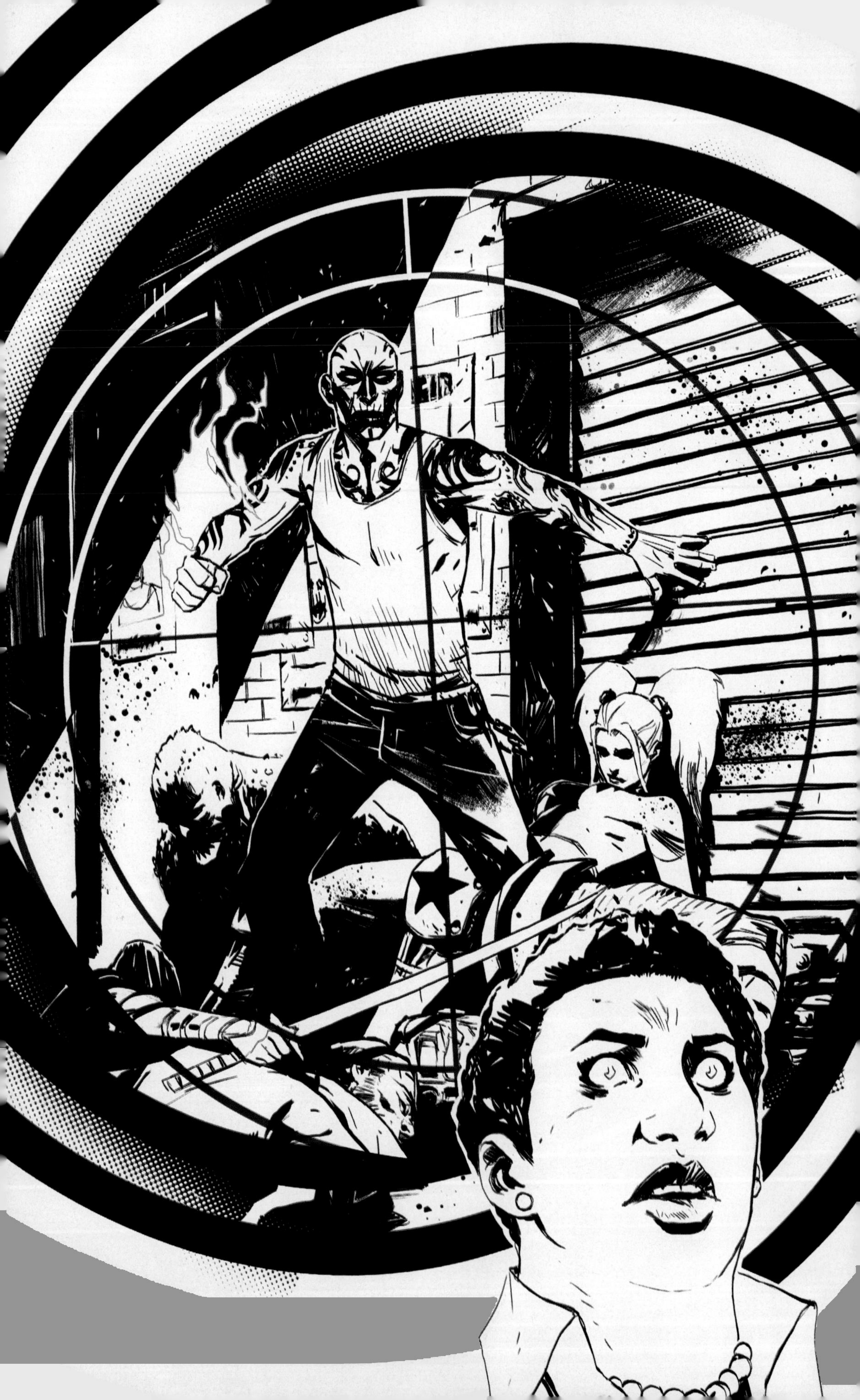

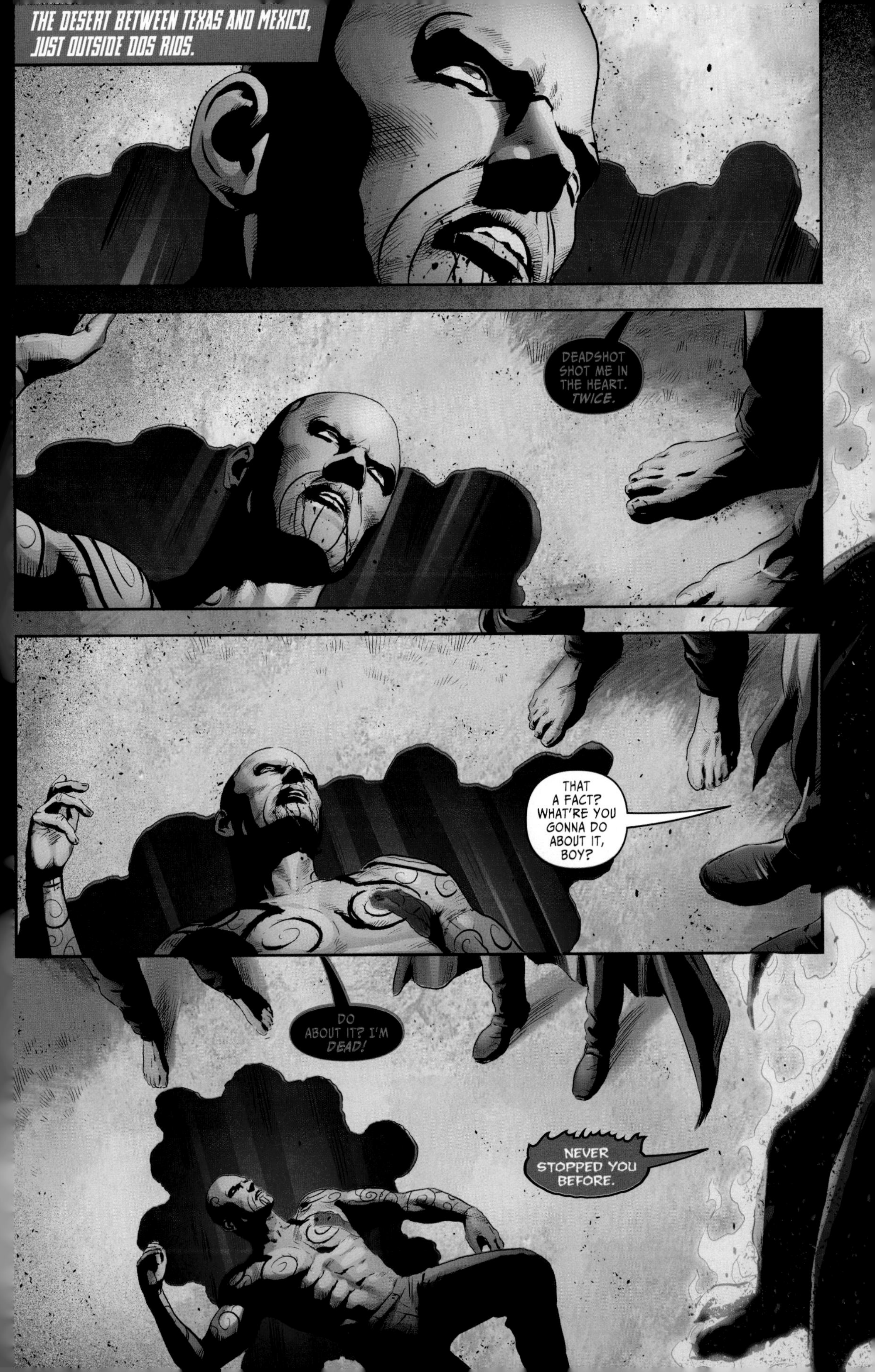

THE DESERT BETWEEN TEXAS AND MEXICO, JUST OUTSIDE DOS RIOS.
DEADSHOT SHOT ME IN THE HEART. TWICE.
THAT A FACT? WHAT'RE YOU GONNA DO ABOUT IT, BOY?
DO ABOUT IT? I'M DEAD!
NEVER STOPPED YOU BEFORE.

DEAD AGAIN!
DEATH HAS NEVER STOPPED EL DIABLO!
CHUTRIEL. FALLEN ANGEL.
LAZARUS LANE. GUNFIGHTER.
EL DIABLO, A.K.A. CHATO SANTANA. SUICIDE SQUAD.

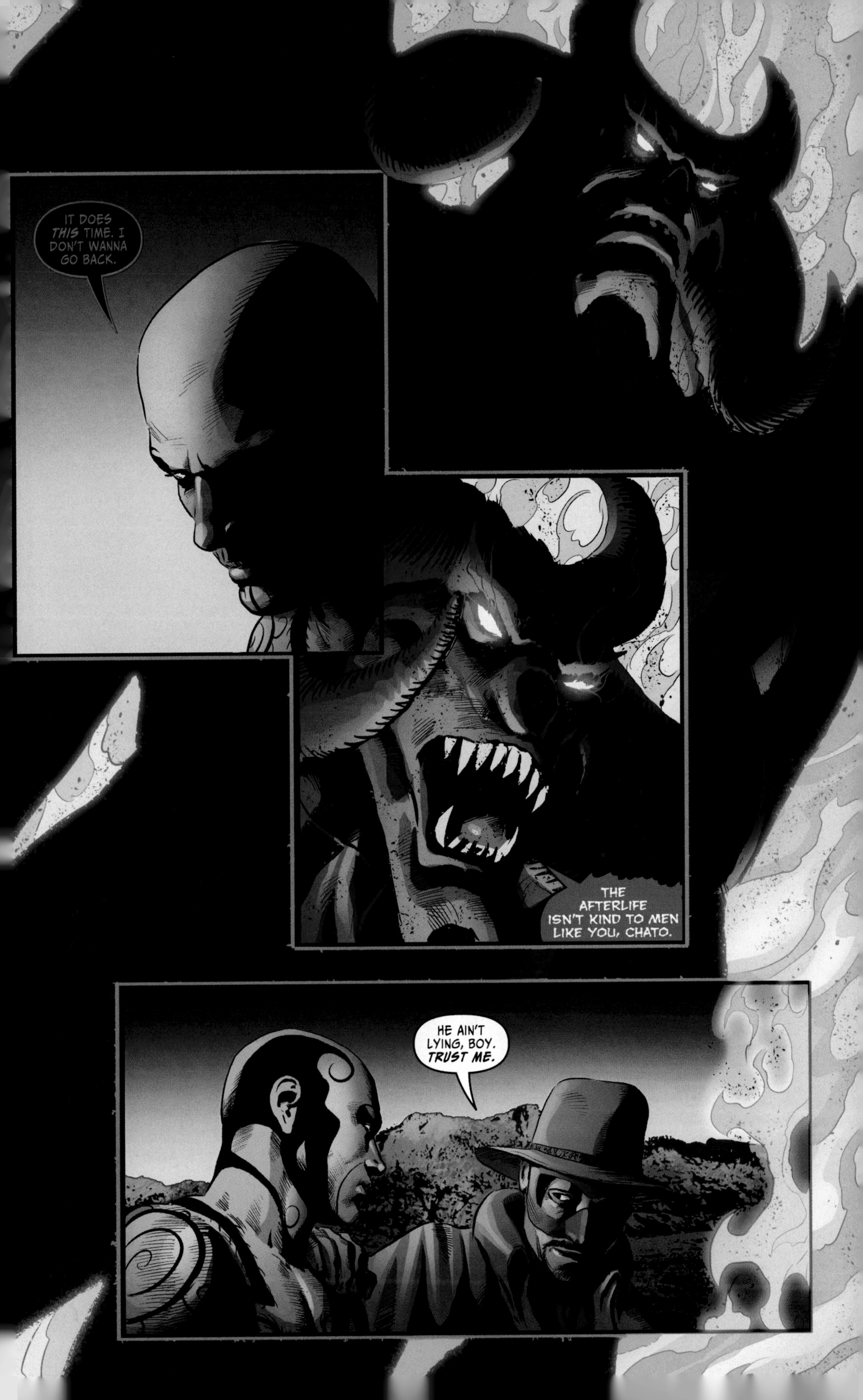
IT DOES *THIS* TIME. I DON'T WANNA GO BACK.
THE AFTERLIFE ISN'T KIND TO MEN LIKE YOU, CHATO.
HE AIN'T LYING, BOY. ***TRUST ME.***

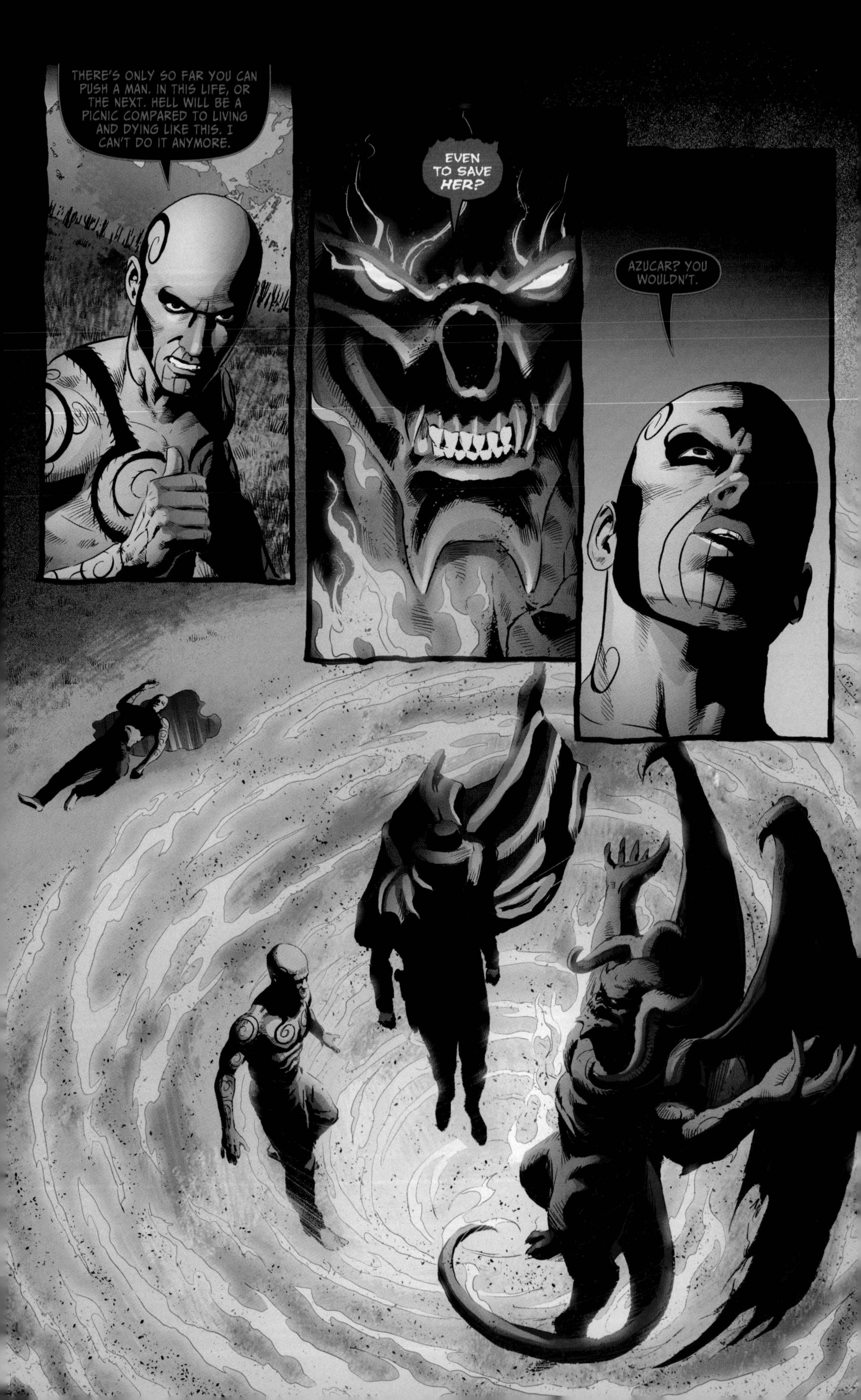
THERE'S ONLY SO FAR YOU CAN PUSH A MAN. IN THIS LIFE, OR THE NEXT. HELL WILL BE A PICNIC COMPARED TO LIVING AND DYING LIKE THIS. I CAN'T DO IT ANYMORE.
EVEN TO SAVE HER?
AZUCAR? YOU WOULDN'T.

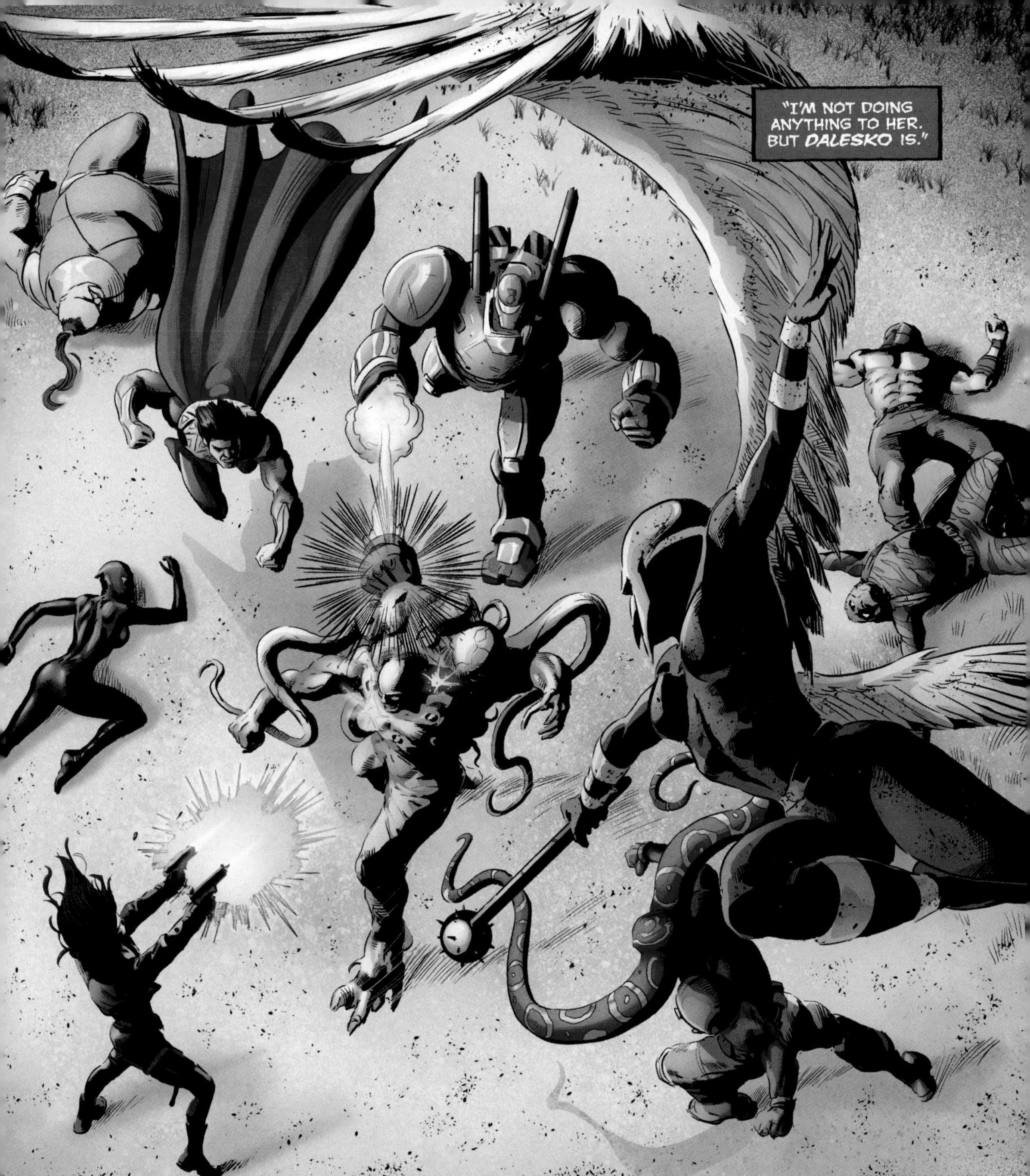
"I'M NOT DOING
ANYTHING TO HER.
BUT DALESKO IS."

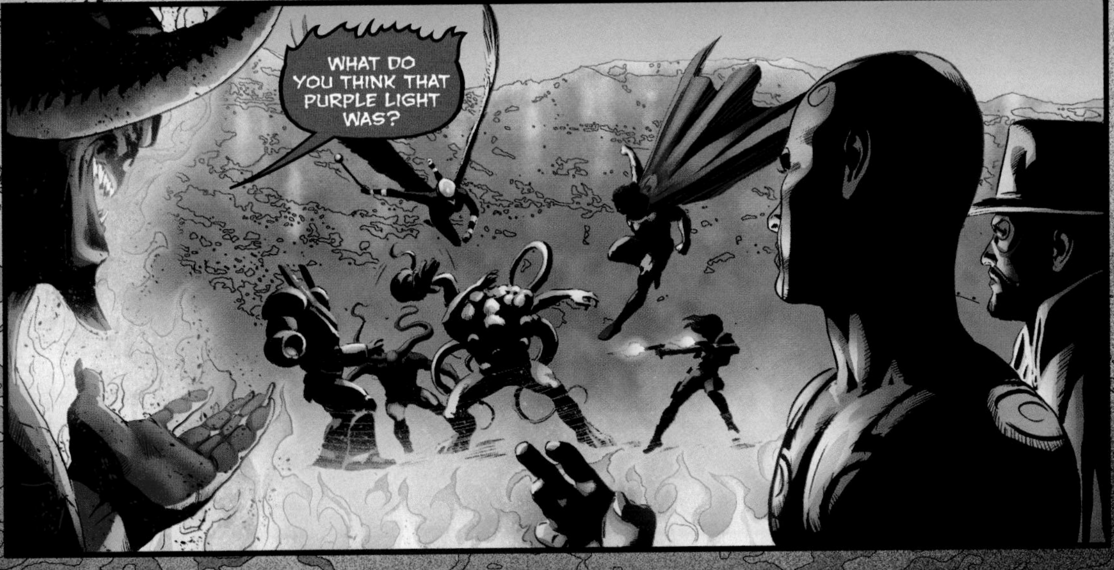
WHAT DO
YOU THINK THAT
PURPLE LIGHT
WAS?

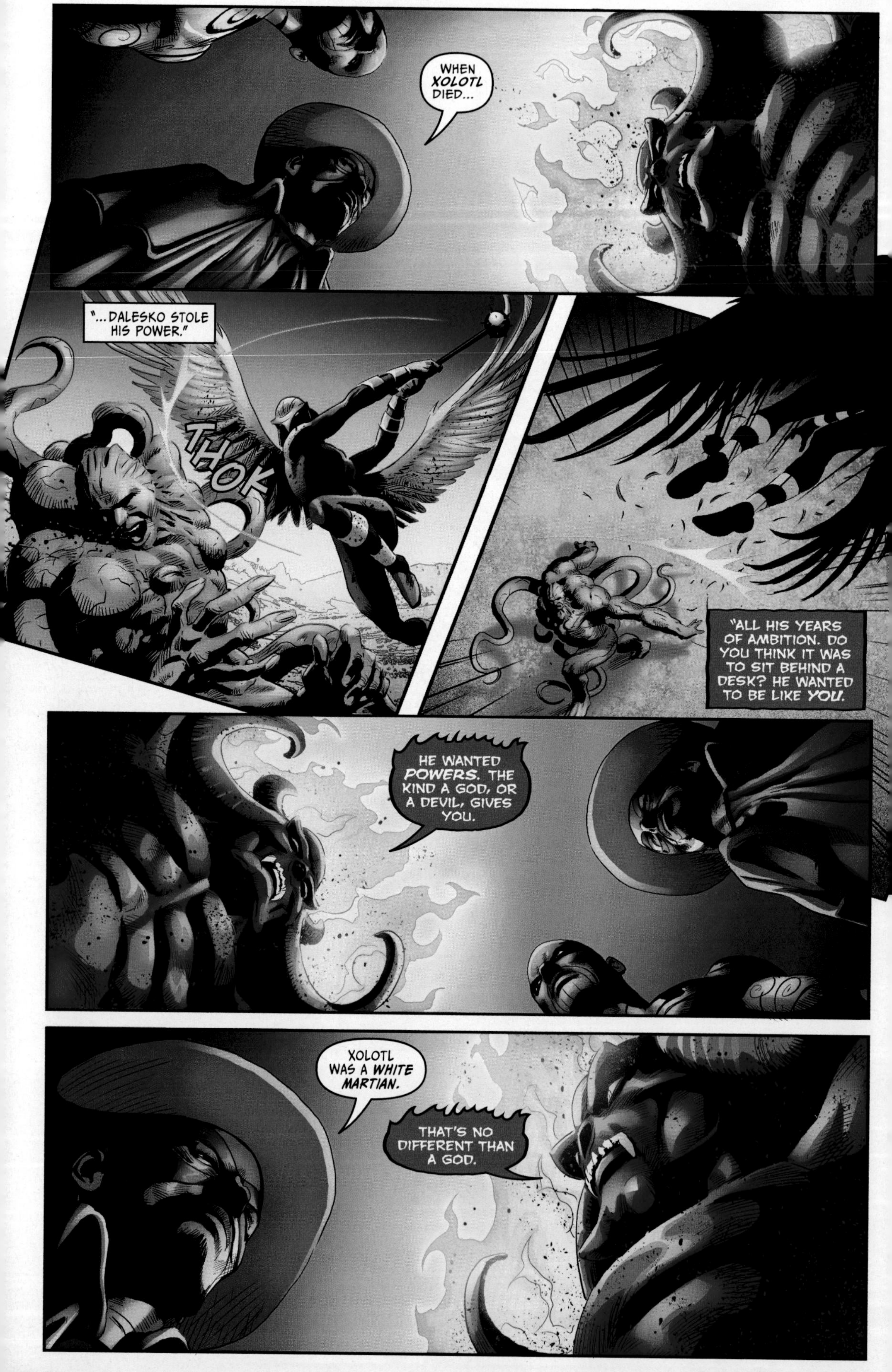
WHEN XOLOTL DIED...
"...DALESKO STOLE HIS POWER."
THOK
"ALL HIS YEARS OF AMBITION. DO YOU THINK IT WAS TO SIT BEHIND A DESK? HE WANTED TO BE LIKE YOU.
HE WANTED POWERS. THE KIND A GOD, OR A DEVIL, GIVES YOU.
XOLOTL WAS A WHITE MARTIAN.
THAT'S NO DIFFERENT THAN A GOD.

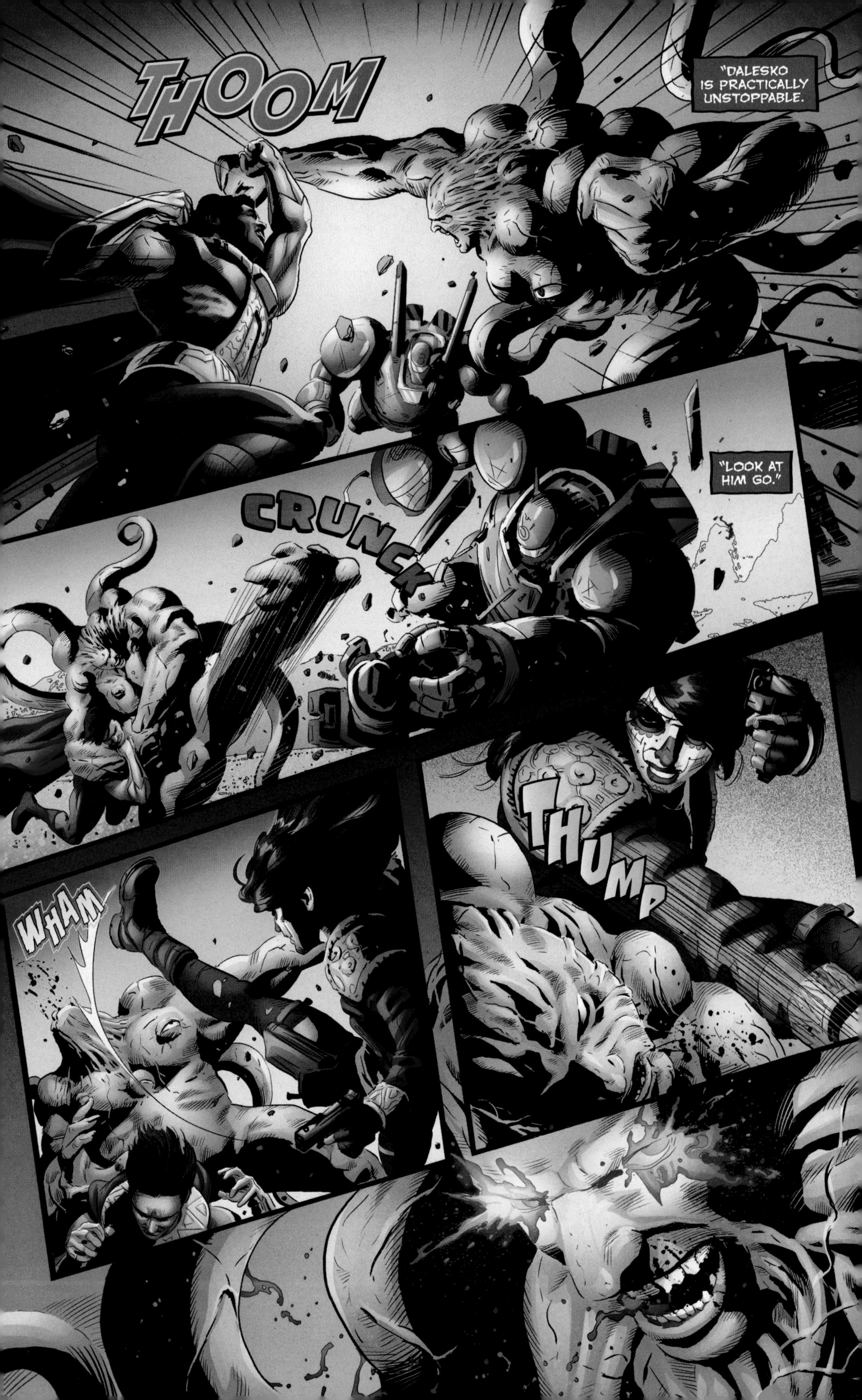
THOOM
"DALESKO IS PRACTICALLY UNSTOPPABLE.
"LOOK AT HIM GO."
CRUNCK
THUMP
WHAM

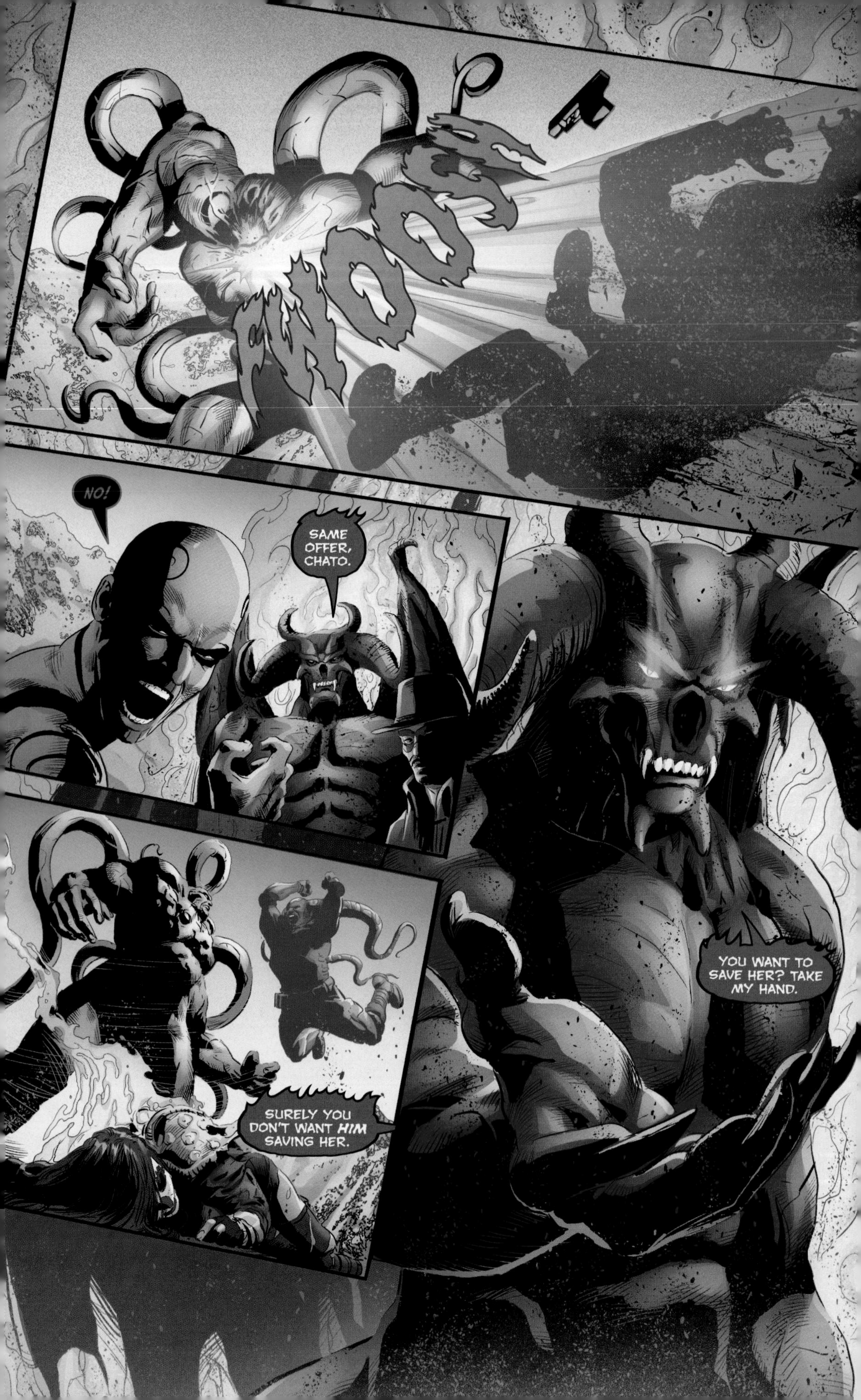
WHOOSH
NO!
SAME OFFER, CHATO.
YOU WANT TO SAVE HER? TAKE MY HAND.
SURELY YOU DON'T WANT HIM SAVING HER.

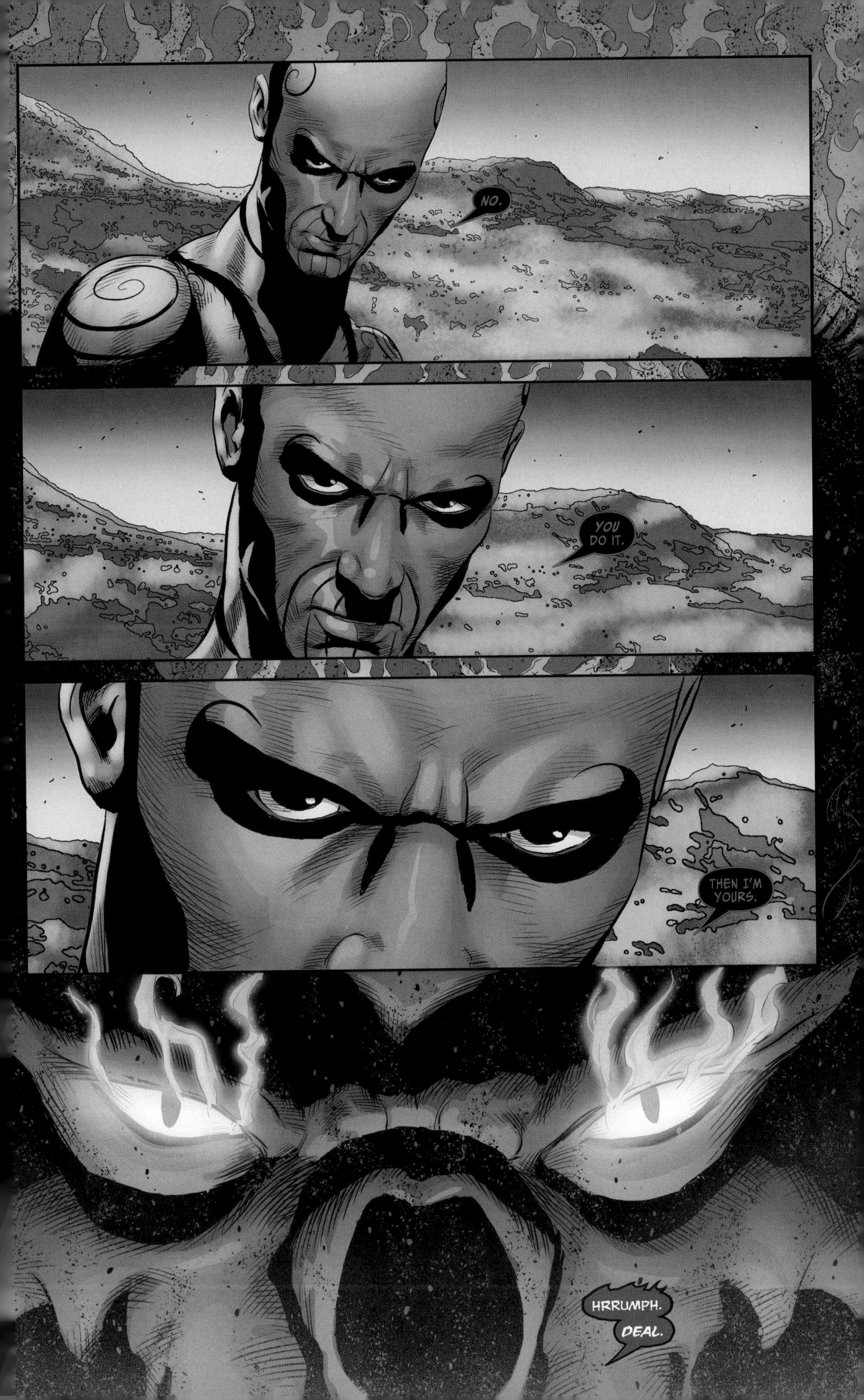
NO.
YOU DO IT.
THEN I'M YOURS.
HRRUMPH.
DEAL.

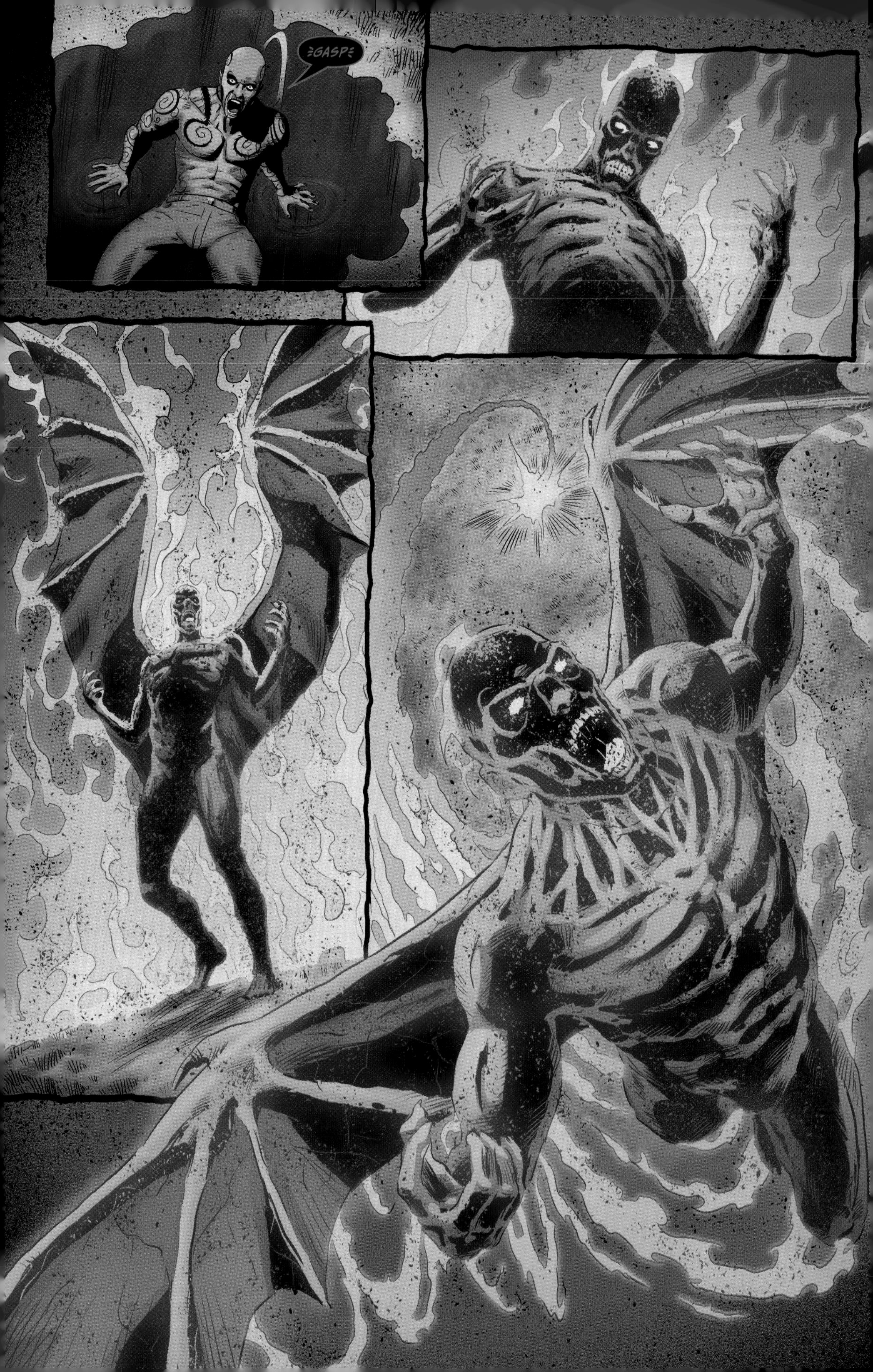
GASP

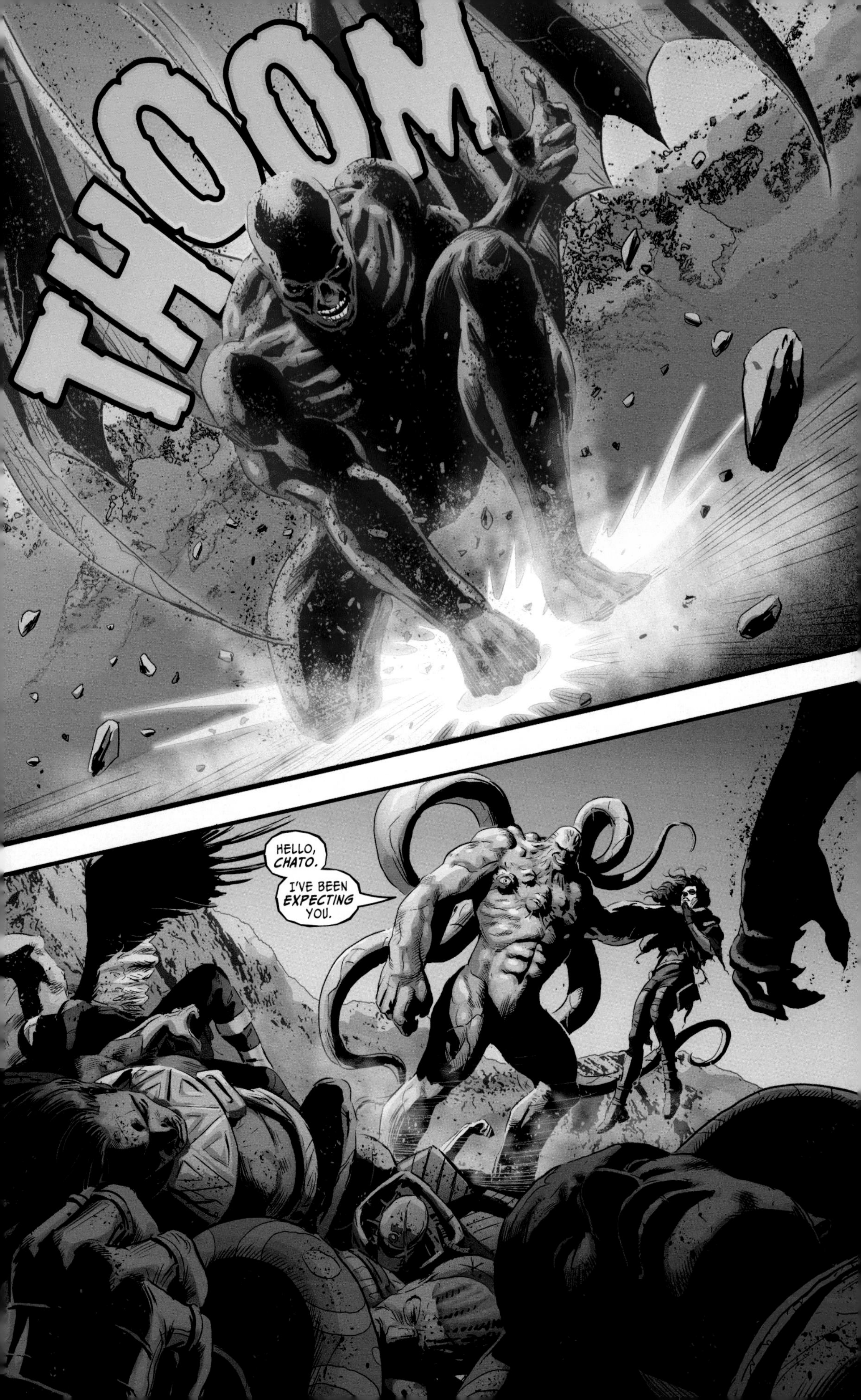
THOOM
HELLO, CHATO.
I'VE BEEN EXPECTING YOU.

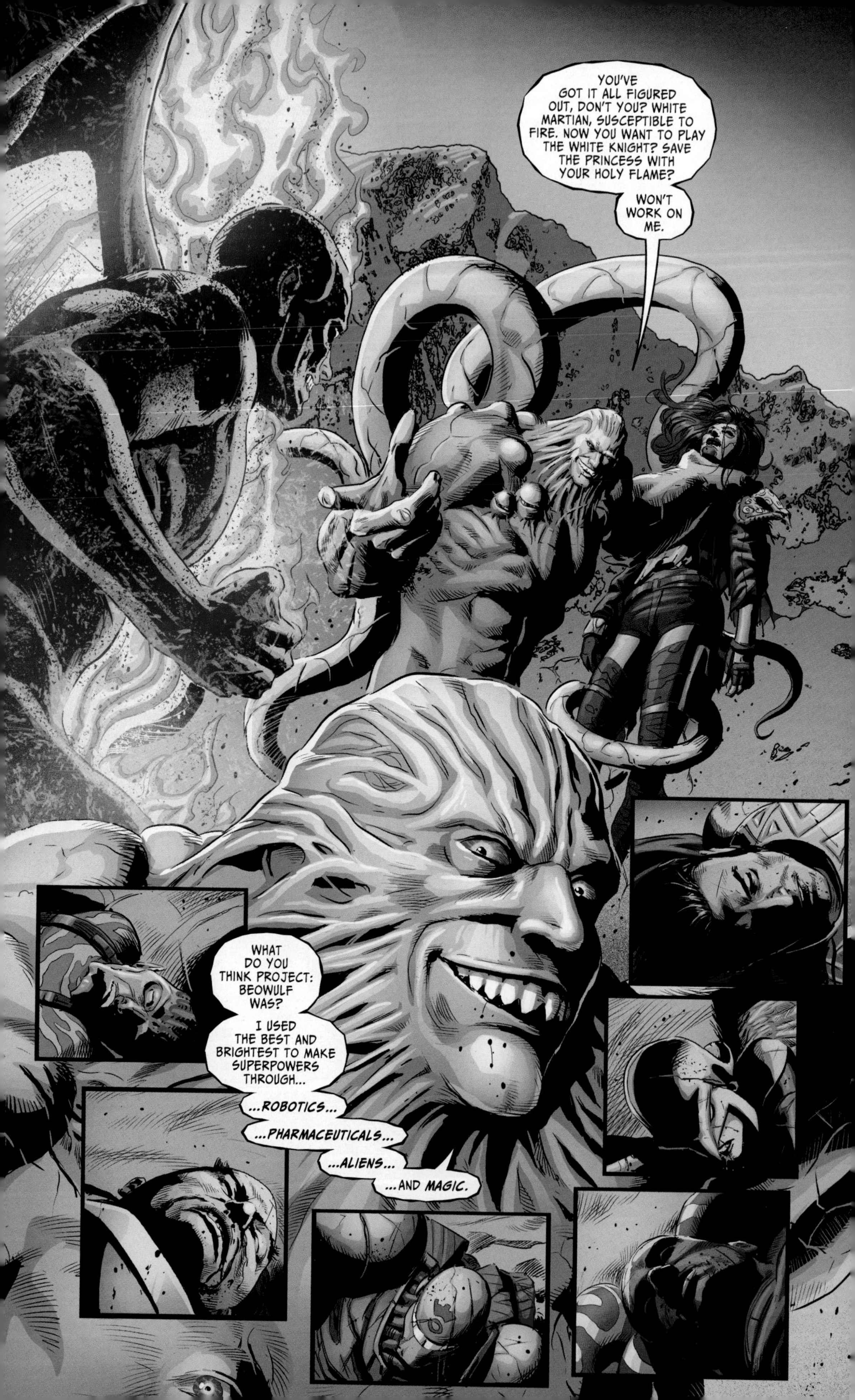
YOU'VE GOT IT ALL FIGURED OUT, DON'T YOU? WHITE MARTIAN, SUSCEPTIBLE TO FIRE. NOW YOU WANT TO PLAY THE WHITE KNIGHT? SAVE THE PRINCESS WITH YOUR HOLY FLAME?
WON'T WORK ON ME.
WHAT DO YOU THINK PROJECT: BEOWULF WAS?
I USED THE BEST AND BRIGHTEST TO MAKE SUPERPOWERS THROUGH...
...ROBOTICS...
...PHARMACEUTICALS...
...ALIENS...
...AND MAGIC.

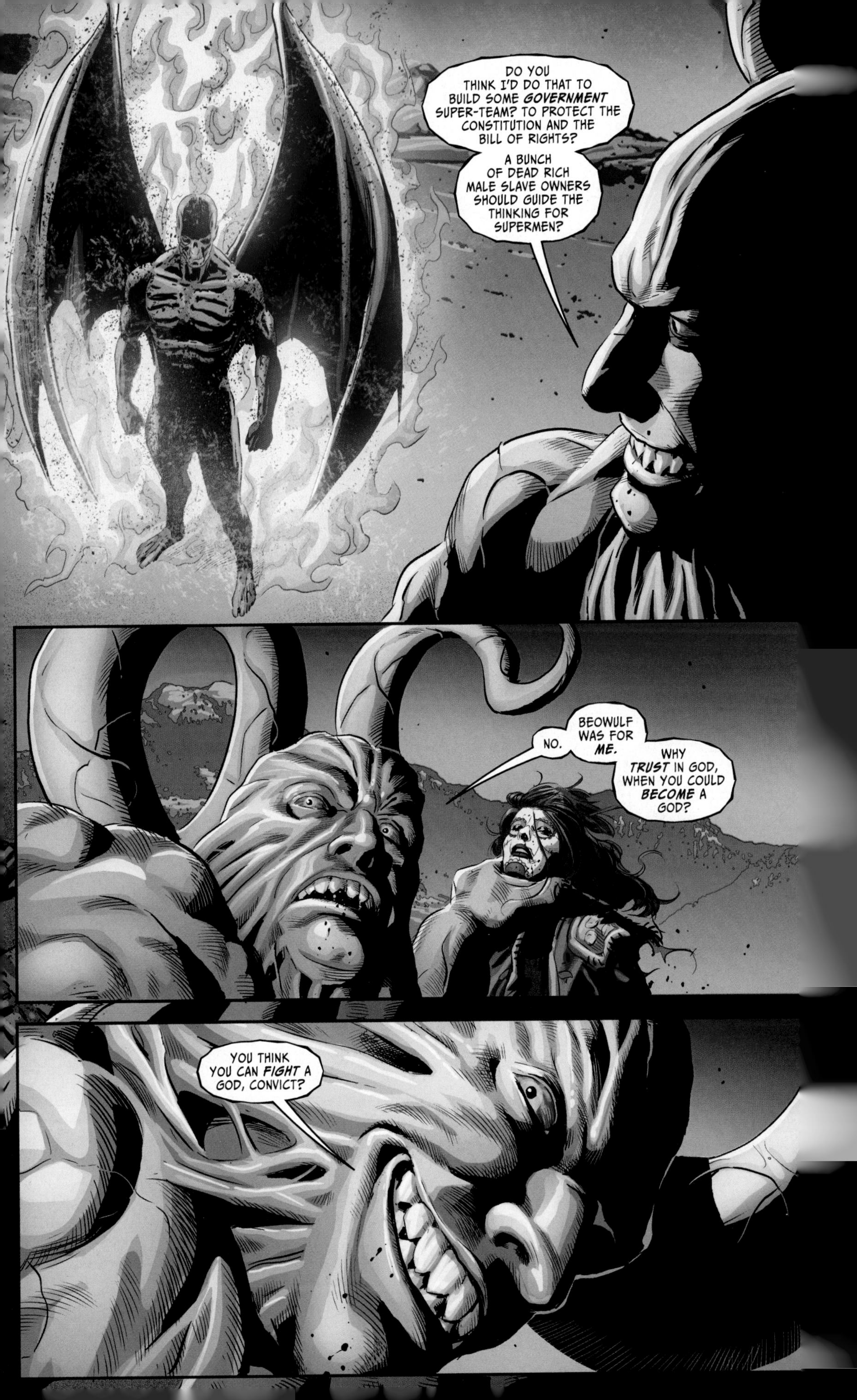
DO YOU THINK I'D DO THAT TO BUILD SOME *GOVERNMENT* SUPER-TEAM? TO PROTECT THE CONSTITUTION AND THE BILL OF RIGHTS?
A BUNCH OF DEAD RICH MALE SLAVE OWNERS SHOULD GUIDE THE THINKING FOR SUPERMEN?
NO.
BEOWULF WAS FOR *ME.*
WHY *TRUST* IN GOD, WHEN YOU COULD *BECOME* A GOD?
YOU THINK YOU CAN *FIGHT* A GOD, CONVICT?

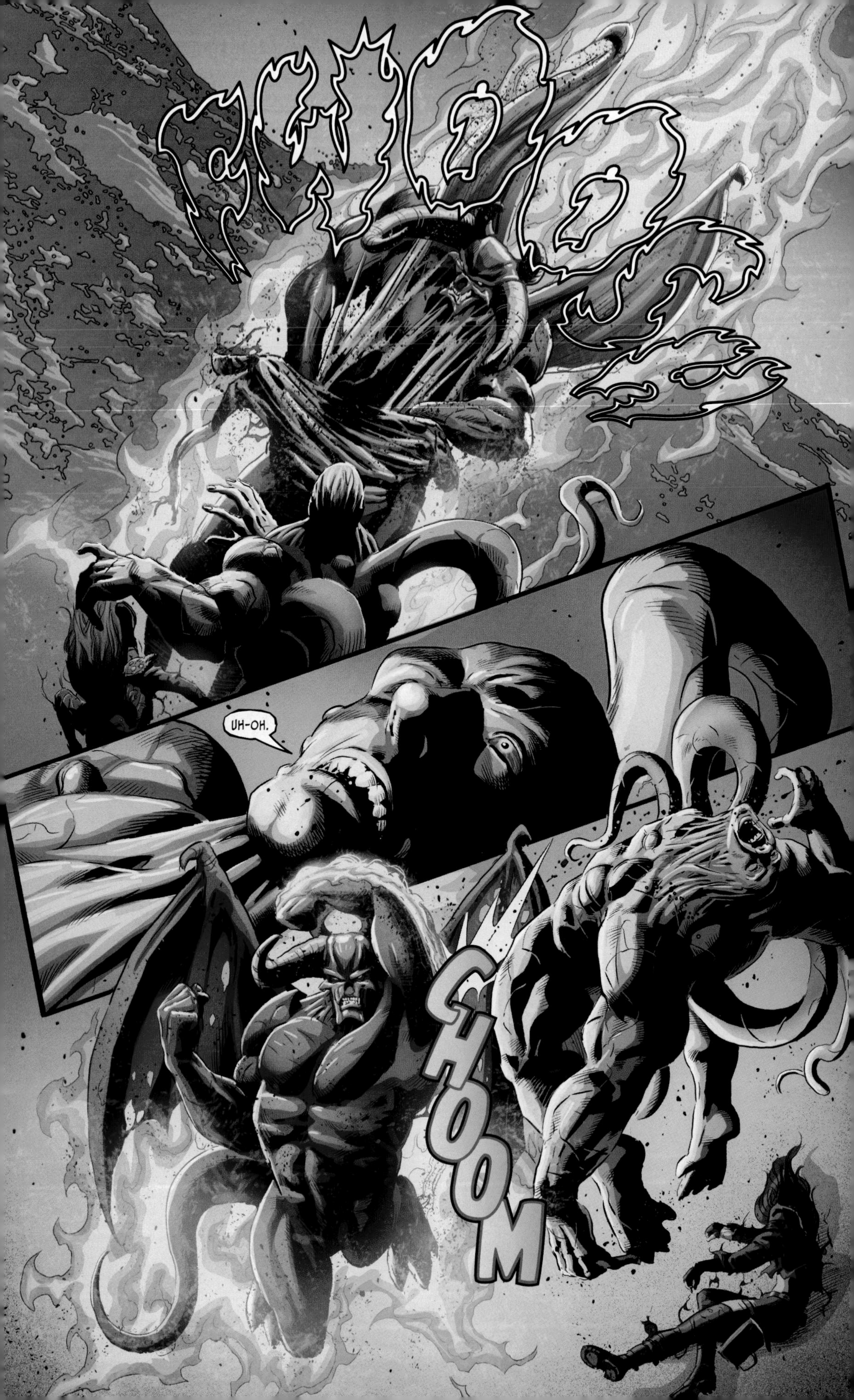
UH-OH.
CHOOOM

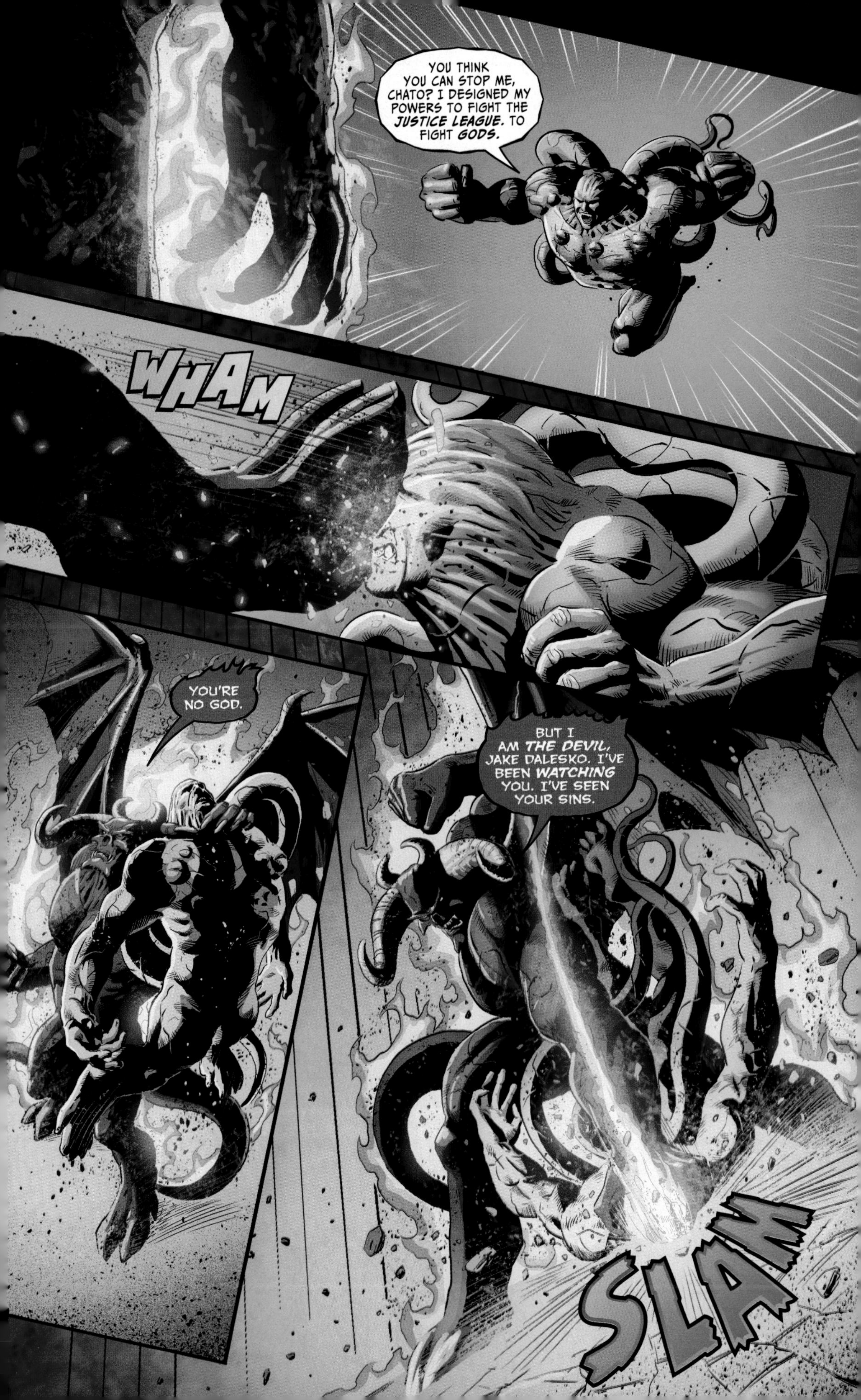

YOU THINK YOU CAN STOP ME, CHATO? I DESIGNED MY POWERS TO FIGHT THE JUSTICE LEAGUE. TO FIGHT GODS.
WHAM
YOU'RE NO GOD.
BUT I AM THE DEVIL, JAKE DALESKO. I'VE BEEN WATCHING YOU. I'VE SEEN YOUR SINS.
SLAM

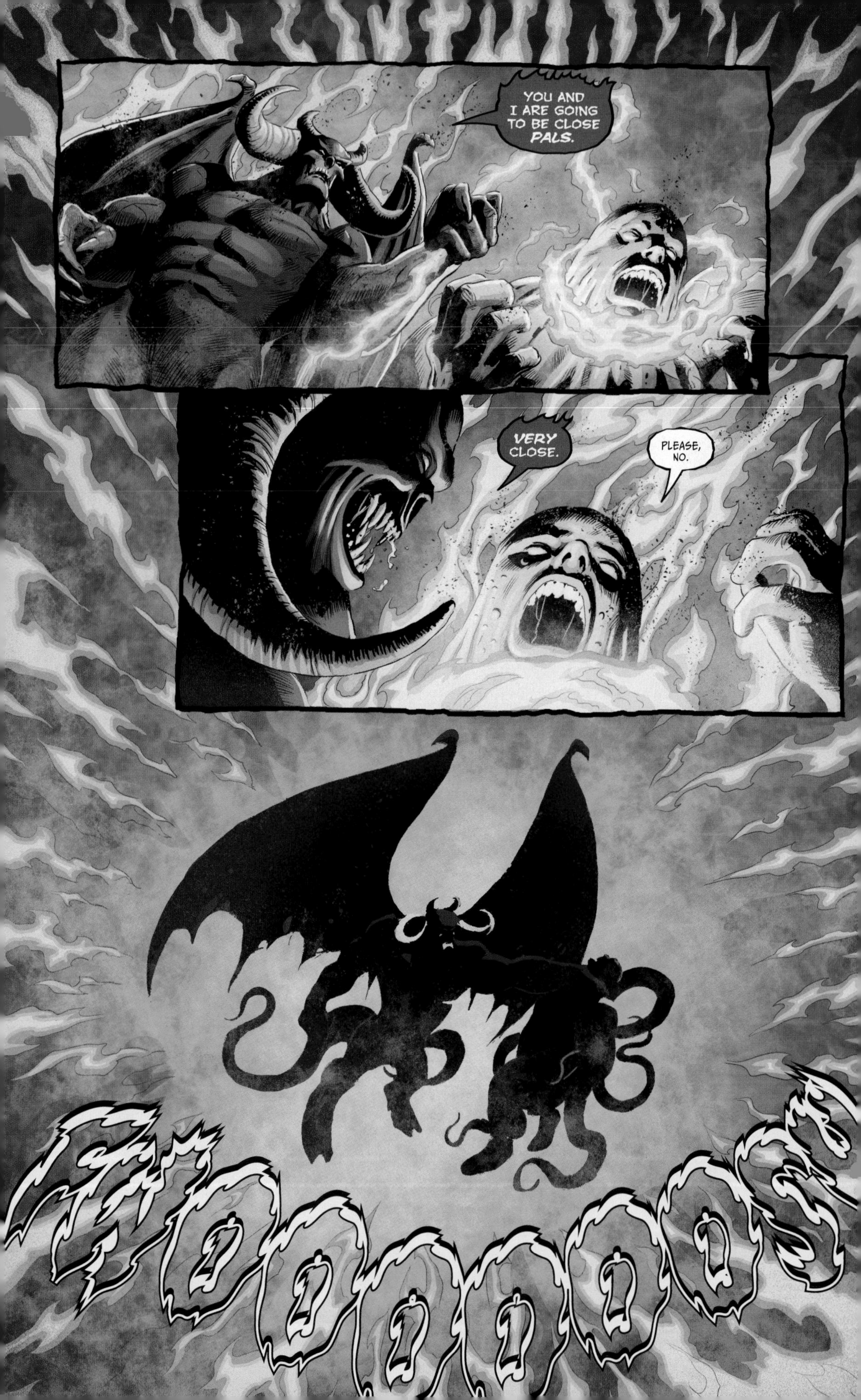
YOU AND I ARE GOING TO BE CLOSE PALS.
VERY CLOSE.
PLEASE, NO.

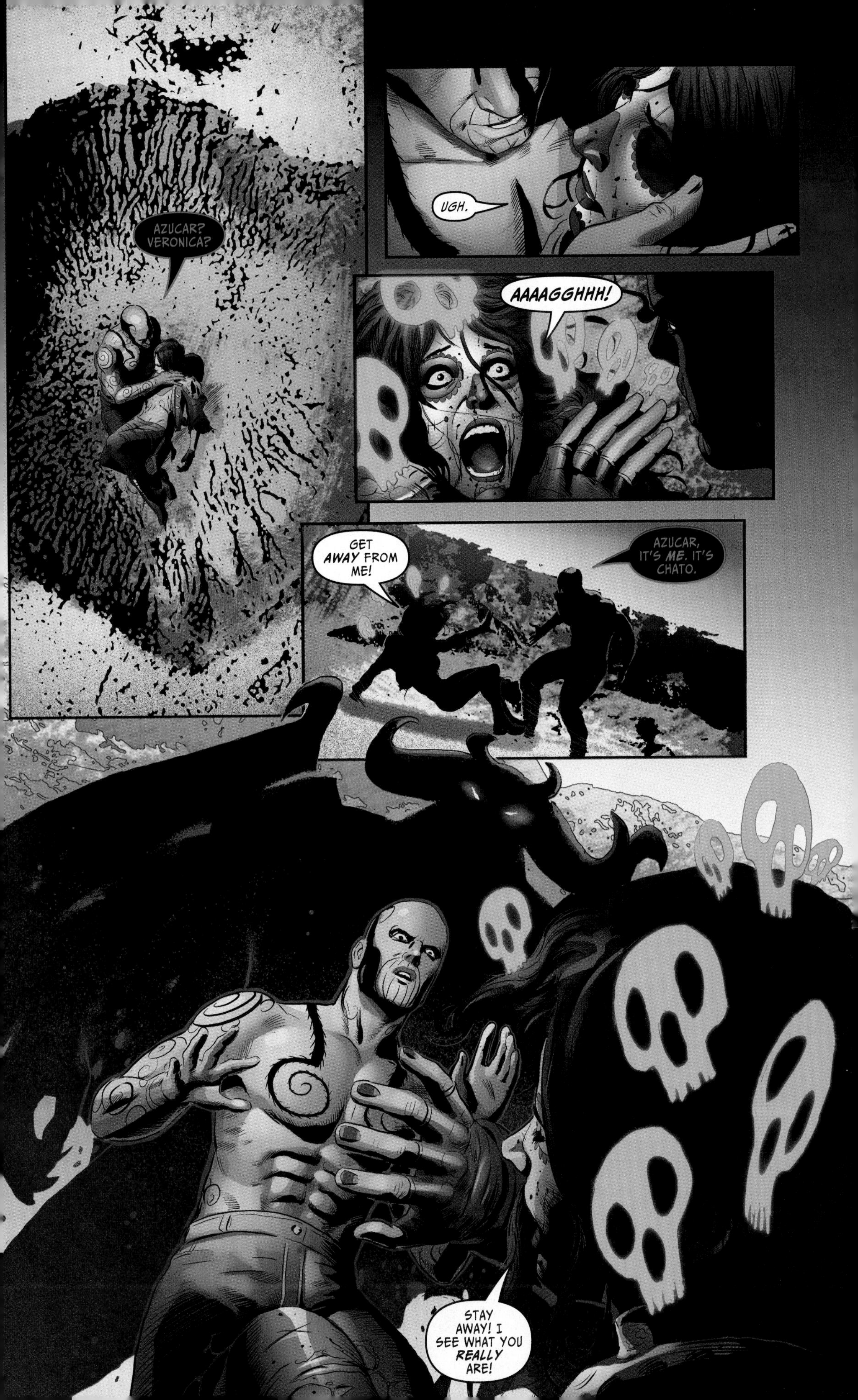
AZUCAR? VERONICA?
UGH.
AAAAGGHHH!
GET AWAY FROM ME!
AZUCAR, IT'S ME. IT'S CHATO.
STAY AWAY! I SEE WHAT YOU REALLY ARE!

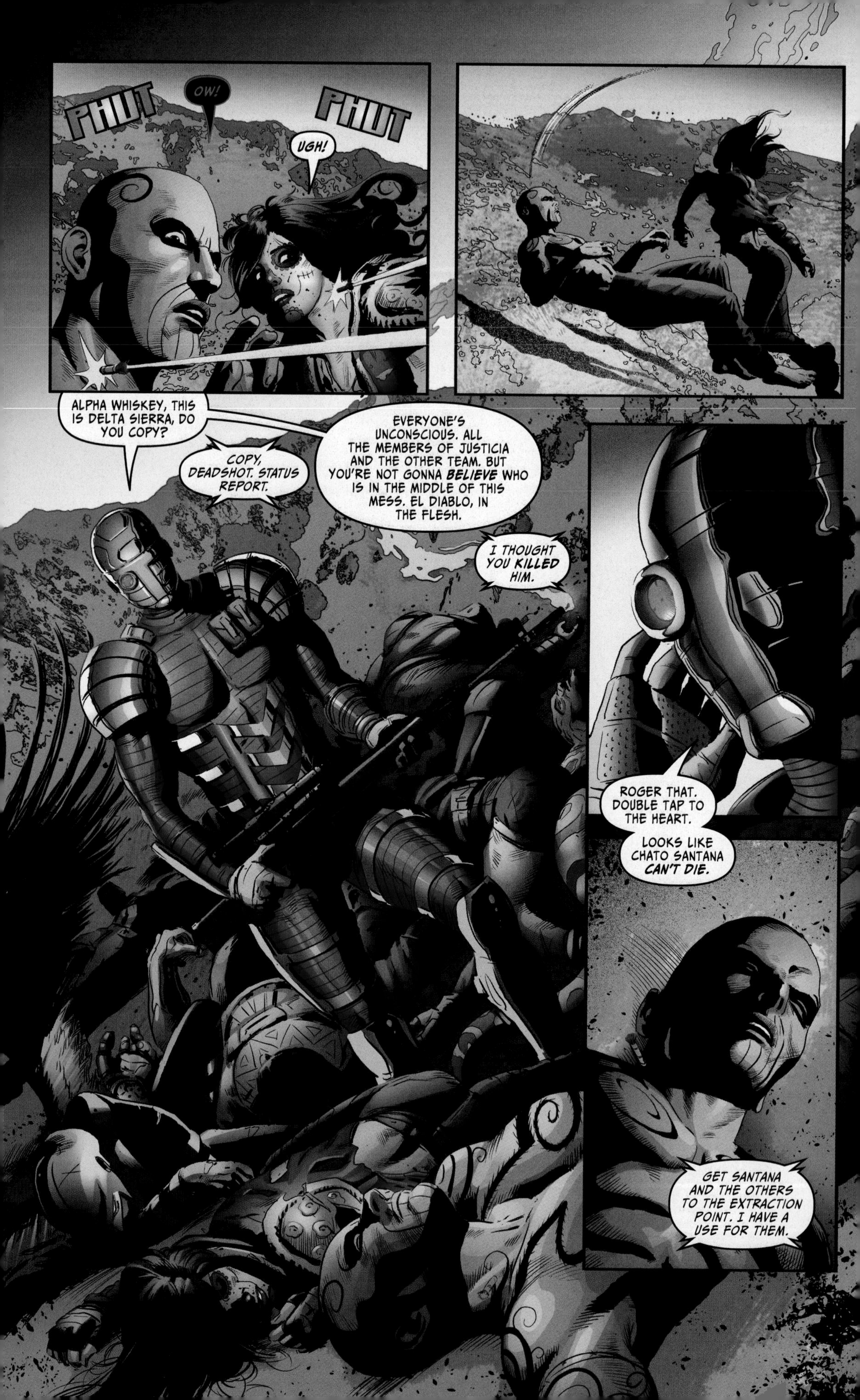
PHUT
OW!
PHUT
UGH!
ALPHA WHISKEY, THIS IS DELTA SIERRA, DO YOU COPY?
COPY, DEADSHOT. STATUS REPORT.
EVERYONE'S UNCONSCIOUS. ALL THE MEMBERS OF JUSTICIA AND THE OTHER TEAM. BUT YOU'RE NOT GONNA BELIEVE WHO IS IN THE MIDDLE OF THIS MESS. EL DIABLO, IN THE FLESH.
I THOUGHT YOU KILLED HIM.
ROGER THAT. DOUBLE TAP TO THE HEART.
LOOKS LIKE CHATO SANTANA CAN'T DIE.
GET SANTANA AND THE OTHERS TO THE EXTRACTION POINT. I HAVE A USE FOR THEM.

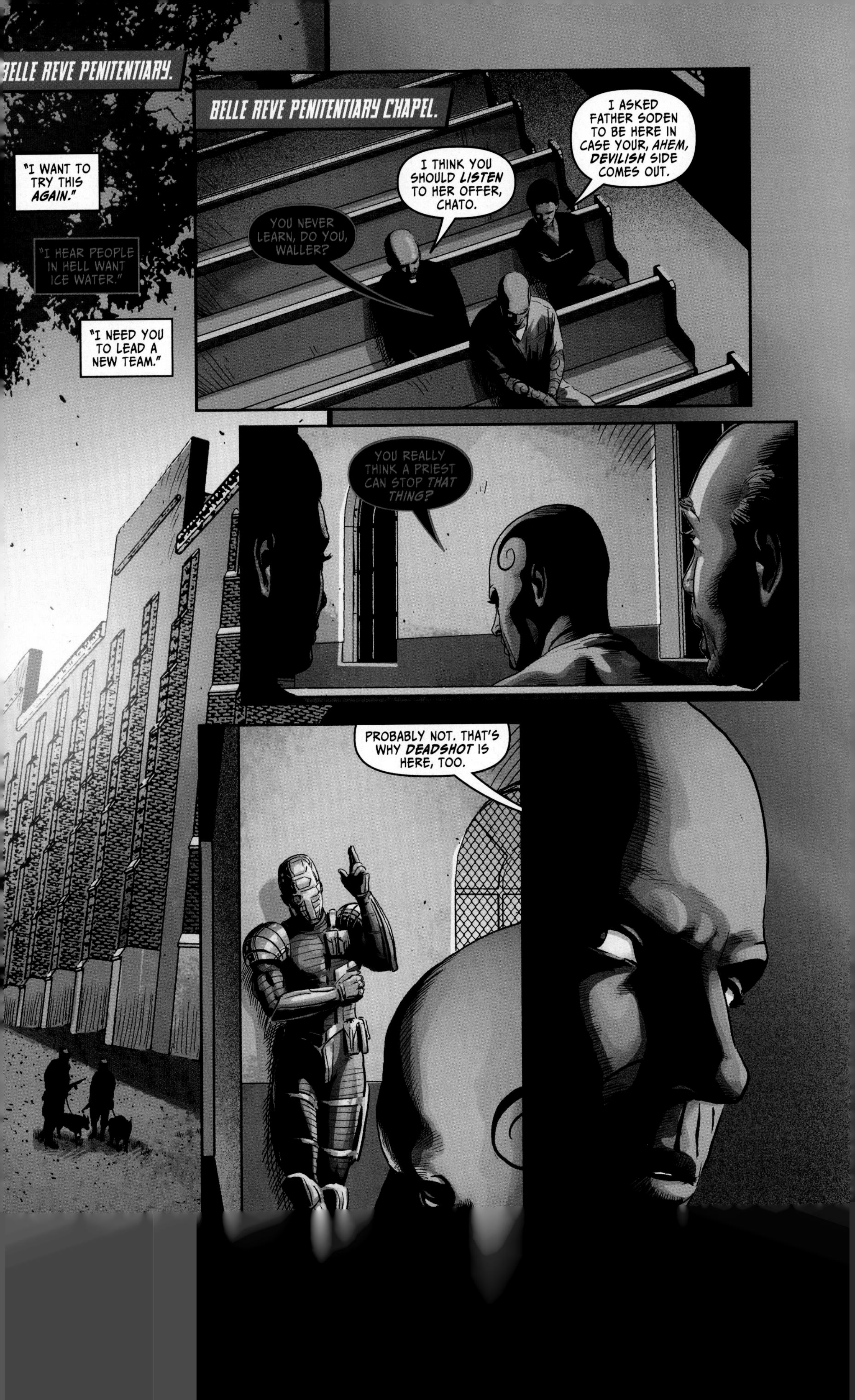
BELLE REVE PENITENTIARY.
"I WANT TO TRY THIS AGAIN."
"I HEAR PEOPLE IN HELL WANT ICE WATER."
"I NEED YOU TO LEAD A NEW TEAM."
BELLE REVE PENITENTIARY CHAPEL.
YOU NEVER LEARN, DO YOU, WALLER?
I THINK YOU SHOULD LISTEN TO HER OFFER, CHATO.
I ASKED FATHER SODEN TO BE HERE IN CASE YOUR, AHEM, DEVILISH SIDE COMES OUT.
YOU REALLY THINK A PRIEST CAN STOP THAT THING?
PROBABLY NOT. THAT'S WHY DEADSHOT IS HERE, TOO.

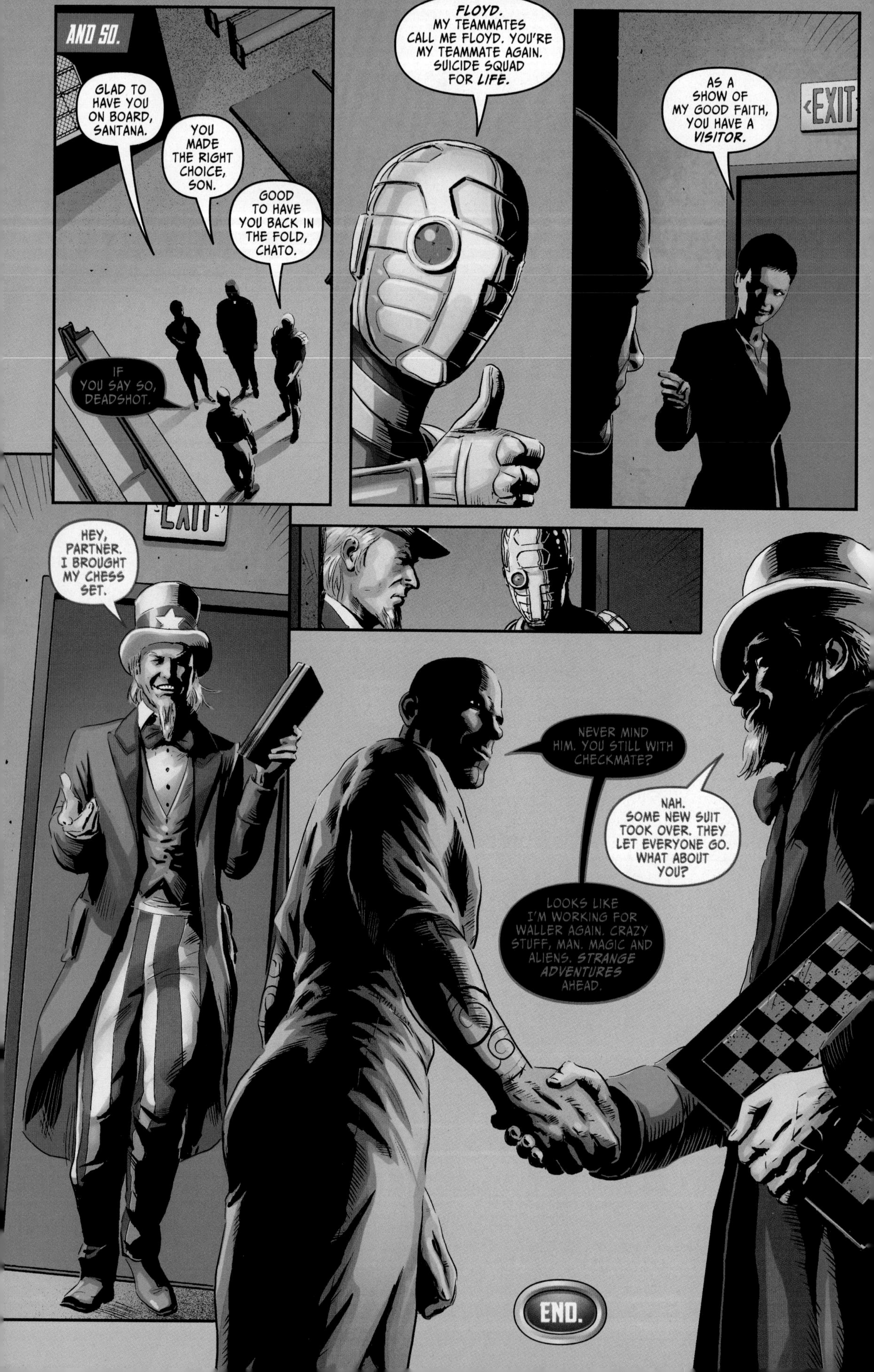
AND SO.
GLAD TO HAVE YOU ON BOARD, SANTANA.
YOU MADE THE RIGHT CHOICE, SON.
GOOD TO HAVE YOU BACK IN THE FOLD, CHATO.
IF YOU SAY SO, DEADSHOT.
FLOYD. MY TEAMMATES CALL ME FLOYD. YOU'RE MY TEAMMATE AGAIN. SUICIDE SQUAD FOR LIFE.
AS A SHOW OF MY GOOD FAITH, YOU HAVE A VISITOR.
EXIT
HEY, PARTNER. I BROUGHT MY CHESS SET.
NEVER MIND HIM. YOU STILL WITH CHECKMATE?
NAH. SOME NEW SUIT TOOK OVER. THEY LET EVERYONE GO. WHAT ABOUT YOU?
LOOKS LIKE I'M WORKING FOR WALLER AGAIN. CRAZY STUFF, MAN. MAGIC AND ALIENS. STRANGE ADVENTURES AHEAD.
END.

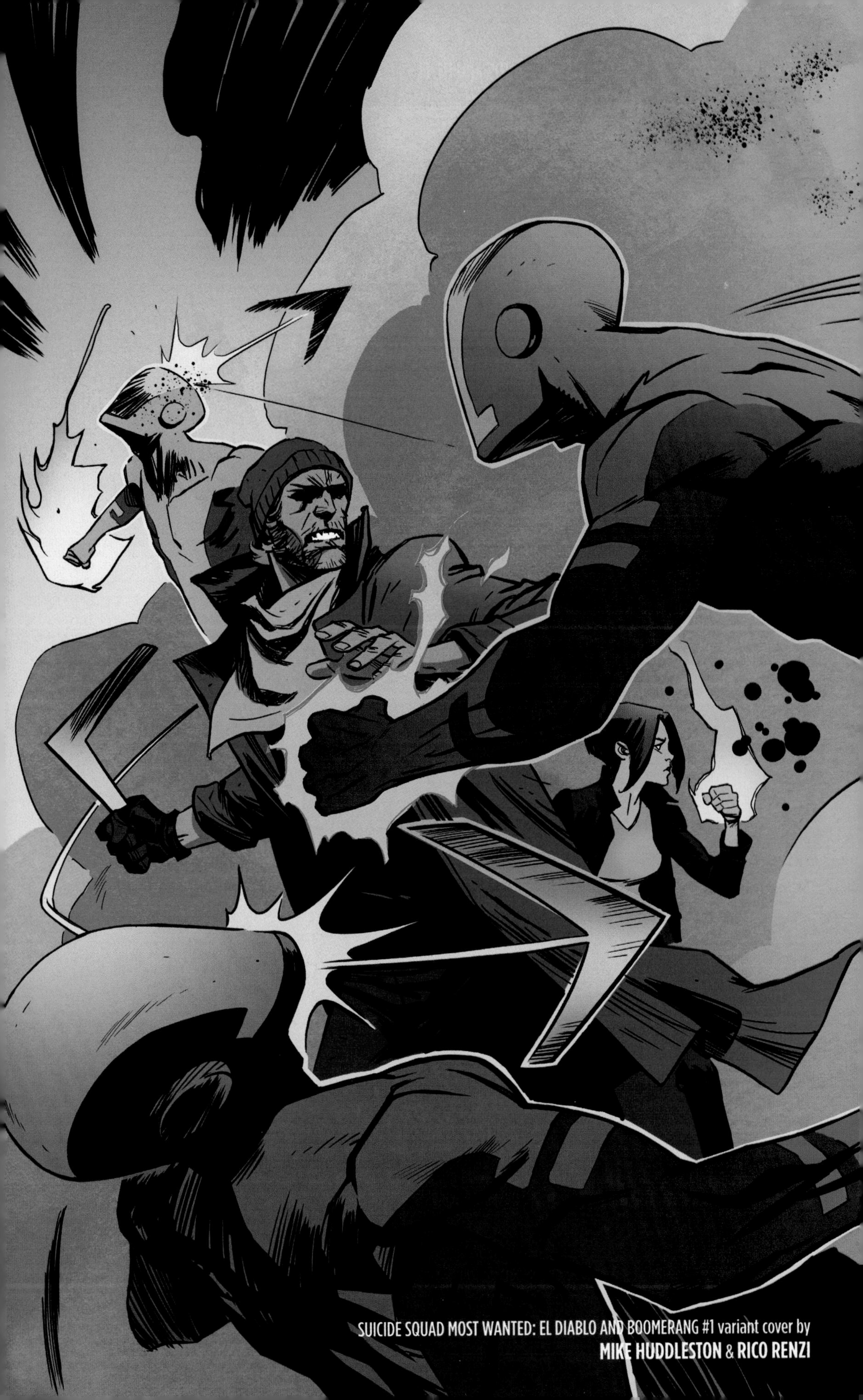

SUICIDE SQUAD MOST WANTED: EL DIABLO AND BOOMERANG #1 variant cover by
MIKE HUDDLESTON & RICO RENZI

XOLOTL CHARACTER DESIGN BY CLIFF RICHARDS and HI-FI

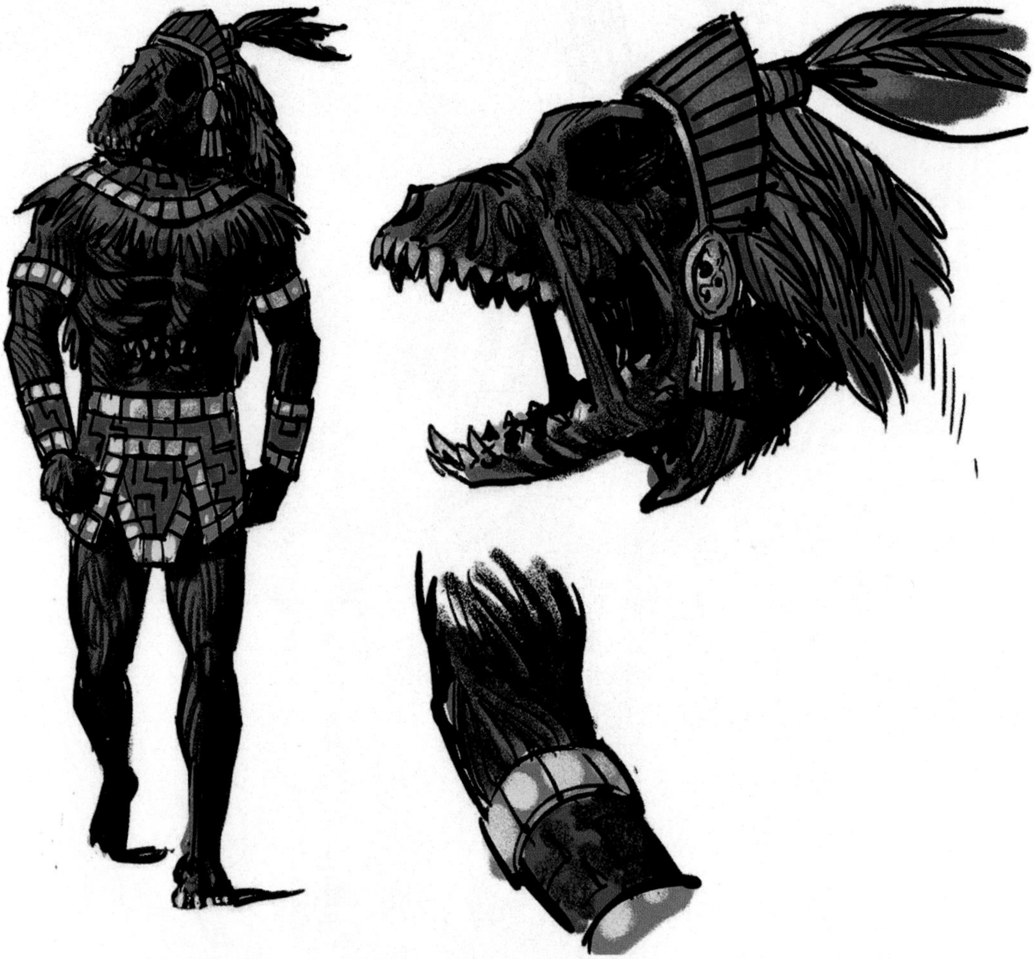

SUICIDE SQUAD MOST WANTED: EL DIABLO AND KILLER CROC #4 COVER SKETCHES BY MIKE HUDDLESTON

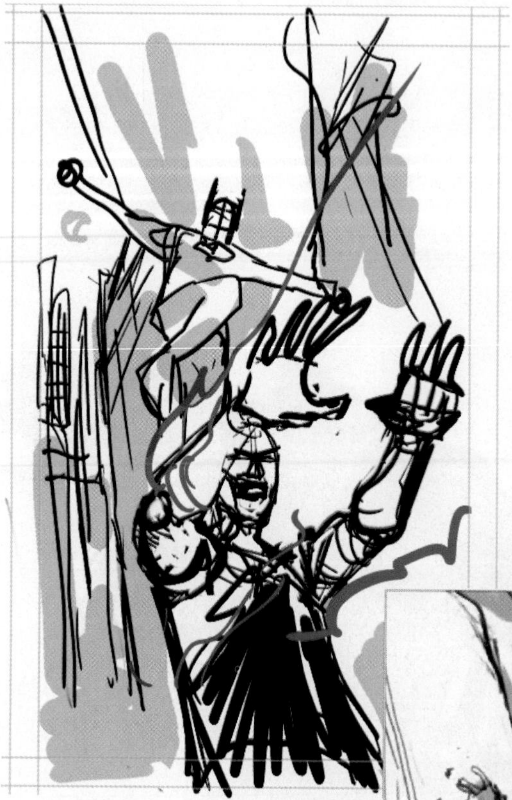

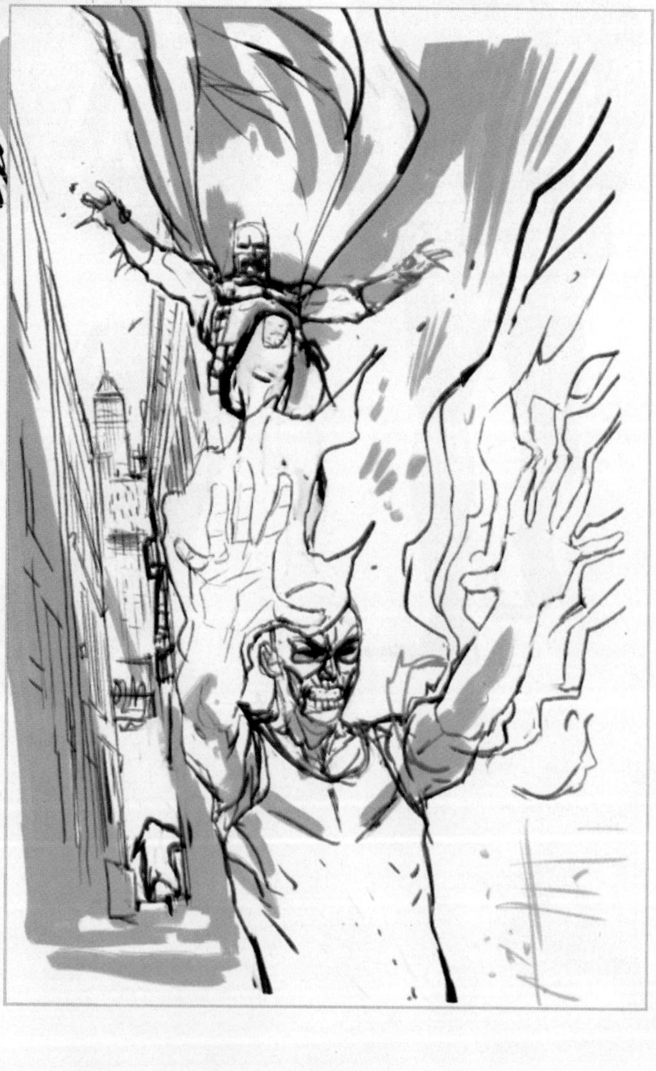

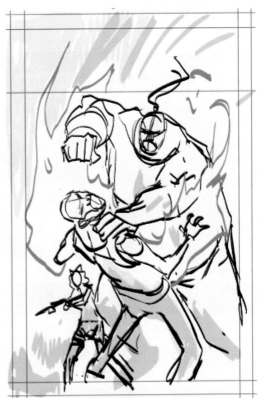

"It's nice to see one of the best comics of the late '80s return so strongly."
– Comic Book Resources

"It's high energy from page one through to the last page." – BATMAN NEWS

DC UNIVERSE REBIRTH

SUICIDE SQUAD

VOL. 1: THE BLACK VAULT

ROB WILLIAMS
with JIM LEE and others

VOL.1 THE BLACK VAULT
ROB WILLIAMS • JIM LEE • PHILIP TAN • JASON FABOK • IVAN REIS • GARY FRANK

VOL.1 THE POISON TRUTH
SIMON OLIVER • MORITAT • ANDRE SZYMANOWICZ

THE HELLBLAZER VOL. 1:
THE POISON TRUTH

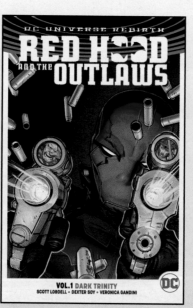

VOL.1 DARK TRINITY
SCOTT LOBDELL • DEXTER SOY • VERONICA GANDINI

RED HOOD AND THE OUTLAWS VOL. 1:
DARK TRINITY

VOL.1 DIE LAUGHING
AMANDA CONNER • JIMMY PALMIOTTI • CHAD HARDIN • JOHN TIMMS

HARLEY QUINN VOL. 1:
DIE LAUGHING

Get more DC graphic novels wherever comics and books are sold!

"A pretty irresistible hook..."
– THE ONION A.V. CLUB

"A CLEVERLY WRITTEN, OUTSTANDING READ FROM BEGINNING TO END." — USA TODAY
THE NEW 52!
SUICIDE SQUAD
VOLUME 1
KICKED IN THE TEETH
ADAM GLASS FEDERICO DALLOCCHIO CLAYTON HENRY

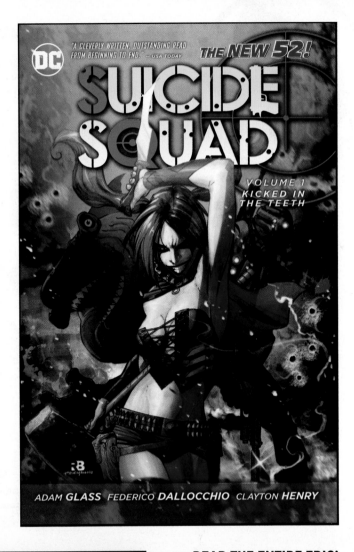

SUICIDE SQUAD

VOL. 1: KICKED IN THE TEETH

ADAM GLASS with
FEDERICO DALLOCCHIO

THE NEW 52!
SUICIDE SQUAD
"A CLEVERLY WRITTEN, OUTSTANDING READ FROM BEGINNING TO END." — USA TODAY
VOLUME 2 BASILISK RISING
ADAM GLASS FERNANDO DAGNINO

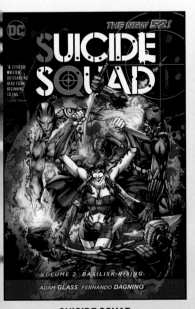

SUICIDE SQUAD
VOL. 2: BASILISK RISING

THE NEW 52!
SUICIDE SQUAD
VOLUME 3
DEATH IS FOR SUCKERS
DEADSHOT
ADAM GLASS HENRIK JONSSON SANDU FLOREA

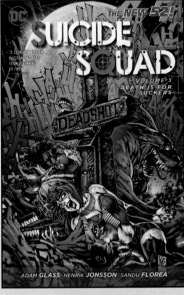

SUICIDE SQUAD
VOL. 3: DEATH IS FOR SUCKERS

READ THE ENTIRE EPIC!

SUICIDE SQUAD VOL. 4:
DISCIPLINE AND PUNISH

SUICIDE SQUAD VOL. 5:
WALLED IN

"A cleverly written, outstanding read from beginning to end."
– USA TODAY

Get more DC graphic novels wherever comics and books are sold!

"Chaotic and unabashedly fun."
– IGN

HARLEY QUINN

VOL. 1: HOT IN THE CITY
AMANDA CONNER
with JIMMY PALMIOTTI
& CHAD HARDIN

**HARLEY QUINN
VOL. 2: POWER OUTAGE**

**HARLEY QUINN
VOL. 3: KISS KISS BANG STAB**

READ THE ENTIRE EPIC!

HARLEY QUINN VOL. 4:
A CALL TO ARMS

HARLEY QUINN VOL. 5:
THE JOKER'S LAST LAUGH

"I'm enjoying this a great deal;
it's silly, it's funny, it's irreverent."
– COMIC BOOK RESOURCES